MEMOIR, LETTERS,

AND

A SELECTION FROM THE POEMS AND PROSE WRITINGS

OF

ANNA LÆTITIA BARBAULD.

VOLUME I.

A L Barbauld

A MEMOIR OF MRS. ANNA LÆTITIA BARBAULD,

WITH MANY OF HER LETTERS.

BY

GRACE A. ELLIS.

"To strew fresh laurels, let the task be mine."
TICKELL.

BOSTON:
JAMES R. OSGOOD AND COMPANY,
LATE TICKNOR & FIELDS, AND FIELDS, OSGOOD, & CO.
1874.

University Press: Welch, Bigelow, & Co.,
Cambridge.

TO

MY MOTHER

I DEDICATE THESE VOLUMES,

INSCRIBING

THIS IMPERFECT, BUT NOT UNFAITHFUL WORK,

WHICH I HOPE MAY PERPETUATE

The Memory

OF A VIRTUOUS AND TALENTED WOMAN, AND AWAKEN NEW INTEREST IN HER LIFE AND WRITINGS,

TO ONE

WHO HAS EVER BEEN TO ME

A FRIEND, A GUIDE, AND AN INSPIRATION,

WITH THE WARMEST FEELINGS OF AFFECTIONATE REGARD.

PREFACE.

THE writing and reading of biographies of very varied lives and different characters have long been the occupation of the ablest writers, and given pleasure and profit to many students of the thoughts, manners, and personal and mental peculiarities of the good and great. All the eminent men and women who have lived and labored in this busy world, and left enduring records of themselves in works which follow them, deserve from some impartial hand a recognition of their career, — a just estimate of their position in their chosen walk of life. Though memory may embalm their names for centuries in the hearts and minds of many generations, it cannot do more than leave vague and uncertain fancies as years roll on, if no extended sketches of their lives and works are given to the world.

Some of the very greatest geniuses the world ever knew have suffered from this neglect, and we have only the merest shadows of men and women given us where we should eagerly study a life-size mental portrait. Dr. Johnson says that only those who have lived with a man or woman should attempt to portray their lives, as they alone are properly qualified to depict the true character and draw well the lights and shades of it. Though this real or fancied advantage which Dr. Johnson considered an absolute necessity, as a condition of success, is not mine, I have ventured to give the world a sketch of Mrs. Barbauld's life in a more extended and particular form than has yet been attempted; and if not found personal enough in its character, the reader must bear in mind that the "inaudible and noiseless foot of Time" has recorded almost half a century since her death.

With the encouragement and advice of my father-in-law, George E. Ellis, D. D., I undertook this Memoir of Mrs. Barbauld, with the care of preparing and editing a Selection from her Poems and Prose Works. In so doing I have received from him valued assistance in the revision of my manuscripts. To my father, James L. Little, Esq., I may here acknowledge my indebtedness for the interest he has manifested in my work throughout the time I have devoted myself to it. In the use of books beyond my own library I have been greatly aided by the friendly care and attention of Justin Winsor, Esq., the able Superintendent of the Public Library, who in every way facilitated my object. To Mr. Hunter, of the Williams Library in London, I also feel indebted for the attention shown me by him while there. And I must here thank Mr. James T. Fields for the friendly thoughts which have manifested themselves in various ways during my preparation of this work.

I wish to call attention to the engraving which Mr. W. H. Forbes has had made for me; and, when finished in the beautiful and perfect style in which the reader sees it, he insisted on my acceptance of it as his contribution towards the book, desiring that I should not mention it; but this I could not consent to do, and must here thank him for the great addition to the value of the Life which this admirable portrait gives.

In alluding to those whose kindness I have experienced, I do not forget those whom I may not name, and would here express my obligations to those of my family and friends who have aided in my little work and lightened my labors. One of my friends thoughtfully undertook and completed the larger part of the copying of the poems.

The nineteenth century has done so much admirable and laborious work in reviving, rescuing from oblivion, and bringing out of their seclusion old books and authors, that one feels no apology is needed for reprinting a portion of the writings of an author once so widely known by her works, and still highly respected for her moral and mental qualities, as Mrs. Barbauld. Her name is among those of the worthies of England that still live in the hearts of the people, and it is as "familiar as household words" in many homes, while her prose works, and much of her poetry, are almost unknown to many readers and quite out of print.

The "Prose Hymns" for children and "Early Lessons" are still used, and of these two little books there have been many editions; I have before me two editions of the "Prose Hymns" which present the extremes of elegance and simplicity. The first is the beautiful edition of the Hymns printed and illustrated in the most perfect manner, and issued by John Murray in 1865. The second is probably the cheapest ever printed, being published by the Sunday School Association at the astonishingly small sum of threepence.

Mrs. Barbauld's name cannot be forgotten while large numbers of these little books are sold and read by young children, and her beautiful verses form a considerable part of our hymn-books, and are justly admired for the true devotion and elegance of style which they display; but one has no just idea of the varied and extensive powers of Mrs. Barbauld, and no thorough study can be made of her works and genius, without a collection of her writings. In forming this Selection I have endeavored to give the public the best of her writings, and as a rule have made use only of pieces of general interest, omitting the greater part of the poems written for particular occasions, and have not used any of her political pamphlets, fine as they are, or her sermons, which appeared after her death in the "Christian Reformer." The pamphlets are powerful productions, but the present interest in them would not justify their reprint; and the sermons are not suited to the plan and scope of this Selection, as they are of a purely religious and didactic style, and hardly interesting to the general reader.

I have placed among her poems several which are not to be found in Miss Aikin's collection. These I have taken from Dr. Aikin's "Collection of Songs," and as they are in no way inferior to her other poems, I insert them in the Poems. What the good taste of Dr. Aikin selected for his excellent book of songs should not be rejected. Ritson has placed some of them in his "Collection of English Songs," giving them an honorable mention.

I have placed among the Miscellaneous Pieces two Essays, one on "Prejudice," the other on "Education"; these first appeared in the "Monthly Magazine," and were much admired at the time. "The Misses," which I think is not known to many readers, was printed after Mrs. Barbauld's death in the juvenile "Forget-me-not" of 1830, a charming annual for children, edited by Mrs. S. C. Hall. This little allegory is the first piece in the "Forget-me-not," and is well entitled to a place of honor, even among the distinguished names which we find in the list of contributors.

It only remains for me to say that, though I feel assured there are many persons better qualified by years and experience to have written the "Life of Mrs. Barbauld," yet it has not been done, and this must be my excuse for assuming the responsibility of it. I believe it to be an honest piece of work, and I hope that care and fidelity may atone for the lack of brilliancy and exciting incidents in the records of a quiet life. As the worthy and quaint old Izaak Walton says, in speaking of his assuming the care of writing the "Life of George Herbert": — "*For these reasons I have undertaken it, and if I have prevented any abler person, I beg pardon of him and my reader.*"

GRACE ATKINSON ELLIS.

2 Commonwealth Avenue, Boston,
January, 1874.

CONTENTS.

CHAPTER I.

Page

Introduction. — Birth and Parentage. — Position of Dissenters. — Early Life. — Education. — Friends and Companions. — Classical Studies. — Love of Nature. — Poetical Taste and Imagination . 1 – 17

CHAPTER II.

Removal to Warrington. — Friends made there. — Mode of Life at the Academy. — Tutors and Scholars. — State of Learning in England at the Universities. — Address to Mrs. Priestley. — Visits Dr. and Mrs. Priestley at Leeds. — Poems written there. — Visits Mr. Turner at Wakefield . . . . 18 – 38

CHAPTER III.

Letters to Family and Friends. — John Aikin, M. D. — His Return to Warrington. — His Literary Productions. — Prepares his Sister's Poems for Publication. — Poems printed in 1773. — Address to the Corsicans. — Miscellaneous Pieces collected and published in 1773. — Remarks of Fox. — Criticism of Dr. Johnson on the Imitation of his Style. — Essay in the "Christian Reformer" . . . . 39 – 53

CHAPTER IV.

Marriage. — Mr. Barbauld's Parentage and Family. — Reply to Mrs. Montague and Others. — Mr. Barbauld settles at Palgrave. — They open a School in that Town. — Success of the Enterprise. — Mrs. Barbauld's Method of Instruction. — Dr. Sayers's Remembrance of the Lessons given by her. — William Taylor of Norwich, one of the

Scholars. — Letters to her Brother, with Account of the School, and her Interest in the Lessons and Amusements of the Boys . . 54–69

CHAPTER V.

Mrs. Barbauld's Letters. — Dr. Johnson's Description of her. — Publishes "Thoughts on the Devotional Taste." — London Society at that Period. — The Eminent Men and Women of the Time. — The Blue-Stocking Club. — Miss More's "Bas Bleu." — Miss More meets Mrs. Barbauld. — Mr. and Mrs. Barbauld offer to adopt one of Dr. Aikin's Children. — The Offer accepted. — "Early Lessons" written by Mrs. Barbauld for his Use. — Letters to Miss Dixon . .. 70–95

CHAPTER VI.

Mrs. Barbauld takes Charge of some Young Scholars. — Writes the "Prose Hymns." — Her Aim in writing them. — Visits London. — Letters to Dr. Aikin. — Visits Norwich. — Peculiarities of the old Town. — Letters to Miss More. — Miss More's Poem on "Sensibility." — Address to Mrs. Barbauld. — Dr. Aikin removes to Yarmouth. — Visit to London in the Christmas Holidays. — Meets many Friends there. — Joseph Johnson, her Publisher. — Miss Burney. — Letters 96–120

CHAPTER VII.

Mr. and Mrs. Barbauld relinquish their School. — They make a Continental Journey. — Letters written to the Family and Friends on this Journey. — Persons whose Acquaintance they make. — They meet John Howard. — Magnetism. — Manners and Customs. — Mode of Travelling 121–164

CHAPTER VIII.

The Barbaulds return to England. — They reside in London for a few Months. — Social Life there. — Removal to Hampstead. — Hampstead and its Inhabitants. — Mrs. Barbauld writes "Address to the Opposers of the Repeal of the Corporation and Test Acts." — Cause of the Act and Occasion for the Repeal. — Final Success of the Advocates of the Measures 165–187

CHAPTER IX.

Mrs. Barbauld's "Poetical Epistle" to William Wilberforce. — Horace Walpole's Remarks on Mrs. Barbauld. — Letters. — Dr. Johnson's Character — Mrs. Barbauld's "Reply" to Mr. Wakefield's Pamphlet on Worship. — She visits Scotland. — Various Impressions of the Highlands. — Mrs. Barbauld writes Essays on Akenside's "Pleasures of the Imagination," and on Collins's Odes. — Meets General Paoli. — Letters . . . . 188 - 211

CHAPTER X.

The Barbaulds visit Bristol. — They meet Dr. Beddoes. — His Character. — They visit Dorking. — Call on Madame D'Arblay. — Her Account of the Visit, and Impression of Mr. and Mrs. Barbauld. — Mr. Rogers's Anecdote of a Poem of Mrs. Barbauld. — Letter from Mrs. Barbauld to Miss More. — She forms a Friendship with the Edgeworths. — Miss Edgeworth's Account of it. — Mrs. Edgeworth's Description of Mr. and Mrs. Barbauld. — Sugar not used by the Opponents of the Slave-Trade. — Character of Dr. Priestley by Mrs. Barbauld. — Address to him by her. — Joanna Baillie. — Her Tragedies. — Dr. Aikin's Description of his Visit to Kibworth 212 - 236

CHAPTER XI.

Removal of the Barbaulds to Stoke Newington. — Cause of it. — Lines to Mrs. Barbauld by Dr. Aikin. — History of the Chapel. — Letters. — The Annual Review. — Mrs. Barbauld edits with Essay a "Selection." — Miss Aikin's Opinion about this Essay. — Diary of Mr. Robinson, and his Introduction to Mrs. Barbauld. — Wordsworth's Admiration of "Life." — His Remarks about Mrs. Barbauld. — Sir Henry Holland's Recollections of Newington Society and Mrs. Barbauld. — She writes the "Life of Richardson." — Anecdotes about it. — Miss Aikin's Letters. — Anecdotes. — Mr. Barbauld's Death. — His Character, by Mrs. Barbauld . . 237 - 264

CHAPTER XII.

Mrs. Barbauld edits "British Novelists." — Prepares a "Selection" for the Young, called "The Enfield Speaker." — Publishes Poem "Eighteen Hundred and Eleven." — Criticisms on this Poem. —

Style of it. — Mr. Robinson's Diary. — Letters. — Social Activity of Mrs. Barbauld. — She meets Scott at Dinner. — Mrs. Farrar's Recollections. — Mrs. Barbauld and Byron's Poem. — Miss Edgeworth's Visit. — Mr. Robinson's Picture of Mrs Barbauld. — Dr. Channing visits her. — Old Age and its Trials. — Loss of her old Friends. — Death of Dr. Aikin. — Mrs. Barbauld's cheerfulness and Patience. — Illness and Death. — Miss Aikin's Estimate of her Character. — Miss Edgeworth's Remarks. — Tablet to Mrs. Barbauld's Memory. — Anecdotes. — Mrs. Barbauld's Poetry. — Her Prose Works. — Her Position in English Literature. — Her Character. — Her Influence. — Her Personal Appearance. — The Justice of the Claims to Respect and Veneration her Life inspires . . 265 - 339

LIFE OF MRS. BARBAULD.

CHAPTER I.

INTRODUCTION. — BIRTH AND PARENTAGE. — POSITION OF DISSENTERS. — EARLY LIFE. — EDUCATION. — FRIENDS AND COMPANIONS. — CLASSICAL STUDIES. — LOVE OF NATURE. — POETICAL TASTE AND IMAGINATION.

IN offering this biography to the public, I feel the difficulty of my self-imposed task, which has become, with the performance of it, a pleasure. I hope that the purpose to place before the present generation the character and the just claims to veneration and respect which the life of Mrs. Barbauld must inspire, may not be wholly unsuccessful; that her noble qualities of mind and heart, her high culture and poetic genius, her pure and simple course of life, may impress themselves upon the reader better than any words of mine can do. Miss Aikin's Memoir of her, from which I have quoted somewhat, appeared in the edition of Mrs. Barbauld's Works published in London in 1825. It is a brief, comprehensive, and very limited sketch of her aunt's life and writings. What she wrote was couched in elegant language, and the criticism is very discriminating and impartial; but she had not the space proper for such an undertaking, and time has given us many more facts of interest connected with Mrs. Barbauld. Many of her contemporaries have left their remembrances and records, and there is much to be gleaned from them of value to the reader of the present day. The biographer of Miss Lucy Aikin herself tells us of her Life of Mrs. Barbauld, and that of her father, John Aikin, M. D.: "Both may be regarded as works of filial piety, for her aunt shared with her father in the reverence and affection with which she regarded the union of virtue and talent. The cast of her own mind fitted her better for sympathizing with the strong practical sense, the liberal views, and the literary diligence of her father, than with the sensibility and poetical elegance of her aunt." Undoubtedly the biographer of Miss Aikin was better able to judge of the cast of her mind than I am, and perhaps the task was not congenial to her, but, at all events, it is more correctly elegant than warm and personal in its nature; but sixty pages of large type were devoted to the Memoir and critical remarks on the Works, while one fair-sized volume was given by her to the life of Dr. Aikin.

Mrs. Barbauld's fame justifies and demands, therefore, more of an extended study of her life and writings than has yet been given them; and, without encroaching on the sacred privacy of a family, it seems as if, with the new materials now at hand, a pleasant and instructive Memoir may be produced.

I have used the letters which were first published in the second volume apart from Miss Aikin's Memoir, and placed them in their proper order in the Life. This gives them an interest which their own merit should claim for them; but in fact they need illustration by and impart an additional value to the biographical sketch of her career. I am able to add to them two which I have found in an early Memoir of Miss Hannah More, and which I think valuable, and worthy of being placed among the others, as showing in a marked degree the enlightened and liberal religious views and sentiments of their writer, and the warm friendship existing between herself and Miss More. Also I insert a brief note to Mr. Wedgwood, which was found among his papers by Miss Meteyard; this gives us a little glimpse of the domestic life of the author, and its cares. There are some extracts from her correspondence which are not very numerous, and make us wish for more; it is to be hoped that time will bring to light, among other good things, more of Miss Barbauld's letters, and particularly those from her to her friend Miss Edgeworth, with whom she corresponded for many years, whose memory is so widely respected as an author, and who would be deeply loved for herself, could she be more known in her private character.

A well-sustained and truthful sketch of the life, character, and writings of an elevated mind, a high-toned and gifted person, is no easy task; and it becomes doubly hard when the materials are rather scanty, the incidents few, and the life was passed quietly amidst the duties and trials of a private and secluded home. The life of Mrs. Barbauld was long, full of days and honor, not without its trials; she bore her part and performed her life work with an admirable and perfect simplicity of purpose. Her character is very beautiful as studied from her own expressions and writings; her poems and prose works are full of the best and purest thought; and her life was a perfectly rounded circle of duties well done, sorrows borne with Christian fortitude, human sympathies and warm affection shown to her family and friends. In the course of her long career she was the friend and intimate of three generations of persons eminent in literature and science, and distinguished for originality of mind, vigor of thought, and power of expression. Her early youth was passed among an unusually intelligent and cultivated group of people. The celebrated Dr. Doddridge was for many years an inmate of her grandfather's house. Her father, John Aikin, D. D., his assistant for a time, was one of the most eminent and learned Dissenting clergymen of his generation. Influenced in her youth by such men, she met in her early womanhood and formed a life-long friendship with Mr.—afterwards Dr.—Joseph Priestley and his wife; and her residence at Warrington, then the seat of the Academy, was in the society of a little community of scholarly and refined men and women, who stimulated her mind, already replete with knowledge, and carefully trained by a fine classical education, to its first indications of genius and expressions of enlarged thought. In her full maturity of mind she met and held converse, more or less intimately, with many of Great Britain's most brilliant thinkers, great writers, and discoverers. Among these contemporaries, the men and women of her day, friends and acquaintances, may be numbered Dr. Priestley; John Howard, the great philanthropist; Dugald Stewart, the eminent Scotch metaphysician; Sir Walter Scott; Miss Hannah More; Mrs. Elizabeth Montague; Madame D'Arblay; Roscoe, the historian and banker; Miss Joanna Baillie; Sir James Mackintosh; Coleridge; Charles Lamb; Wordsworth; Rogers, the banker-poet; Miss Maria Edgeworth. Many more great names might be added. Henry Crabb Robinson was one of her great admirers, and justly enthusiastic in his warm expressions of friendship. To him, and others who knew her, we owe little reminiscences of the charms of her conversation, her fine personal appearance, and the womanly virtues and sweetness of character which were so truly her greatest attraction, notwithstanding her high literary reputation and just claims to respect as an author.

Mrs. Barbauld's life was not like that of a gifted man whose statue bears a brief inscription to this effect, — "Too short for friendship, not for fame"; hers was an active and busy one, and she left the impress of her thought and best efforts on many young minds at a most sensitive and receptive age. With genius and powers of mind uncommon in her sex, cultivation of the highest order, womanly charms and accomplishments which fitted her for the most brilliant society and the highest walks of literature, what Dr. Johnson has stated in his observations on the character and writings of Dr. Watts is not less true of her, — that she "condescended for children to lay aside the scholar, the philosopher, and the wit, and to write little poems of devotion and systems of instruction adapted to their wants and capacities, from the dawn of reason through its gradations of advance in the morning of life." Her very remarkable capacity as a writer for children of the most charming prose hymns ever produced at any time has almost obscured her other manifestations of genius as one of England's ablest minds, and an ornament to her sex and age. Whether she is considered as a powerful prose writer on various subjects which received broad and liberal treatment in clear and beautiful English from her able mind; as a sweet singer of the ever-changing and many aspects of life which drew from her, in turn, true pathos, sweet and pure sentiment, inspiring and elevating verse, devotional songs of the highest strain of worship; or as a writer of the fascinating and simply unsurpassed hymns for children, — she merits our respectful admiration and honest emulation as one who used her talents, and did a high and noble work in her day.

Anna Lætitia Aikin, the subject of this sketch, was born in the obscure little village of Kibworth Harcourt, in Leicestershire, England, June 20, 1743. She was the eldest child and only daughter of her parents, John Aikin, D. D., and his wife Jane, who was a daughter of the Rev. John Jennings, of Kibworth. Her father was the son of a Scotchman who was settled in London as a shopkeeper. He had originally been destined for a business life, and had been for some time a French clerk in a city counting-house, where his health was affected by the confinement and the air of London. He was therefore sent into the country for his health, and placed "for a time with Dr. Doddridge, who succeeded Dr. Jennings in his academy at Kibworth, and removed it later to Northampton." Feeling a strong inclination for the life of a scholar, he sought and obtained his father's consent to his giving up a business career, and began to prepare himself for the ministry. After he had completed his studies at the University of Aberdeen, he became Dr. Doddridge's assistant in his academy at Northampton. Soon after his acceptance of this position he was chosen by a Dissenting congregation at Leicester to be their minister; but, when entering on his new position, a lung disease attacked him, rendering his performance of the duties he had assumed impossible, and he was forced to abandon all thoughts of preaching. He was obliged by his complaint to resign his future prospects in his chosen work, and, being without advancement, became a teacher for life. After being for a short time in partnership with a Mr. Lee, who kept a school for boys, he married Miss Jennings, and opened a school of his own at Kibworth, which soon became well known and very successful. Gilbert Wakefield, who afterwards had an intimate knowledge of the mind and thoughts of Dr. Aikin at Warrington, said of him, "He was a gentleman whose endowments as a man and as a scholar it is not easy to exaggerate by panegyric; . . . . his intellectual attainments were of a very superior quality indeed. His acquaintance with all true evidences of revelation, with morals, politics, and metaphysics, was most accurate and extensive. Every path of polite literature had been traversed by him, and traversed with success. He understood the Hebrew and French languages to perfection, and had an intimacy with the best authors of

Greece and Rome, superior to what I have ever known in any Dissenting minister from my own experience."

Macaulay, in his History, refers to the position of the Dissenting clergy, and their comparatively independent circumstances after the accession of William and Mary. The agitation about the passage of the Comprehension Bill and the repeal of the Test Acts causes him to speak of the opposition and failure of these measures, and why they did not pass. He says: "Even those Presbyterian ministers whose scruples the Comprehension Bill was expressly intended to remove were by no means unanimous in wishing it to pass. The ablest and most eloquent preachers among them had, since the Declaration of Indulgence had appeared, been very agreeably settled in the capital and other large towns, and were now about to enjoy, under the sure guaranty of an Act of Parliament, that toleration which under the Declaration of Indulgence had been illicit and precarious. The situation of these men was such as the great majority of the divines of the Established Church might well envy. Few, indeed, of the parochial clergy were so abundantly supplied with comforts as the favorite orator of a great assembly of nonconformists in the city. The voluntary contributions of his wealthy hearers, aldermen and deputies, West India merchants and Turkey merchants, wardens of the Company of Fishmongers, and wardens of the Company of Goldsmiths, enabled him to become a land-owner or a mortgagee. The best broadcloth from Blackwell Hall and the best poultry from Leadenhall Market were frequently left at his door. His influence over his flock was immense. Scarcely any member of a congregation of Separatists entered into a partnership, married a daughter, put a son out as apprentice, or gave his vote at an election, without consulting his spiritual guide. On all political and literary questions the minister was the oracle of his own circle. It was popularly remarked, during many years, that an eminent Dissenting minister had only to make his son an attorney or physician; that the attorney was sure to have clients, and the physician to have patients. While a waiting-woman was generally considered as a helpmeet for a chaplain in holy orders of the Established Church, the widows and daughters of opulent citizens were supposed to belong in a peculiar manner to nonconformist pastors. One of the great Presbyterian rabbies, therefore, might well doubt whether, in a worldly view, he should be benefited by a comprehension. He might indeed hold a rectory or a vicarage, when he could get one. But in the mean time he would be destitute; his meeting-house would be closed; his congregation would be dispersed among the parish churches; if a benefice were bestowed on him, it would probably be a very slender compensation for the income which he had lost. Nor could he hope to have, as a minister of the Anglican Church, the authority and dignity which he had hitherto enjoyed. He would always, by a large portion of the members of that church, be regarded as a deserter. He might, therefore, on the whole, very naturally wish to be left where he was." In Brown's "Amusements, Serious and Comical," he treats the Presbyterian divines very abusively; of their preaching he says that it "brings in money, and money buys land; and land is an amusement they all desire, in spite of their hypocritical cant. If it were not for the quarterly contributions, there would be no longer schism or separation." He asks how it can be imagined that, while "they are maintained like gentlemen by the breach, they will ever preach up healing doctrines." Hawkins, in his Life of Dr. Johnson, relates some curious instances of the influence exercised by the popular Dissenting ministers. Addison, in a paper in the Spectator, "The Journal of the Retired Citizen," has indulged in some exquisite pleasantry on this subject. "The Mr. Nisby whose opinions about the peace, the Grand Vizier, and laced coffee, are quoted with so much respect, and who is so well regaled with marrow-bones, ox-cheek, and a bottle of Brook's and Hellier, was John Nesbit, a highly popular preacher, who about the time of the Revolution became pastor of a Dissenting congregation in Hare Court, Aldersgate Street." The quotations and anecdotes might be multiplied to prove the superiority and worldly advantages of the lot of Dissenting clergymen; but, whatever their condition may have been for a time, and in the great metropolis among the city merchants, the salaries and emoluments of the preachers of the sect, and their worldly position, were far from being so enviable as Macaulay would have his reader believe, at the time of which we read. Dissent was, and always has been, unfashionable, and confined to the middle classes in England. Respectability and industry, wealth and influence, were not wanting in their ranks; but, as a rule, the Dissenters were of the middle class, and their various disabilities under the law kept them from aspiring to rank and honor, which they could not conscientiously receive and enjoy. The position of Miss Aikin, therefore, was bounded by certain arbitrary customs, and she inherited a condition which gave her "neither poverty nor riches," as the daughter of a Dissenting clergyman whose health obliged him to resign his only chance for wealth.

Miss Aikin was descended, on her mother's side, from an ancient and respectable family, the Wingates of Bedfordshire. She showed at a very early age an extraordinary capacity for learning, and great mental powers. Her mother wrote of her in a letter which still exists: "I once, indeed, knew a little girl, who was as eager to learn as her instructors could be to teach her, and who, at two years old, could read sentences and little stories in her *wise* book roundly, without spelling, and in half a year more could read as well as most women; but I never knew such another, and, I believe, never shall." The good lady was quite distressed, in later years, that she could not make her granddaughter, Miss Lucy Aikin, learn as readily, and seems to have left a lasting impression of her sternness on the child, who in her Reminiscences laments the difference between her aunt's early development and her own; she says that Mrs. Barbauld "could read with ease before she was twenty months old." This very unusual display of mental strength and precocious genius did not at all exhaust her intellect, and we find her pursuing a classical education with great interest and avidity. Mrs. Cappe, in her valuable Memoir of her excellent husband, relates that Mr. Cappe passed the year 1748, previous to entering as a student under Dr. Doddridge, with Dr. Aikin, receiving from him preparatory instruction; and while an inmate of his family he had great pleasure in observing many early indications of his daughter's talent. His attention was attracted by the child, then but five years of age. One day as the Doctor and he were conversing on the passions, the former observed that joy, accurately defined, cannot have place in a state of perfect felicity, since it supposes an accession of happiness. "I think you are mistaken, papa," said a little voice from the opposite side of the table. "Why so, Lætitia?" "Because in the chapter I read to you this morning in the Testament it is said, there is more joy in heaven over one sinner that repenteth, than over ninety and nine just persons that need no repentance." This appears to have brought the worthy Doctor's definitions to a termination for the time. Her excellent mother personally instructed her in all the domestic branches of a woman's education, and made her a proficient in the household arts, in which too often women without literary tastes for compensation and those gifted mentally are alike singularly deficient.

Her studies were pursued under the parental roof entirely, and she enjoyed peculiar advantages from the care of cultivated parents, and their refined and elevating influence. But, while fortunate in her surroundings in these respects, she was almost without companions of her own age. At the time when the young and light-hearted are allowed and encouraged to mingle with friends and playfellows, she was quite alone, without any suitable associates of her own age, sex, and position. The small village of Kibworth afforded so little society for her that she was thrown upon her own resources for occupation and amusement. Her brother John was three years younger than herself, so that she was brought up among people of mature years, which tended to give her mind a more serious cast than was natural, or perhaps desirable. In after life she often referred her want of ease and a feeling of constraint in society to this cause, and probably with good reason. Her mother was unusually strict in her oversight of her, that her daughter might not become too masculine in her tastes, left as she was almost entirely to her for female companionship in the large academy for boys, of which her father was the master. Being a woman of keen perceptions and good understanding, she saw, undoubtedly, the strong and almost masculine mind of her daughter, and wished to temper judiciously the powerful traits of character and understanding she displayed with feminine graces and accomplishments, thus making her in after life the noble specimen of womanly perfection which she was. The very loneliness and restraint of these early years had a marked effect in strengthening and developing her mind, and concentrating in an unusual degree her thought and power of expressing herself. Wordsworth speaks of the inward eye,

> "Which is the bliss of solitude";

and like all true poets, thinkers, and lovers of nature, she found

> "Tongues in trees, books in the running brooks,
> Sermons in stones, and good in everything."

Nature inspired her, and, born with the heart of a poet,

she drew pleasure and the keenest enjoyment from the observation and study of the simple, yet ever-varying, face of that great world of beauty which unrolls before us all its vast and boundless pages for those who love it.

Miss Aikin says of her aunt's life at this time: "Her recollections of childhood and youth were, in fact, not associated with much of the pleasure and gayety usually attendant upon that period of life; but it must be regarded as a circumstance favorable, rather than otherwise, to the unfolding of her genius, to have been thus left to find or make in solitude her own objects of interest and pursuit. The love of rural nature sank deep into her heart; her vivid fancy exerted itself to color, to animate, and to diversify all the objects which surrounded her; the few but choice authors of her father's library, which she read and reread, had leisure to make their full impression, — to mould her sentiments, and to form her taste; the spirit of devotion, early inculcated upon her as a duty, opened to her by degrees an exhaustless source of tender and sublime delight; and while yet a child she was surprised to find herself a poet." Among her other advantages for self-improvement, she enjoyed one rather peculiar for a woman, — an excellent classical education, very rare at that day, when a strong prejudice almost prevented women from gaining any thorough knowledge of the learning of the ancients, and in most cases confined them to the simplest rudiments of the English branches. Grand exceptions, of course, there were to this rule, as the career of Mrs. Barbauld and many of her sister authors proves; but as a predominant condition the education of women was very poor at that time in England. Her father was justly proud of her mental activity, breadth of thought, and industry, and at last yielded his own unwillingness to teach her what he considered the unfeminine branches of knowledge, because of her great wish to learn. Under his good instruction she became proficient in the Latin, French, and Italian languages, and made some progress in the study of the Greek authors. She was early a thorough student and admirer of the writers of the best and most vigorous English, and her own works indicate plainly her love and careful reading of these classic models. She was not afraid to express what she strongly felt, the truest admiration for Addison and others of the so-called Augustan Age of English literature; and to the influence of these great minds we trace her fine style, her classic and powerful language, her early development of poetic talent, and her eloquent, forcible prose. Her mind was naturally well balanced and strong, her views liberal, her fancy keen; native wit and animation also threw their charm over her work; but her taste was formed, and her mental grasp enlarged by the judicious studies of her childhood and youth.

CHAPTER II.

REMOVAL TO WARRINGTON. — FRIENDS MADE THERE. — MODE OF LIFE AT THE ACADEMY. — TUTORS AND SCHOLARS. — STATE OF LEARNING IN ENGLAND AT THE UNIVERSITIES. — ADDRESS TO MRS. PRIESTLEY. — VISITS DR. AND MRS. PRIESTLEY AT LEEDS. — POEMS WRITTEN THERE. — VISITS MR. TURNER AT WAKEFIELD.

SO passed the earlier years of Miss Aikin; and, happily for her, when longer seclusion and quiet might have depressed her naturally good spirits, and injured the brightness of her fancy, wit, and vivacity of thought, she was removed to a more animated scene, congenial with her social and literary tastes. By the invitation of the trustees of the Dissenting Academy at Warrington, her father assumed the position of classical tutor at that Institution. This change of residence and society happened when his daughter was fifteen years of age, and the next fifteen years of her life were mostly passed in that town. The Academy numbered among its trustees, tutors, and scholars, names celebrated in literature, art, and the sciences. Lord Willoughby of Parham was for a time, as representative of one of the oldest Presbyterian families in the kingdom, president of its board of trustees. Here Priestley, addressed later on as "Patriot, and Saint, and Sage" by Coleridge, first displayed his great mental endowments, and engaged in a variety of publications of his observations and researches, which announced to the world the extent and originality of his thought and varied accomplishments.

As one of those intimately connected with Miss Aikin at this period of their lives, and always the object of her affectionate and respectful admiration, a brief sketch of Dr. Priestley may not be misplaced here. Born in an obscure village, near Leeds, where his father was a small woollen-cloth manufacturer, Joseph Priestley was precluded by the very moderate circumstances of his parents from receiving a thorough education, but was enabled to fit himself fairly for the position of a Dissenting clergyman. His active mind and powerful grasp of thought soon carried him into an extended course of study, and he began while at Warrington to show the wonderful scope and breadth of intellect he possessed. In 1767 he left Warrington to fill the pulpit of a chapel at Leeds; and the chemical researches he there began were of the utmost importance and value, laying the basis of all after discoveries in the chemical properties of gases, and the foundation of that branch of the science known as pneumatic chemistry. To him the world is indebted for the discovery and analysis of a number of the gases now known. He had an extraordinary versatility of mind, and the most intense love of truth in all its manifestations, natural or moral. Whether he is viewed as a pneumatic chemist, a theologian, an electrician, an historian, or a politician, his writings show him as an ardent lover of the great and beautiful in nature and mankind. He became the subject of sharp persecution for his sympathy with the earlier manifestations of the French Revolution, which could not have been the result of anything but the lowest prejudices and party spirit; and the ill-treatment he received, the actual violence with which his property was utterly destroyed at the Birmingham riot, when he with his family were forced to flee for their lives, at last drove him to America, where he died in 1804.

The elder Dr. Aikin was at first the classical tutor, and later filled the theological chair at the Academy, after the death of its able and excellent incumbent, Dr. John Taylor of Norwich, — a man widely known and respected for his piety and learning. Gilbert Wakefield, a learned and able scholar and critic, well known as the translator of Lucretius, was tutor after Dr. Priestley left, in his place. He was graduated at Jesus College, Cambridge, and ordained as a deacon in the Established Church. Feeling conscientious scruples, he became a Dissenter, greatly to his own loss in a worldly point of view. He wrote and published some very bold and offensively radical pamphlets, and, finally, a "Reply to some Parts of the Bishop of Landaff's Address" drew upon him the charge of sedition. He was arrested, and imprisoned for two years; his publisher also being punished for printing a seditious work. This treatment he did not long survive, his health being affected by the confinement. He fell a victim to fever soon after his release. Dr. Enfield, a warm friend of the younger Dr. Aikin, by him addressed, —

> "O friend, to whose clear sight the mystic roll
> Of wisdom lies displayed, —"

was another of the able and scholarly men who made the Academy the seat of such learning and repute as it enjoyed for a time. It numbered among its scholars the political economist Malthus, Dr. Estlin of Bristol, "a learned scholar and divine," the Martineaus and Taylors of Norwich, John Wedgwood of Etruria, son of the great potter, and afterwards one himself, Dr. Percival of Manchester, Dr. Farr, the translator of Hippocrates, and John Aikin, M. D., who were among those pupils of the establishment that made themselves distinguished by their talents and learning in the walks of literature.

Warrington is one of the oldest towns in Lancashire, and was originally a Roman station. It is situated on the north bank of the Mersey. Miss Aikin, in her poem, "The Invitation," addressed to a friend, has described so well and fully the surrounding objects of beauty, and her love of the place, that I need only say it is at the present time very much the same in its general aspect as she saw it more than a hundred years ago, with the exception of a large town which has grown up round the Warrington Junction of the North-western Railroad, that runs near the old town. The old town remains much as it was, and is rather a sleepy, dull place. During the civil wars Warrington was the scene of two severe conflicts. From the press of this town the first newspaper in the county was issued, and it also boasted that the first stage-coach in the country was started from it. John Howard's work on Prisons was printed at the Warrington Press, as were also the most of Miss Aikin's earlier works, the first writings of Thomas Roscoe, the works of Dr. Ferrier, Gibson, and others. In 1757 an academy was established there, which rapidly rose into celebrity under the able direction and care of the tutors whose names have been mentioned, and others. The Academy was broken up in the year 1786, and from its ruins a college was started at York, then removed to Manchester, and now has several branches, of which that in London is one,—the Manchester New College. This institution is in Gordon Square, London, and is presided over by the Rev. James Martineau, D. D., known as one of the ablest thinkers and brilliant and powerful writers of the present time, who holds the office of

Principal, filling likewise the professorship of Philosophy. The chair of Hebrew language and literature is ably filled by his son, Professor Russell Martineau, who follows in the footsteps of his father, and will sustain the family reputation for scholarship and learning.

From the Transactions of the Historical Society of Cheshire and Lancashire I take some interesting facts about this Academy, with which Miss Aikin was identified in early life, and which she celebrated in the following lines, testifying her genuine love for and interest in the place,—

> "Mark where its simple front yon mansion rears,
> The nursery of men for future years."

These are taken from her poem describing Warrington, and inviting her friend to visit her, of which I have just spoken. The buildings were "simple" indeed, even poor; and the real strength of the Academy lay, not in the beauty of the architecture nor the extent of the buildings, but in the able, self-denying, and devoted tutors. Mr. Seddon, the originator of it, "did not scruple some stout puffing" on its behalf. Mrs. Barbauld, after her marriage and settlement at Palgrave, receiving one of his official statements, wrote to her brother, Dr. Aikin, then residing at Warrington, in the practice of his profession, "Who hath believed our report?" The Academy was in existence twenty-nine years, but the management and discipline exercised by the tutors not being equal to their instruction, the Presbyterians, who had taken an active and important part in its origin and maintenance, fell off, not being satisfied with the way the affairs of the institution were administered. New buildings were contracted for and built without proper means of meeting the debt thus assumed, and this was another unfortunate and ill-judged arrangement bringing trouble with it. The debt was finally paid by subscriptions raised by the friends of the Academy; and among them we find the name of Josiah Wedgwood of Etruria, whose son John had entered there as a student in 1782–83. Reform in other directions, for various reasons, appears to have been considered, after many efforts, an impossibility, and the close of the midsummer session of 1786 saw also the termination of the Warrington Academy. Mrs. Barbauld wrote of the new buildings, when she addressed Dr. Enfield on his revisiting Warrington in 1789, when she says, —

> "Lo there the seats where science loved to dwell,
> Where Liberty her ardent spirit breathed."

Dr. Priestley, in his own Memoir, alludes to his residence at Warrington, and says of it: "I was singularly happy there in the society of my fellow-tutors, and of Mr. Seddon, the minister of the place. We drank tea together every Saturday, and our conversation was equally instructive and pleasing. I often thought it not a little extraordinary, that four persons who had no previous knowledge of each other should have been brought to unite in conducting such a scheme as this, all being zealous Necessarians as we were." Again he writes of his life there: "Though all the tutors in my time lived together in the most perfect harmony, though we all exerted ourselves to the utmost, and there was no complaint of want of discipline, the Academy did not flourish." And he appears to have cherished most happy recollections of this peaceful circle and the quiet life he enjoyed there. Dr. Aikin was succeeded by Dr. Priestley in his tutorship of *Belles-Lettres* and the classics, when he took the chair of theology made vacant by the death of Dr. Taylor. Mr. Seddon, the minister of the town, was also the tutor of *Belles-Lettres* for a time, and resident manager of the establishment under the title of *Rector Academiæ.* He was succeeded in his office, at his death, by Dr. Enfield. Mr. Seddon, in writing to Dr. Aikin in regard to his removal from Kibworth to Warrington, after his appointment there, gives a curious passage in his letter, which shows how very difficult and disagreeable travelling was in England a hundred years and more since.

Mr. Seddon's letter is dated March 11, 1758. "Mr. Holland has given us some reason to hope that you will come over to Warrington in the Easter week, in order to take a view of your future situation; if so, give me leave to recommend the following plan. I'll suppose you set out from Kibworth on Sunday afternoon; as you intend travelling by post-chaises, you 'll easily reach Loughborough, or perhaps Derby, that night; the next night you may come to Offerton, which is about a mile short of Stockport, where I am with Mrs. Seddon, and will be ready to receive you, and wait upon you to Warrington; you will do well to come prepared for riding, for you will not meet with any carriages at Stockport, nor are the roads to Warrington proper for them; when you get to a place called Bullock's Smithy, about two miles short of Stockport, inquire for Offerton. Mr. Roe, late of Birmingham, now lives there, and we shall be glad to see you. If you 'll write to me time enough, and be particular enough in your time, I will endeavor to meet you with my own chaise, or send a servant for that purpose."

All these elaborate preparations for comfort in so short a journey show how very difficult and tedious travelling was at that period; and when it is considered that the approach to Warrington, the seat of a large academy, was by a road too bad for carriages, one realizes something of the discomfort involved.

The society at Warrington was enlivened and adorned by a number of brilliant and accomplished ladies, among whom Miss Aikin shone and was warmly loved. Miss

Lucy Aikin says of her aunt at this time: "The fifteen succeeding years passed by her at Warrington comprehended probably the happiest, as well as the most brilliant, portion of her existence. She was at this time possessed of great beauty, distinct traces of which she retained to the latest period of life. Her person was slender, her complexion exquisitely fair, with the bloom of perfect health; her features were regular and elegant, and her dark blue eyes beamed with the light of wit and fancy."

"A solitary education," says the same authority, "had not produced on her its most frequent ill effects, pride and self-importance; the reserve of her manners proceeded solely from bashfulness, for her temper inclined her strongly to friendship and social pleasures, and her active imagination, which represented all objects tinged with hues 'unborrowed of the sun,' served as a charm against that disgust with common characters and daily incidents which so frequently renders the conscious possessor of superior talents at once unamiable and unhappy." Her warmest attachment seems to have been placed in Mrs. Priestley, whom Dr. Priestley had married in 1762. He describes her in his Memoirs as "a woman of an excellent understanding, much improved by reading; of great fortitude and strength of mind; and of a temper in the highest degree affectionate and generous, feeling strongly for others and little for herself." Miss Aikin passed much time with this superior and cultivated woman; she wrote to her and of her, —

"Oft the well-worn path to her abode
At early dawn with eager steps I've trode
And with unwilling feet returned at eve,
Loath its approach unheeded to believe.
No cold reserve, suspicion, silent care,
Or dark, unfriendly passions enter there;
But pleasing fires of lively Fancy play,
And Wisdom mingles her serener ray!"

The "Address" to Mrs. Priestley, of which these lines form only a small part, was never published, and they are taken from the manuscript poem which was thrown into the chaise at the time Dr. and Mrs. Priestley left Warrington for Leeds in 1767. This is believed to be her earliest poetical work, at least of any importance or length. Miss Lucy Aikin, in one of her letters to a friend long afterwards, in speaking of Warrington and its society, says, "Both *bout rimés* and *vers de société* were in fashion with the set. Once it was their custom to slip anonymous pieces into Mrs. Priestley's work-bag. One copy of verses, a very eloquent one, puzzled all guessers for a long time; at length it was traced to Dr. Priestley's self. Somebody was bold enough to talk of getting up private theatricals. This was a dreadful business. All the wise and grave, the whole tutorhood, cried out, It must not be! All the students, the Rigbys, and, I must add, my aunt, took the prohibition very sulkily; and my aunt's 'Ode to Wisdom' was the result." In one of Mrs. Barbauld's letters to her friend Miss Belsham, she herself alludes to the gayety and brightness of the little circle, and wishes her there to make one of their merry group. The elder students and the young ladies met in a pleasant and social way, which gave life and animation to the place. She writes, "We have a knot of lasses just after your own heart,— as merry, blithe, and gay as you would wish them, and very smart and clever; two of them are the Miss Rigbys."

Simplicity of life and manners, combined with intellectual pursuits and tastes, made Warrington during this period a charming residence for one of Miss Aikin's genius and love of literature and society. Though struggling with poverty and the annoyance attendant on straitened means, the tutors were men of learning, refinement, and good reputation, and the students were young men of good families and position, and while they were inmates of the tutors' houses behaved in a quiet and dignified manner. Miss Lucy Aikin wrote in another letter: "I have often thought with envy of that society. Neither Oxford nor Cambridge could boast of brighter names in literature or science than several of these Dissenting tutors,—humbly content, in an obscure town, and on a scanty pittance, to cultivate in themselves and communicate to a rising generation those mental acquirements and moral habits which are their own exceeding great reward. They and theirs lived together like one large family, and in the facility of their intercourse they found large compensation for its deficiency in luxury and splendor."

Gibbon in his Autobiography gives a picture of the state of learning and the want of discipline at Oxford, which makes one question whether much more cannot be said for the industrious and worthy tutors at Warrington. He writes of his life at Magdalen College: "I spent fourteen months at Magdalen College; they proved the fourteen months the most idle and unprofitable of my whole life; the reader will pronounce between the school and the scholar, but I cannot affect to believe that Nature had disqualified me for all literary pursuits." And in confirmation of the singular want of supervision and instruction he received, the historian quotes another great authority, Dr. Adam Smith, who states that in the University of Oxford the greater part of the public professors have for these many years given up altogether even the pretence of teaching. "Incredible as the fact may appear, I must rest my belief on the positive and impartial evidence of a master of moral and political wisdom, who had himself resided at Oxford." Gibbon adds, "Of the state of discipline occasioned by the position of the

Oxford professors, who are secure in the enjoyment of a fixed stipend, without the necessity of labor or the apprehension of control . . . . Dr. —— well remembered that he had a salary to receive, and only forgot that he had a duty to perform. Instead of guiding the studies and watching over the behavior of his disciple, I was never summoned to attend even the ceremony of a lecture; and, excepting one voluntary visit to his rooms during the eight months of his titular office, the tutor and his pupil lived in the same college as strangers to each other." When it is remembered that Gibbon was even in early youth an intense lover of learning, and yet that "the want of experience, of advice, and of occupation, soon betrayed me into some improprieties of conduct, ill-chosen company, late hours, and inconsiderate expense, — a tour to Bath, a visit into Buckinghamshire, and four excursions to London in the same winter," what must be thought of the state of the University? and how did the boys who did not love learning, and aspire to classical study and composition as Gibbon did in the midst of these wild and lawless frolics, conduct themselves? The pupils of Warrington Academy, being in a large house by themselves, and no longer under the care of the different tutors, with whom they previously boarded, were much more at liberty, and many unpleasant practical jokes were the consequence; some being of such a nature as to bring discredit to the establishment, and seriously injure its reputation for order and quiet.

The West Indian scholars shocked the tutors by their lawlessness, violence, and Southern habits of indolence; they were wont to bewail their native islands, and declare that the earliest request of a planter's child was for "a young nigger to kick." This set was very unruly, and in time broke up the Academy by their insolence and insubordination. Archibald Hamilton Rowan, afterwards the notorious Irish rebel, was one of the students at the Academy. It was in his defence that Curran made his famous eulogium of the British law in these words: "The law which proclaims even to the stranger and the sojourner, the moment he sets his foot on British earth, that the ground he treads is holy, and consecrated by the genius of universal emancipation." His biographer says that, while being rusticated for misconduct at the University, he was sent to Warrington; and in after years he had been heard to say, "that Lætitia Aikin, afterwards Mrs. Barbauld, was his first love. A declaration indicative of his taste and discrimination; for in mental and personal accomplishments few, if any, could vie with that excellent lady."

She appears to have been much admired, and justly so, by all who knew her, even in the morning of life, when with most minds that early period is devoted to trifles "light as air," which may amuse, but can hardly be the incentive of admiration. She was gifted with great personal and mental charms, an unusual and rare union of strength, elegance and versatility of mind, and wit and fancy in conversation and writing. Her beauty of face and figure gave her an added attraction for those who were so happy as to have her personal acquaintance. She had a remarkable facility and taste for taking silhouette portraits, and took the students, tutors, her family and friends, in this style. Many of these likenesses are still preserved by her family. There is a very affectionate "Address" to her brother, on his removing from Warrington to pursue his medical studies at Aberdeen; this is in manuscript, now in possession of her family, and was accompanied by three profiles of her father, mother, and herself.

The lines addressed by Miss Aikin to Mrs. Priestley, from which I have quoted, were followed by many more, and some of her finest poems were written during her life at Warrington. In 1769, Miss Aikin visited Dr. and Mrs. Priestley at Leeds, and with them and other friends in the neighborhood passed the larger part of that summer. During this visit she wrote many beautiful poems, several of them being suggested by incidents which occurred to call them forth and rouse her fancy. "The Mouse's Petition," which is a well-known and favorite production of its author, owed its origin to the following circumstances, which may interest the reader. The story is well related by Mr. William Turner, in a brief contemporaneous notice of Mrs. Barbauld at the time of her death. I use his words: "Dr. Priestley, from the vicinity of his residence to a large brewery, had been led to notice the suffocating vapor which is extricated in the process of fermentation (now so well known as the carbonic acid gas, but then denominated by Dr. Black fixed air, and by Dr. Rutherford nephitic air); this circumstance, happily for science, further led him to that train of discoveries which gave rise to pneumatic chemistry, and immortalized his name among philosophers. In the midst of these investigations Miss Aikin found him. He was then, as he says in his letter to Gibbon he afterwards continued to be at Birmingham, *totus in illis.* In the course of these investigations the suffocating nature of various gases required to be determined, and no more easy or unexceptionable way of making such experiments could be devised, than the reserving of these little victims of domestic economy, which were thus at least as easily and as speedily put out of existence as by any of the more usual modes. It happened that a captive was brought in after supper, too late for any experiment to be made with it that night, and the servant was desired to set it by till the next morning. Next morning it was brought in after breakfast, with its petition twisted among the wires of its cage." We need hardly add that the poetical genius of the mouse prevailed, and in virtue of its kind friend's petition it was set free, perhaps to learn wisdom and shun traps.

Dr. Priestley wrote in his Memoirs: "Mrs. Barbauld has told me that it was the perusal of some verses of mine that first induced her to write anything in verse; so that this country is in some measure indebted to me for one of the best poets it can boast. Several of her first poems were written while she was in my house, on occasions that occurred while she was there." This *jeu d'esprit* will connect her with the great student of pneumatic chemistry as a friend, and indicates the tenderness of her feeling and fancy. But there were higher flights of imagination and poetry, and nobler themes for her vivid perception of the sublime and beautiful, and one of these gave rise to her beautiful poem, "The Address to the Deity." This was probably one of those which Dr. Priestley thought of when he wrote these lines in his "Memoir." This grand and highly devotional poem was written under peculiar circumstances. Miss Aikin was then visiting at the house of the Rev. Mr. Turner, minister of a Dissenting congregation in Wakefield, near Leeds, and in connection with whom some of Dr. Priestley's publications on his researches were carried on. In the following extract from Dr. Priestley's Preface to his two discourses, the first on "Habitual Devotion" and the other on "The Duty of not Living to Ourselves," first published in 1782, he states: "To the former of these discourses the public are already under considerable obligations, though they have been ignorant of it, as it was the occasion of that excellent poem of Mrs. Barbauld's entitled 'An Address to the Deity,' which was composed immediately after the first delivery of it before an assembly of ministers at Wakefield, in Yorkshire, in the year 1769. Were I to inform my readers how soon the poem appeared after the delivery of the discourse, it would add much to their idea of the powers of the writer. I could make the same observation with respect to several other pieces, and some of the most admired in that collection." He then quoted from it several portions of the poem which he considered peculiarly suitable and appropriate for the purpose, and so closed his Preface. Many years after Mrs. Barbauld's death, Miss Lucy Aikin, in writing to her friend Dr. Channing, of Boston, U. S. A., says, "I have a vivid memory of Priestley, the friend of my father, the dearer and more intimate friend of my aunt, Mrs. Barbauld. . . . . My aunt has said of him, with as much truth as brilliancy, that he followed truth as a man who hawks follows his sport, — at full speed, straight forward, looking only upward, and regardless into what difficulties the chase may lead him."

When Miss Aikin left the friendly and hospitable home of Mr. Turner, she placed in the hands of his little son, a child seven years of age, the writer of the sketch to which I refer and have already quoted from, "an ivory memorandum-book, on the leaves of which, after she was gone, were found written the following lines." They contain a beautiful tribute to the virtues and character of the elder Mr. Turner, and are so pretty and playfully impressive that he printed them: —

"Accept, my dear, this toy, and let me say,
The leaves an emblem of your mind display.
Your youthful mind, uncolored, pure, and white,
Like crystal leaves, transparent to the sight,
Fit each impression to receive whate'er
The finger of instruction traces there.
O, then transcribe into the shining page
Each virtue that adorns your tender age;
And grave upon the tablet of your heart
Each lofty science and each useful art!

"But, with the likeness, mark the difference well,
Nor think complete the hasty parallel.
These leaves by folly scrawled, or foul with stains,
A drop of water clears with little pains;
But from a blotted *mind* the smallest trace
Not seas of bitter tears can e'er efface, —
The spreading mark forever will remain,
And rolling years but deepen every stain.

"Once more one difference let me still explain:
The vacant leaves thus ever will remain,

Till some officious hand the tablet fill
With sense or nonsense, prose or rhyme, at will.
Not so your mind without your forming care;
Nature forbids an idle vacuum there;
Folly will plant her tares without your toil,
And weeds spring up in the neglected soil.

"But why to you this moralizing strain?
Vain is the precept, and the caution vain, —
To you, whose opening virtues bloom so fair,
And well reward the prudent planter's care, —
As some young tree, by generous juices fed,
Above its fellows lifts its towering head,
Whose proud, auspicious shoots incessant rise,
And every day grows nearer to the skies.

"Yet should kind heaven thy opening mind adorn,
And bless thy noon of knowledge as thy morn, —
Yet were thy mind with every science blest,
And every virtue glowing in thy breast,
With learning, meekness, and with candor, zeal,
Clear to discern, and generous to feel, —
Yet should the graces o'er thy breast diffuse
The softer influence of the polish muse, —
'T is no original, the world will tell,
And all your praise is but to copy well.

CHAPTER III.

Letters to Family and Friends. — John Aikin, M.D. — His Return to Warrington. — His Literary Productions. — Prepares his Sister's Poems for Publication. — Poems printed in 1773. — Address to the Corsicans. — Miscellaneous Pieces collected and published in 1773. — Remarks of Fox. — Criticism of Dr. Johnson on the Imitation of his Style. — Essay in the "Christian Reformer."

MISS AIKIN says of her aunt's letters that they "were certainly never intended by herself to meet the public eye"; she adds, however, that it was "impossible not to be influenced also by the desire of thus communicating to those admirers of Mrs. Barbauld's genius who did not enjoy the advantage of her personal acquaintance a just idea of the pointed and elegant remark, the sportive and lambent wit, the affectionate spirit of sympathy, and the courteous expressions of esteem and benevolence, which united to form at once the graces of her epistolary style and the inexpressible charm of her conversation." Her first letter placed before the reader is dated 1771, and is addressed to her life-long friend, Miss Belsham, afterwards Mrs.

Kenrick. The letters are certainly charming, and full of life and spirit; several of them have in them allegorical tales and *jeu d'esprit* in their writer's best and inimitable manner, and all add much to her reputation for mind, heart, and the highest degree of culture and elegance. Cheap postage had not reduced letter-writing to the slight and hasty work now given it as a rule, and a letter might be as elaborate as possible without exciting either surprise from the receiver or apology from the writer for its length. Letters of that time have therefore, and always must have, an interest for the public, as the natural, full, and personal record of feelings and events, and as first impressions of men and women. If an ordinary letter-writer can so interest, what shall be said of the fascination and attraction which a superior mind and animated fancy throw over a correspondence? The letters of Mrs. Barbauld deserve to rank with the first and best the world has yet seen, and the only thing to be regretted is the limit to their number. Those we have must, however, afford excellent specimens of her style, and undoubtedly are among the best and choicest of her letters, and were kept by her friends with that feeling.

LETTER TO MISS E. BELSHAM, AFTERWARDS MRS. KENRICK.

LONDON, February, 1771.

Believe me, my dear Betsy, my heart has some time reproached me for being in your debt. . . . . I am much obliged to you for your kind invitation to Bedford; certainly, few things would give me more pleasure than conversing with my Betsy; but it will not be in my power to reach Bedford this time. I have already been so long from home that they begin to be impatient for my return, and I would not trespass too far upon their goodness, who, I am sensible, in some measure deny themselves in being without me.

Patty and I are now with Mrs. K. She and I are great walkers, and in fine weather often stroll about almost all the morning; but we have very little to do with visiting any public places except the playhouses, where we have been three or four times. Last night we saw the "West-Indian," a very pretty play, as we thought on reading it; but the characters are so ill cast, that we had not half the pleasure in seeing it. One part, indeed, the Irishman, was excellently done, but that was the only one; I think they seem to want actors very much for easy, genteel characters, which are more difficult to support than mimicry or strong-marked passions. The chaste and delicate sensibilities of a young, unpractised heart, or the decorums of a virtuous character, must be very difficult to assume; and, indeed, there are so many qualifications requisite to make a perfect actor, it is almost a pity one possessed of them should follow the profession; nor is it surprising there should be but one upon the stage at once. . . . . I admire Mrs. K. beyond most women I know, that, engaged as she is by matrimonial connections, she is not engrossed by them, but has a heart as open to every other endearing relation and friendly sentiment as ever. It is not true, what Dr. Fordyce insinuates, that women's friendships are not sincere; I am sure it is not. I remember when I read it I had a good mind to have burnt the book for that unkind passage. I hope the doctor will give us our revenge, as he has begun his sermons to young men; they were advertised in the papers. Was it not a piece of parade unbecoming a preacher? It would be difficult to determine whether the age is growing better or worse; for I think our plays are growing like sermons, and our sermons like plays.

In the year 1771, John Aikin, M. D., returned to Warrington to settle himself there as a physician, and he soon discovered the merit and beauty of his sister's poems. Dr. Aikin even then displayed the correct taste, habits of application, and literary industry which are his best claims to respect and notice at the present time. Without the bright fancy, playful wit, and poetic genius of his sister, he was an excellent writer, a careful compiler, and an essayist of good judgment, critical taste, and ability. He was also an able editor, and brought into notice, preparing with care and discrimination, many valuable and now standard works. He did some very good work in interesting the young in nature by his books on natural objects, of which he was a keen observer, and on which he was a pleasant writer. His "Medical Memoir" appeared in the year 1780, and with his principal work, "The General Biographical

Dictionary," is of permanent value. For several years he edited the "Monthly Magazine," and contributed to it a variety of essays and articles marked by his good taste, sound judgment, and liberality of view and opinion. His "Evenings at Home" must not be forgotten in speaking of larger works. This book made a little fortune, it is believed, for its original publisher, and has gone through very many editions, being one of the most enduringly popular juvenile volumes ever produced. This was written for the instruction and amusement of his own family, and in his labor of love Mrs. Barbauld participated; but the larger share of it was his own.

To Miss Belsham.

Warrington, January, 1772.

I heard not long ago a piece of news which pleases me beyond measure. Can you guess what it is? Mrs. Lewin tells me that my dear Betsy intends coming to Lancashire soon. I hope these her good intentions will speedily be put in execution. If we had you here, Patty and I should be as happy as the day is long. We have a knot of lassies just after your own heart, — as merry, blithe, and gay as you would wish them, and very smart and clever; two of them are the Misses Rigby. We have a West-Indian family, too, that I think you would like; a young couple who seem intended by nature for nothing but mirth, frolic, and gayety. I say nothing of our young men, as I would not flatter you with the hopes of any conquest, for the aforesaid damsels have left no hearts to conquer.

You who love so dearly to puzzle other people, I have a puzzle for you. Can you find a number of words that will take in all the letters of the alphabet and no more? We have all been trying at it, with Mr. Enfield's assistance, a long time; if you can accomplish it, we kiss the hem of your garment.

Soon after Dr. Aikin's return to Warrington, he undertook the selection, revision, and arrangement of his sister's poems for the press; and, when all the preparatory steps had been taken, finding her still reluctant to appear before the public as an author, he himself procured the paper for the book, and had it put into type. It soon appeared, and the result fully justified his anticipations, for the book went through four editions in the first year of its publication, 1773; the first edition being in quarto, the other three being issued in octavo form. I have before me a copy which formed one of the first edition; it is a handsome quarto volume, and bears the imprint of the Warrington Press, though published by Joseph Johnson of St. Paul's Churchyard,— one who should be remembered as a kindly and encouraging man of business, and an excellent friend to many authors of the day. The work was dedicated to Lady Mary West, in compliance with the fashion of the time, which almost demanded such tribute to titled patronage; and we must not wonder at an almost unknown and comparatively friendless author recognizing this custom, when we call to mind the weary waiting of the great Dr. Johnson for the smile of Lord Chesterfield on his Dictionary, and his at last freeing himself from patronage by the indignation he felt at the neglect and contemptuous treatment he received in his noble would-be patron's waiting-room. The book contains many of her short poems, and one longer and more powerful in its theme and treatment, — that on Corsica. Numerous editions of the poems attest to the popularity of the collection, and we are told by Miss Lucy Aikin that the critics treated it favorably, and gave it their meed of praise.

The poem on Corsica was written in 1769. James Boswell had recently made his visit to that island, as he tells us in his Life of Dr. Johnson; and the fruits of his visit were embodied in this volume, published by him after his return, entitled "Corsica," a work which gained for him a considerable amount of notice in literary circles in London, and gave him for many years the name of "Corsica Boswell" among those who knew him personally and by repute. Miss Aikin begins her poem, —

"Hail, generous Corsica! unconquered isle!
The fort of freedom; that amidst the waves
Stands like a rock of adamant, and dares
The wildest fury of the storm."

Continuing her apostrophe to the island and islanders, she then alludes to the traveller: —

"Such were the working thoughts which swelled the breast
Of generous Boswell, when with nobler aim
And views beyond the narrow, beaten track
By trivial fancy trod, he turned his course
From polished Gallia's soft, delicious vales,
From the gray reliques of imperial Rome,
From her long galleries of laureled stone,
Her chiseled heroes and her marble gods,
Whose dumb, majestic pomp yet awes the world
To animated forms of patriot zeal;
Warm in the living majesty of virtue;
Elate with fearless spirit; firm; resolved;
By fortune nor subdued, nor awed by power."

She then describes the beauty and grandeur of the island, its

"Mountains, brown with solemn shade
Of various trees, that wave their giant arms
O'er the rough sons of freedom";

the impetuous streams that rush down their sides; the

"Deep indented shores,
And pointed cliffs, which hear the chafing deep
Incessant foaming round their shaggy sides";

the luxuriant vegetation which clothes this lovely but unhappy island, torn with strife,

"With living verdure; savage forests awful deep,"

and the herds of cattle which roam them untamed and

free; all these wild, majestic, natural objects attract the spirit of freedom.

> "Liberty,
> The mountain Goddess, loves to range at large
> Amid such scenes, and on the iron soil
> Print her majestic step. For these she scorns
> The green enameled vales,"

and softer scenes of other Southern climes, and marked

> "This isle emerging like a beauteous gem
> From the dark bosom of the Tyrrhene Main"

for her own possession and seat of abode.

The long, unequal struggle for freedom is related, how, "still unquelled,"

> "Her genuine sons —
> A broken remnant from the generous stock
> Of ancient Greece, from Sparta's sad remains"—

have maintained the hard conflict for liberty with

> "Haughty Genoa and ambitious Gaul."

She feels confident of their ultimate success and victory over their oppressors, and sees in Paoli

> "The Man
> Born to exalt his own, and give mankind
> A glimpse of higher natures";

and she closes a glowing tribute to him with these lines, —

> "The man devoted to the public, stands
> In the bright records of superior worth
> A step below the skies; if he succeed,

The first fair lot which earth affords, is his;
And if he falls, he falls above a throne.
When such their leader, can the brave despair,
Freedom the cause, and Paoli the chief!"

"A British muse" bids them to hope, and urges them to patience and boldness, painting the fruits of perseverance and final victory, and indicates to them, if their cause is gained, the long years of prosperity to the country and fame to him who led them in their attempt.

"Some muse,
More worthy of the theme, shall consecrate
To after-ages, and applauding worlds
Shall bless the godlike man who saved his country."

Here occurs a sudden break in the poem, and after the failure of the efforts of the islands to throw off their galling foreign yoke, Miss Aikin continued it:—

"So vainly wished, so fondly hoped the Muse:
Too fondly hoped. The iron fates prevail,
And Cyrnus is no more. Her generous sons,
Less vanquished than o'erwhelmed, by numbers crushed,
Admired, unaided fell. So strives the moon
In dubious battle with the gathering clouds,
And strikes a splendor through them; till at length
Storms rolled on storms involve the face of heaven
And quench her struggling fires. Forgive the zeal
That, too presumptuous, whispered better things,
And read the book of destiny amiss.
Not with the purple coloring of success
Is virtue best adorned: the attempt is praise.

There yet remains a freedom, nobler far
Than kings or senates can destroy or give;
Beyond the proud oppressor's cruel grasp
Seated secure, uninjured, undestroyed;
Worthy of gods: — the freedom of the mind."

The length alone of this fine and inspiring address to the Corsicans prevented its being placed among the other Works; but the extracts I have given will show its style and spirit.

The poem, "The Groans of the Tankard," was called forth by the remark of a gentleman who was dining with her father, Dr. Aikin, and commented on the degradation to which he subjected a large old family tankard which stood upon the sideboard filled with water, after having so many years been used for more generous liquors. His remarks on the noble old vessel and its modern usage occasioned the verses, supposed to be the groans it uttered at its unhappiness.

To Miss Belsham.

Warrington, January 1, 1773.

Not in charity with me, forsooth! So you would pretend you never received a letter from me a great while ago, in answer to your last! A letter, madam, written with such purity of style, such admirable brevity and perspicuity, that I am confident there was not a sentence of it you would wish omitted, or that the severest critic would object to.

Well, if you will fancy I am still in your debt, I must make haste and get out of it as fast as I can.

We are preparing to celebrate the birthday of — a prince, shall I say? why not? a king, if you please, since he has more power than any monarch in the universe, and we all expect blessings from him of more value than the Indies; perhaps, indeed, we may expect too much from him, for it is natural to hope for everything under the auspices of a new king; and, however we may have been disappointed by his predecessors, we fondly flatter ourselves that the young sovereign will crown all our hopes, and put us in possession of all our wishes. Blessings, invaluable ones, he certainly has in his disposal; but if we have wasted the bounties of his predecessors, would it not become us to mingle a tear to their memories with the joy which his accession inspires? May the present reign, however, be happy to you and me and all of us; long, I dare not add, except in good actions, because, young as the prince is, it is no presumption to say that his days are numbered; the astronomers have already cast his nativity, nor is it in the power of all the sons of Adam to prolong beyond the appointed term, though but for an hour, the life of — the New Year.

The success of Miss Aikin's poems induced her to collect her prose articles; and with her brother she published a small volume in 1773, under the title of "Miscellaneous Pieces in Prose," by J. and L. Aikin. Miss Lucy Aikin says that several of these essays were wrongly attributed to Mrs. Barbauld, while some of hers were supposed to be the work of her brother; and she especially mentions the fragment "Sir Bertrand," which was ascribed to her, though in reality it was by Dr. Aikin. This error was the result of their having printed the articles intentionally without distinguishing them by their signatures. This plan led to some curious mistakes. Rogers in his "Table-Talk" gives an anecdote apropos: "At a dinner-party where I was, Fox met Aikin. 'I am greatly pleased with your *Miscellaneous Pieces*, Mr. Aikin,' said Fox (alluding to the volume written partly by Aikin and partly by his sister, Mrs. Barbauld). Aikin bowed. 'I particularly admire,' continued Fox, 'your essay, *Against Inconsistency in our Expectations*.' 'That,' replied Akin, 'is my sister's.' 'I like much,' returned Fox, 'your essay, *On Monastic Institutions*.' 'That,' answered Aikin, 'is also my sister's.'" Mr. Rogers adds, "Fox thought it best to say no more about the book." In fact, Dr. Aikin's share in the book was the least important and valuable one; the finest and most interesting articles were Miss Aikin's, and rather threw his into the shade by their greater brilliancy, depth of thought, and strength of reasoning.

The essays which were her work are as follows: "On Monastic Institutions"; "An Inquiry into those Kinds of Distress which excite Agreeable Sensations," with a tale; "Seláma, An Imitation of Ossian"; "Against Inconsistency in our Expectations"; "The Hill of Science"; "An Essay on Devotional Taste"; "On Romances," which last was professedly an imitation of Dr. Johnson's thought and mode of expression. He himself, in talking with Boswell, said he felt this to be the best attempt made by any one to imitate his peculiar style. Boswell had observed to him that Dr. Hugh Blair had "animadverted on the Johnsonian style as too pompous, and had attempted to imitate it by giving a sentence of Addison" in the manner of Johnson. He then cited the original passage and Dr. Blair's alteration in it; this did not please Dr. Johnson, who rejoined, "Sir, these are not the words I should have used. No, sir; the imitators of my style have not hit it. Miss Aikin has done it the best; for she has imitated the sentiment as well as the diction." Mr. Croker, in a foot-note to his edition of Boswell, adds that the imitation was "probably in an essay, 'Against Inconsistency in our Expectations'"; but we have Miss Lucy Aikin's authority for naming the essay "On Romances" as her aunt's imitation of the great essayist and dictionary-maker.

In the "Christian Reformer" for 1853, there appeared a short essay by Miss Aikin, entitled "The Vision of Anna, the Daughter of Haikim (an unedited parable)." This first appeared in the "Christian

Miscellany" in 1792. It is there called "A Chapter of Modern Apocrypha," and was written in the year 1773. The occasion of this now almost unknown production of its author was the disapprobation expressed by thirteen Scotch Presbyterian ministers, in 1773, at the renewal of an application to Parliament by the Protestant Dissenting ministers. These men denied the need of help or of freedom from Subscription to the Establishment, and the writer represents them in this parable as the Little Sister who loved not the Light, and sat by preference in darkness. This pointed and spirited little article would have formed an appropriate companion to the author's eloquently indignant "Address to the Opposers of the Repeal of the Corporation and Test Acts." At present the subjects of these articles no longer interest the public, though the treatment of the theme is forcible, impressive, and animated.

CHAPTER IV.

MARRIAGE. — MR. BARBAULD'S PARENTAGE AND FAMILY. — REPLY TO MRS. MONTAGUE AND OTHERS. — MR. BARBAULD SETTLES AT PALGRAVE. — THEY OPEN A SCHOOL IN THAT TOWN. — SUCCESS OF THE ENTERPRISE. — MRS. BARBAULD'S METHOD OF INSTRUCTION. — DR. SAYERS'S REMEMBRANCE OF THE LESSONS GIVEN BY HER. — WILLIAM TAYLOR, OF NORWICH, ONE OF THE SCHOLARS. — LETTERS TO HER BROTHER, WITH ACCOUNT OF THE SCHOOL, AND HER INTEREST IN THE LESSONS AND AMUSEMENTS OF THE BOYS.

IN May, 1774, Miss Aikin married the Rev. Rochemont Barbauld; an event which made an important change in her pursuits, and gave her an active and rather arduous and engrossing participation in the education, mental activity, and growth of thought of very young children. Mr. Barbauld was descended from a French Protestant family settled in England. During the persecutions of the Protestants by Louis XIV., his grandfather, "then a boy, was carried on board a ship, enclosed in a cask, and conveyed to England." He settled himself in that country, married there, and had a son who took orders in the Established Church. On the marriage of one of the daughters of George II. to the Elector of Hesse, he received an appointment as chaplain in her household, went with her in the pursuance of his duties, and made one of her establishment at Cassel. His son Rochemont was born and passed his early life there. On the return of his father to England, when the household of the Electress was broken up, he went with him, remaining a year in Paris on their way to England. After their arrival he was sent by his father to the academy at Warrington. There he first met Miss Aikin, and soon became interested in her. The rather unwise course of his father in sending a son, who he hoped would follow in his footsteps by entering the Established Church, to a Dissenting academy, was attended by the natural consequence, that he became a Dissenter, and could not conscientiously fulfil his father's expectations and anticipations for his future career in the Church of England. He changed his views, and began to fit himself for the position of a Presbyterian preacher. For some time want of advancement in his profession delayed his marriage ; but, on receiving a call from a small Dissenting congregation at Palgrave, near Diss, in Suffolk, he accepted it, and also undertook the care and management of a boarding-school for boys. This arrangement soon proved most satisfactory, and their ultimate success was complete. Before their marriage, while their plans were uncertain, and they were considering what might be done to increase the small income which he would receive as a preacher, a proposal was made by some friends of Miss Aikin who were interested in her future career, and they offered her a project for consideration. These persons were advocates of a more extended and elevated system of education for women, and invited the co-operation of Miss Aikin in their plan, under their patronage and support. Well aware that the name of Miss Aikin would be a sufficient and undoubted guaranty for its success, from her high reputation for good judgment, intelligence, and noble principles, they applied to her to assume the charge and instruction of an academy or college for young ladies. Among the proposers of this scheme was Mrs. Elizabeth Montague.

In a letter of reply to them, Miss Aikin gave them her own views on higher education for women, and some of the objections to the system of study proposed for them, with great good sense and simplicity. At the present day some of her reasons against a more extended course of learning for women may not be equally cogent; but her statement is worthy of note as the opinion of a finely educated, intelligent, intellectual woman, who was an ornament to her age and sex. On the whole, with slight modifications, her reasoning is as just and sound for the present time as it was then, and is deserving of calm consideration as the view of a thoroughly educated woman on the subject. Her objections to the plan naturally influenced the advocates of it, and it was abandoned as impracticable. I give her answer to the proposal.

"A kind of literary academy for ladies (for that is what you seem to propose), where they are to be taught in a regular, systematic manner the various branches of science, appears to me better calculated to form such characters as the *Précieuses* or the *Femmes sçavantes* of Molière than good wives or agreeable companions. Young gentlemen, who are to display their knowledge to the world, should have every motive of emulation, should be formed into regular classes, should read and dispute together, should have all the honors, and, if one may say so, the pomp of learning set before them, to call up their ardor. It is their business, and they should apply to it as such. But young ladies, who ought only to have such a general tincture of knowledge as to make them agreeable companions to a man of sense, and to enable them to find rational amusement for a solitary hour, should gain these accomplishments in a more quiet and unobserved manner; subject to a regulation like that of the ancient Spartans, the thefts of knowledge in our sex are only connived at while carefully concealed, and, if displayed, punished with disgrace. The best way for women to acquire knowledge is from conversation with a father, a brother, or a friend, in the way of family intercourse and easy conversation, and by such a course of reading as they may recommend. If you add to these an attendance upon those masters which are usually provided in schools, and perhaps such a set of lectures as Mr. Ferguson's, which it is not uncommon for ladies to attend, I think a woman will be in a way to acquire all the learning that can be of use to those who are not to teach or engage in any learned profession. Perhaps you may think that, having myself stepped out of the bounds of female reserve in becoming an author, it is with an ill grace I offer these sentiments; but, though this circumstance may destroy the grace, it does not the justice, of the remarks; and I am fully convinced that to have a too great fondness for books is little favorable to the happiness of a woman, especially one not in affluent circumstances. My situation has been peculiar, and would be no rule for others.

"I should likewise object to the age proposed. Their knowledge ought to be acquired at an earlier period; geography, those languages it may be proper for them to learn, grammar, etc., are best learned from about nine to thirteen or fourteen, and will then interfere less with other duties. I should have little hopes of cultivating a love of knowledge in a young lady of fifteen, who came to me ignorant and untaught; and if she has laid a foundation, she will be able to pursue her studies without a master, or with such a one only as Rousseau gives his Sophie! It is too late then to *begin* to learn. The empire of the passions is coming on, a new world opens to the youthful eye; those attachments begin to be formed which influence the happiness of future life; the care of a mother, and that alone, can give suitable attention to this important period. At this period they have many things to learn which books and systems never taught. The grace and ease of polished society, with the established modes of behavior to every different class of people; the detail of domestic economy, to which they must be gradually introduced; the duties, the proprieties of behavior, which they must practise in their own family, in the families where they visit, to their friends, to their acquaintance; lastly, their behavior to the other half of their species, with whom before they were hardly acquainted, and who then begin to court their notice, the choice of proper acquaintance of that sex, the art to converse with them with a happy mixture of easy politeness and graceful reserve, and to wear off by degrees something of the girlish bashfulness without injuring virgin delicacy. These are the accomplishments which a young woman has to learn from fourteen or fifteen till she is married, or fit to be so; and surely these are not to be learned in a school. They must be learned partly at home, and partly by visits in genteel families; they cannot be taught where a number are together; they cannot be taught without the most intimate knowledge of a young lady's temper, connections, and views in life, nor without an authority and influence established upon all the former part of her life. For all these reasons, it is my full opinion that the best public education cannot at that period be equally serviceable with — I had almost said — an indifferent private one.

"My next reason is, that I am not at all qualified for the

task. I have seen a great deal of the manner of educating boys, and know pretty well what is expected in the care of them; but in a girls' boarding-school I should be quite a novice; I never was at one myself, have not even the advantage of younger sisters; indeed, for the early part of my life I conversed little with my own sex. In the village where I was, there were none to converse with; and this, I am very sensible, has given me an awkwardness in many common things which would make me most peculiarly unfit for the education of my own sex. But suppose I were tolerably qualified to instruct those of my own rank; consider that *these* must be of a class far superior to those I have lived amongst and conversed with. Young ladies of that rank ought to have their education superintended by a woman perfectly well-bred, from whose manner they may catch that ease and gracefulness which can only be learned from the best company; and she should be able to direct them, and judge of their progress in every genteel accomplishment. I could not judge of their music, their dancing, and, if I pretended to correct their air, they might be tempted to smile at my own; for I know myself remarkably deficient in gracefulness of person, in my air and manner, and in the easy graces of conversation. Indeed, whatever the kind partiality of my friends may think of me, there are few things I know well enough to teach them with any satisfaction, and many I never could learn myself. These deficiencies would soon be remarked when I was introduced to people of fashion; and were it possible that, notwithstanding, I should meet with encouragement, I could never prosecute with any pleasure an undertaking to which I should know myself so unequal; I am sensible the common boarding-schools are upon a very bad plan, and believe I could project a better, but I could not execute it."

Miss Aikin's intelligence and learning were equalled only by her modesty, which makes it evident that a high degree of culture is not incompatible with womanly refinement and graces. But there can be no doubt she greatly undervalued her own capacity and fitness for this undertaking, which she declined partly because of that, and also on the ground of the impracticability and the questionable wisdom of the proposed plan. Her natural refinement, the deep and thorough studies of her youth, all her varied charms of mind and manner, her fine conversation, her bright, playful fancy and wit, her love of the young, her talent for teaching, — which is rare in combination with great power of expression and habits of study, — all eminently marked her as one peculiarly gifted by nature and culture for the instruction and development of mental and moral qualities in the young. The lighter accomplishments, which she stated her ignorance of, were those most easily acquired from a shorter study of them; and, had she felt her fitness for the position, it is to be believed her school would have formed an era in the history of woman's education.

Horace Walpole, in writing to the Countess of Ossory, in 1774, adds, in a postscript to his letter, "Miss Aikin has been here this morning (she is just married); she desired to see the Castle of Otranto (Strawberry Hill); I let her see all the antiquities of it." This glimpse of London, and the beauties and wonders of the great city and its surrounding attractions, Mrs. Barbauld probably had before she settled with her husband at Palgrave, where they opened a boarding-school for boys which had the united attention and care of Mr. and Mrs. Barbauld. Their school soon became a success. Undoubtedly, the fact of Mrs. Barbauld's high character, fine talents, culture, and her good literary reputation for classic study and taste, made her personal superintendence and teaching highly valued as a guaranty for its superiority and attractions over most institutions of that kind.

To Dr. Aikin.

Palgrave, 1774.

Thanks to my dear brother for his letter, and the copy of verses, which Mr. B. and I admire much. As to your system, I do not know what to say; I think I could make out just the contrary with as plausible arguments: as thus, Women are naturally inclined not only to love, but to all the soft and gentle affections, all the tender attentions and kind sympathies of nature. When, therefore, one of our sex shows any particular complacency towards one of yours, it may be resolved into friendship; into a temper naturally caressing, and those endearing intercourses of life which to a woman are become habitual. But when man, haughty, independent man, becomes sensible to all the delicacies of sentiment, and softens his voice and address to the tone of *les manières douces*, it is much to be suspected a stronger power than friendship has worked the change. *You* are hardly social creatures till your minds are humanized and subdued by that passion which alone can tame you to "all the soft civilities of life." Your heart requires a stronger fire to melt it than ours does; the chaste and gentle rays of friendship, like star-beams, may play upon it without effect; it will only yield to gross material fire. There is a pretty flight for you! In short, women, I think, may be led on by sentiment to passion; but men must be subdued by passion before they can taste sentiment. Well! I protest I think I have the best of the argument all to nothing. I 'll go ask Mr. Barbauld. Yes; he says my system will do. I beg I may have Dr. E.'s opinion upon it, as I take him to be a pretty casuist in these affairs. I hope I am by this time richer by a nephew or niece: if it is a boy, I claim it; if a girl, I will be content to stay for the next. I am afraid *my poor child* * is tossing upon the waves, for I have not heard yet of its arrival in London; and I cannot help feeling all a parent's anxiety for its fate and establishment in the world; several people here are so kind as to inquire after it, but I can give them no satisfaction.

* Her Devotional Pieces, sent from Norfolk, by sea, to be printed at Warrington. — EDITOR.

Mr. and Mrs. Barbauld were peculiarly fortunate in their scholars. Two of the eight with whom they began their school were highly gifted by nature, and under Mrs. Barbauld's fostering influence and almost maternal care their minds rapidly developed. One of these boys was Sir William Gell, and the other was William Taylor, of Norwich, well known in after life as the author of a very able and valuable work on English Synonymes, and by his admirably faithful and spirited translations from the German, his version of the Iphigenia in Tauris, and Leonore from Bürger, with other poems which have made him eminent as a man of mind and culture. He was one of the first thorough students of the language, writings, and advanced thought of Germany; and he opened for England that wide field of study and speculation before comparatively unknown and unexplored. Miss Lucy Aikin, in writing of him many years after the time of his residence at Palgrave to one of her friends, speaks of him as one of Mrs. Barbauld's most brilliant scholars. She says, "Of his youth I can only speak traditionally; but I know that high hopes were conceived of him by those who knew him in his boyhood, and especially by her whom I have heard him name with gratitude 'the mother of his mind,' — Mrs. Barbauld. His talent for poetry was early discovered by her." In his memoir of Dr. Sayers, of Norwich, author of "Dramatic

Sketches of Northern Mythology," also a scholar at Palgrave, Mr. Taylor has left a record of the impressions of his friend as to the value and interest derived from Mrs. Barbauld's careful and improving instructions. "Among the instructions bestowed at Palgrave, Dr. Sayers has repeatedly observed to me that he most valued the lessons of English composition, superintended by Mrs. Barbauld. On Wednesdays and Saturdays the boys were called in separate classes to her apartment: she read a fable, a short story, or a moral essay, to them aloud, and then sent them back into the school-room to write it out on their slates in their own words. Each exercise was separately overlooked by her; the faults of grammar were obliterated, the vulgarisms were chastised, the idle epithets were cancelled, and a distinct reason was always assigned for every correction; so that the arts of inditing and criticising were in some degree learnt together. Many a lad from the great schools, who excels in Latin or Greek, cannot write properly a vernacular letter, for want of some such discipline." This description of one of the methods of teaching followed by Mrs. Barbauld is interesting and worthy of record, as indicating the early impression and lasting influence made by a well-trained and cultivated mind in its contact with the young and impressible natures under its charge.

Mrs. Barbauld also taught the usually dull and

rather unattractive study of geography, and made it extremely pleasant, and the vehicle of so much that stimulated and interested the minds of her pupils that this lesson became a source of enjoyment to them, as she related, in connection with the simple details of the position of places, the natural history, manners, and customs of the people, and so much of the history of each country as she thought suited to the comprehension and youth of those whom she taught. Miss Aikin says: "A public examination of the boys was always held at the close of the winter session; at the termination of the summer one they performed a play; and upon Mrs. Barbauld principally devolved — together with the contrivance of dresses and decorations, and the composition of prologues, epilogues, and interludes — the instruction of the young exhibitors in the art of declamation. In this branch she likewise excelled; and the neglected though delightful arts of good reading and graceful speaking were nowhere taught with more assiduity and success." The name of Sir William Gell, the eminent antiquarian, celebrated as the explorer of the Plain of Troy, and also for his large and valuable work on Pompeii, and the explorations there, must not be omitted in mentioning the boys under Mrs. Barbauld's care. He was one of her youngest scholars in the infant class, for whose use she wrote the "Prose Hymns."

PALGRAVE, Sept. 9, 1775.

I give you joy with all my heart, my dear brother, on the little hero's appearance in the world, and hope he will live to be as famous a man as any of his namesakes. I shall look upon you now as a very respectable man, as being entitled to all the honors and privileges of a father of three children. I would advise you to make one a hero, as you have determined; another a scholar; and for the third, — send him to us, and we will bring him up a Norfolk farmer, which I suspect to be the best business of the three. I have not forgot Arthur, and send you herewith a story for his edification; but I must desire you to go on with it. When you have brought the shepherd Hidallan a sheet further in his adventures, send him back to me, and I will take up the pen: it will be a very sociable way of writing, and I doubt not but it will produce something new and clever. The great thing to be avoided in these things is, the having any plan in your head: nothing cramps your fancy so much; and I protest to you I am entirely clear from that inconvenience.

Pray, can you tell me anything about Crashaw? I have read some verses of his, prefixed to Cornaro's Treatise, so exceedingly pretty that I am persuaded he must have written more, and should be glad to see them: I would transcribe the verses, but I think you have Cornaro in your library.

Be it known to you, that Palgrave Seminary will soon abound with poets, even as the green fields abound with grasshoppers. Our usher is a poet profest; and two of the lads have lately exercised their pens the same way, and not amiss. One especially has written two or three pieces, which, if I am not deceived by the partiality I cannot help feeling for the little urchins, I may say are really clever for a boy of twelve years old. Now I am upon poetical subjects, I must tell you that a young clergyman in this neighborhood is writing a play, which he did us the honor to submit to our criticism. The subject is the resistance of the Chilese to the Spaniards, by which they recovered their independence. I am afraid I gave him very wicked advice; for I recommended it to him to re-convert his Indian from Christianity to heathenism, and to make his chiefs a little more quarrelsome.

I believe the Devotional Pieces have met with the fate of poor Jonah, and been swallowed up by some whale, — perhaps out of pity and compassion, to save them in his jaws from the more terrible teeth of the critics. St. Anthony, I think, preached to the fishes; perhaps I may have the same honor. I should as soon hope to inspire a porpoise with devotion, as a turtle-eater.

You must know I find one inconvenience in franks; one never knows when to have done. In a common letter you fill your sheet, and there 's an end; but with a frank you may write on and on forever: I have tried two pens already. But I will write no more to you: I will write to poor Patty, who wants amusement, — so farewell! Go and study your Greek, and do not interrupt us.

And how do you do, my dear Patty? let me take a peep at this boy. Asleep, is he? Never mind; draw the cradle-curtain softly, and let me have a look. Upon my word, a noble lad! dark eyes, like his mother, and a pair of cheeks! You may keep him a few months yet, before you pack him up in the hamper; and then I desire you will send him with all speed; for you know he is to be mine. . . . .

May every blessing attend you and yours, and all the dear society at Warrington!

CHAPTER V.

MRS. BARBAULD'S LETTERS. — DR. JOHNSON'S DESCRIPTION OF HER. — PUBLISHES "THOUGHTS ON THE DEVOTIONAL TASTE." — LONDON SOCIETY AT THAT PERIOD. — THE EMINENT MEN AND WOMEN OF THE TIME. — THE BLUE-STOCKING CLUB. — MISS MORE'S "BAS BLEU." — MISS MORE MEETS MRS. BARBAULD. — MR. AND MRS. BARBAULD OFFER TO ADOPT ONE OF DR. AIKIN'S CHILDREN. — THE OFFER ACCEPTED. — "EARLY LESSONS" WRITTEN BY MRS. BARBAULD FOR HIS USE. — LETTERS TO MISS DIXON.

FROM these accounts of the life at Palgrave we learn how much Mrs. Barbauld personally interested herself in the studies, pleasures, and pursuits of the boys; how they were cared for and sympathized with by her kind heart and the intuition which prompted her to the study and understanding of each mind and its capacity, and how singularly happy those children appear to have been who came under her charge. Each lesson was in itself a study to her; and she must have devoted herself to each branch she taught, to have so successfully adapted her thoughts to the ability and identified herself with the growth of the young minds dependent on her for their development. From those of her own letters which have already been dated from Palgrave, and which speak of her life and the varied occupations there, the reader will gain a good idea of her own thoughts and opinion on the subject, and readily see why, during her residence in that place, she did not do more literary work. She appears to have had her hands, heart, and head full, and no time to spare from the engrossing and absorbing cares she assumed, and which she accomplished so ably and faithfully. Her letters are bright and animated, full of life and spirit, and one finds in them many excellent thoughts, lively sallies of wit, and little allegories and fables. They also record first impressions of new books and old ones just read, of men and women whom she met, and the varied events of the day. She wrote forcibly, simply, and to the point. Though her letters are often full of the trifles which make up the sum of life, yet the style and sentiments of their writer are as evident in these chronicles of her daily existence as in any of her most studied and elaborate works. They extend over a long period, and form quite a memoir of her pursuits, tastes, and friendships. In her letters from Palgrave we can see how busily she was occupied, and her apology to her brother for not writing because of the varied duties of "making up beds; secondly, scolding my maids, preparing for company; and, lastly, drawing up and delivering my lectures on geography," shows how the active housekeeper, full of work and hospitality, and the thoughtful, intelligent teacher met in her person. The prosperity of the school was unusual, and must have been highly gratifying to Mr. and Mrs. Barbauld, who were intensely interested in their life and work. In the following letter, the same from which I have quoted, she tells Dr. Aikin that the school will number twenty-seven pupils before vacation, and two more are to enter at Midsummer.

DEAR BROTHER, — I doubt not but you have been grumbling in your gizzard for some time, and muttering between your teeth, "What is this lazy sister of ours about?" Now, to prove to you that I am not lazy, I will tell you what I have been about. First, then, making up beds; secondly, scolding my maids, preparing for company; and, lastly, drawing up and delivering lectures on geography. Give me joy of our success, for we shall have twenty-seven scholars before the vacation, and two more have bespoke places at Midsummer; so that we do not doubt of being soon full; nay, sir, I can assure you it is said in this country, that it will soon be a favor to be on Mr. Barbauld's list: you have no objection, I hope, to a little boasting.

I thank you, my dear brother, for so kindly drawing your pen in my defence. An admirer of Popery! Heaven help their wise heads! when it was one of my earliest aversions. But this I see, that in religious and political affairs, if a person does not enlist under a party, he is sure to meet with censure from party. I had not seen the charge till I had your letter; we had had the Review too, but I had read it carelessly. If they do not insert your letter, I should be glad to see it.

Yes, Sterne's letters are paltry enough, and so are Lady Luxborough's, which we ran through in the course of an afternoon. I am afraid the public will be satiated with letters before we publish our correspondence. I could make a neat pocket-volume or two of yours, and of Mr. Barbauld's a quarto. Adieu, yours ever.

In Dr. Burney's "Recollections of Dr. Johnson," he says that, after Mrs. Barbauld's "Early Lessons" appeared, Dr. Johnson was very severe in his remarks on her, and growled out the following criticism: "Miss Aikin was an instance of early cultivation, but in what did it terminate? In marrying a little Presbyterian parson, who keeps an infant boarding-school, so that all her employment now is

'To suckle fools, and chronicle small beer.'

She tells the children, 'This is a cat, and this is a dog, with four legs and a tail; see there! you are much better than a cat or a dog, for you can speak.' If I had bestowed such an education on a daughter, and had discovered that she thought of marrying such a fellow, I would have sent her to the Congress."

Some friend, perhaps Boswell, had evidently goaded

Dr. Johnson to this ridiculous and foolish expression of his ignorance of the real importance of Mr. and Mrs. Barbauld's position and the excellent work they did in their school. Mrs. Piozzi in her Reminiscences of the Doctor says, in mentioning those who wrote for children, a class of writers for whom he had a special dislike, "Mrs. Barbauld, however, had his best praise, and deserved it; no man was ever more struck than Mr. Johnson with voluntary descent from possible splendor to painful duty." This seems worthy of him in his better moods, and is surely a just and proper recognition of her merits as one who could write or could refrain from it, if duty called her to other work less attractive and showy, but still important and worthy of her powers.

The time of Mrs. Barbauld, though it was very much occupied by her school duties, was not entirely engrossed by them, and in her leisure hours she accomplished some literary work. The volume given to the public in the year 1775, called "Devotional Pieces compiled from the Psalms of David, with Thoughts on the Devotional Taste," was an evidence of her industry, but hardly added anything to her reputation for taste or literary skill. As a selection, the "Thoughts on the Devotional Taste" was not generally liked, and did not escape some criticism then and later, when the Essay was reprinted among her miscellaneous pieces.

To Dr. Aikin.

"Yes, I was somewhat lazy in writing, I confess; but upon my word I could not tell how to help it, so busy was I; and, by the way, I think I have sometimes been as long without hearing from Warrington. Well! we will all mend if we can.

"Mr. Barbauld thanks you for your elegant 'Pliny,' which he intends to make a school-book immediately after vacation. Your 'Tacitus,' too, seems a very good scheme, and we hope to see it in time. But I own I cannot help wishing you would undertake some original work, either of fancy or elegant criticism; you have the powers for both. I think we must some day sew all our fragments together, and make a *joinerianna* of them. Let me see: I have half a ballad, the first scene of a play, a plot of another, all but the catastrophe, half a dozen loose similes, and an eccentric flight or two among the fairies.

"Did I tell you the boys are going to act the First Part of Henry IV., and I am busy making paper vandykes, and trimming up their hats with feathers? Do you know that we make a trip to Holland this vacation?"

A brilliant circle of women celebrated as poets, wits, and votaries of literature in its various departments, were contemporaries of Mrs. Barbauld, and she lived to see and to know, as they came forward, many of the great lights of the present century. Among her earliest friends was Mrs. Elizabeth Montague, whose house in Hill Street was a "court for the votaries of the Muses," and Montague House, Portman Square, her later more palatial residence, was equally the centre of attraction for those whom she admitted to her circle of visitors. She gathered round her all the eminent men and women of the day, honoring those distinguished by well-known productions, and was as ready to extend the hand of welcome to rising, obscure, and struggling genius. For many years she gave an annual feast to all the chimney-sweeps of London. This noted act of kindness was only one of the many generous deeds of Mrs. Montague that were known, and a great many of her benevolences she did in private, only the receiver being aware of her generosity. Even Dr. Johnson was mollified by her aid of his blind *protégée* and inmate, Miss Williams, and for a time forgave Mrs. Montague her wit, popularity, and social successes, and found her house pleasant, or, as Boswell would say, "not unpleasant," in imitation of Dr. Johnson's style. After an evening passed at Mrs. Montague's, which was characterized by the brilliancy of the conversation, ease of manners, and the talents of the guests who met there, Boswell asked Dr. Johnson if he was "not highly gratified by his visit." "No, sir," said he, "not highly gratified, yet I do not recollect to have passed many evenings with fewer objections."

Miss More, in her poem, *Bas Bleu*, celebrated the names and fame of the three leaders of London society at that period, who had so changed the tone of the gatherings which they admired by their simplicity of dress, intelligent conversation, and the banishment of cards, that many, who possessed neither the taste to enjoy nor the talents to adorn such a superior order of society, scornfully called them the *blue stockings.* In this little tribute of respect and friendly admiration, Miss More praised the successful efforts of her three intimates, Mrs. Vesey, Mrs. Boscawen, and Mrs. Montague, whose attempts to banish the excessive card-playing had been the theme of much conversation, and the cause of a great change in London society. The poem was addressed to Mrs. Vesey, who was one of the first leaders of a certain set, and managed by her talent and tact to break up the usual formality of a *circle,* then the common mode of sitting in a conversation party. And she did so by inducing people to talk together in little separate groups. One can easily fancy how few people would find it either a possible or a pleasant feat to converse while placed in a large circle round a room. She was the wife of the Hon. Agmondesham Vesey, an Irish gentleman, and one of Mr. Burke's friends, on whose recommendation he was admitted to Johnson's Literary Club. Mrs. Boscawen was another celebrated woman of fashion, talent, and culture. She was warmly eulogized by Miss More in her poem on "Sensibility," and there, after animated and good portraits of some of the other distinguished women of the day, including Mrs. Barbauld, she attributed to the spirit of sensibility and the warmth of friendship of this lady her great influence and attractions, —

> "'T is this, whose charms the soul resistless seize,
> And gives Boscawen half her power to please."

The example and influence of these ladies was excellent in banishing cards and gambling; when

> "Society, o'errun
> By whist, that desolating Hun,"

was in great need of reform and improvement; for this she gives —

> "The vanquished triple crown *to you* [Mrs. Vesey],
> *Boscawen* sage, bright *Montague*,
> Divided fell. Your cares in haste
> Rescued the ravaged realms of taste."

The names of these ladies indicate some of the brightest social ornaments of their country, and should not be forgotten among those contemporaries of Mrs. Barbauld who made London the centre of attraction for those who enjoyed conversation, literature, cultivation, and refinement. The English drawing-room then first asserted its just claims to respect and admiration as a social, literary, and refining influence; and the deservedly high character then attributed to these women of taste and culture, who first gave it the reputation it still enjoys, has grown greater with succeeding years.

Miss Elizabeth Carter was another of the noted women of the time, celebrated as the translator of Epictetus. She, by her example and influence, raised the standard of woman's education, in proving that it was not impossible for them to engage in highly intellectual and deep studies, and also to be domestic in their tastes. Her friend Miss Talbot having written, after the translation of Epictetus was finished, asking her to prepare a Life to be published with the Works, she replied: "Whoever that somebody or other is who is to write the Life of Epictetus, seeing I have *a dozen shirts to make*, I do opine, dear Miss Talbot, that it cannot be I." Mrs. Delany, the friend and correspondent of Swift in early life, was among these high-toned, talented women. She was distinguished by George III. and his queen, who did themselves as much honor as they did her by their kindly attentions to her in her extreme old age. She was the life-long friend of the Duchess of Portland, in her childhood known as Prior's "noble, lovely little Peggy," and of whom Miss More wrote later, "Her attractions owe nothing to her rank." Mrs. Delany's Life and Letters reveal her as a talented, amiable, and womanly character, the centre of a large circle of friends and relations. Miss More repeats Burke's remark on Mrs. Delany's extreme sensibility in old age, and her unusual warmth of feeling, "that she was almost the only person he ever saw, who at eighty-eight blushed like a girl." Miss Burney, the gossiping, lively chronicler of her own and other people's doings, from King George and Queen Charlotte down to some of the humblest of their subjects, was one of the noted women of the day; and "little Fanny Burney," as Dr. Johnson affectionately called her, was welcomed and made much of in London society as the authoress of "Evelina," a novel which had interested and amused many, and puzzled them thoroughly as to its unknown writer and unheralded appearance. From her diary I extract some notices of Mrs. Barbauld, who met her quite early in her literary career, and then renewed the acquaintance many years after; of which meeting Madame D'Arblay (Miss Burney) tells her father, noting the pleasure it gave her.

Miss Hannah More's name and high repute as an authoress, and the promoter of so large a number of good works, makes it almost unnecessary to enlarge upon her character; but it is a pleasant fact that this excellent woman and Mrs. Barbauld were warm and affectionate friends. They were perhaps, without exception, the most eminent women of their time, certainly in their order of mind and chosen train of thought without rivals; and their position in life was not dissimilar, both being interested in the instruction of the young in early years. Though differing widely on matters of religious belief and church institutions, — Miss More representing the conservative element, and Mrs. Barbauld being essentially inclined to the largest liberality of view and the utmost freedom of thought and expression of opinion, — yet they had many mutual interests and feelings; and their acquaintance, which began in 1776, grew into a warm and enduring friendship broken only by Mrs. Barbauld's death. Miss More, in one of her first visits to London after her entrance into the great world of literature and fashion as an author, in writing home to her sister of her numerous invitations and engagements, told her of a dinner "with the female Mæcenas of Hill Street" (Mrs. Montague), where she met, among "other distinguished people," friends and associates of that lady, "Mrs. Barbauld." Their intimacy dated from this evening. In the next year she wrote to her sister from Norfolk, where she was then making a visit: "I went to Mrs. Barbauld's on Thursday, intending only to spend one day; but the Muses are such fascinating witches that there is no getting away from them. Mrs. Barbauld and I have found out that we feel as little envy and malice towards each other as though we had neither of us attempted to 'build the lofty rhyme,' though she says this is what the envious and malicious can never be brought to believe."

Dear Brother, — To my sister and yourself Mr. Barbauld and I have a request to make, in which, though perhaps it may be rather singular, we are very seriously in earnest; and therefore, whether you grant or deny, we hope you will neither laugh at us nor take it amiss. Without further preface, it is this. You enjoy a blessing Providence has hitherto denied to us, — that of children: you have already several, and seem very likely to have a numerous family. As to ourselves, having been thus long without prospect of any, it is, to say the least, very uncertain whether that hope, which most, I believe, form when they marry, will ever be fulfilled. Some, indeed, say to us, that, considering how large a family we have of others' children, 't is rather fortunate we have none of our own. And true it is, that, employed as we are in the business of education, we have many of the cares and some of the pleasures of a parent; but the latter very imperfectly. We have them not early enough to contract the fondness of affection which early care alone can give; we have them not long enough to see the fruit of our culture; and we have not enough the disposal of them to follow our own plans and schemes in their education. We wish for one who might be wholly ours; and we think that if a child was made ours by being given young into our hands, we could love it, and make it love us, so well as to supply in a great measure the want of the real relationship. We know there are many instances of people who have taken the greatest satisfaction in, and felt the highest fondness for, children who by some accident have been thrown upon their arms. Why, then, should not we seek out and choose some object of such an affection? and where can we better seek it than in a brother's family?

Our request, then, in short, is this: that you will permit us to adopt one of your children, — which of them, we leave to you; that you will make it ours in every sense in which it is possible to make it; that you will transfer to us all the care and all the authority of a parent; that we should provide for it, educate it, and have the entire direction of it as far into life as the parental power itself extends. Now I know not what to say to induce you to make us such a gift. Perhaps you will entirely deny it, and then we must acquiesce; for I am sensible it is not a small thing we ask, nor can it be easy for a parent to part with a child. This I would say: from a number, *one* may more easily be spared. Though it makes a very material difference in happiness whether a person has children or no children, it makes, I apprehend, little or none whether he has three or four, five or six; because four or five are enough to exercise all his whole stock of care and affection. We should gain, but you would not lose. I would likewise put you in mind that you would not part with it to strangers; the connection between you and it would not be broken off; you would see it (I hope), hear of it often; and it would be taught to love you, if it had not learnt that lesson before. Our child must love our brother and sister. Its relation to you is likewise a presumption that we shall not be wanting in that love for it which will be necessary to make it happy. I believe both Mr. Barbauld and myself are much disposed to love children, and that we could soon grow fond of any one who was amiable and entirely under our care. How, then, can we fail to love a child for whom at setting out we shall have such a stock of affection as we must have for yours? I hope, too, we should have too right a sense of things to spoil it; and we see too much of children to indulge an over-anxious care. But you know us well enough to be able to judge in general how we should educate it, and whether to your satisfaction. Conscience and affection, I hope, would unite in inciting us to fulfil an engagement we should thus voluntarily take upon ourselves, to the best of our abilities.

Our situation is not a certain one, nor have we long tried it; but we have all the reason in the world to hope that, if things go on as they have hitherto done, we should be able to provide for a child in a decent and comfortable manner.

Now, my dear brother and sister, if you consent, give us which of your boys you please: if you had girls, perhaps we should ask a girl rather; and if we might choose amongst your boys, we could make, perhaps, a choice; but that we do not expect you will let us. Give us, then, which you will; only let him be healthy, inoculated, and as young as you can possibly venture him to undertake the journey. This last circumstance is indispensable: for if he were not quite young, we should not gain over him the influence, we could not feel for him the affection, which would be necessary; besides, if at all able to play with our pupils, he would immediately mix with them, and would be little more to us than one of the school-boys. Do not, therefore, put us off by saying that one of yours when he is old enough shall pay us a visit. To see any of yours at any time would, no doubt, give us the highest pleasure; but that does not by any means come up to what we now ask. We now leave the matter before you: consider maturely, and give us your answer.

O no! I never promised to fill this second sheet.

Good by to you.

Mr. and Mrs. Barbauld desired to adopt one of Dr. Aikin's children, as they had none of their own, and in her letter to him on this subject, just copied, she so fully expressed her own feelings that comment is unnecessary upon the interest and pleasure with which she anticipated the care and education of the little boy whom her brother committed to her charge. In the following letter she gives full utterance to her gratitude and joy at the kindness and confidence shown her by her brother, and tells him how much she appreciates also the forbearance and generosity of Mrs. Aikin, who naturally dreaded the parting which must come between her child and herself. The little boy whom they adopted was named Charles Rochemont Aikin. He received devoted attention and parental affection from Mr. and Mrs. Barbauld, and in their declining years was a source of comfort and pride to them. They received him into their home at the age of two years, and for the future Mrs. Barbauld made his education her especial care and study. For his use she wrote the

"Early Lessons," which were justly regarded as admirable, and truly original in style and simplicity. The plan formed a new era in the thought and execution of the works prepared especially for the young, making her name widely known and loved by all who had the best interests of childhood at heart. Dr. Aikin, writing to his sister in the year 1770, spoke of this work for children in the following terms: "The little book you have sent for Charles is what a person of real genius alone could have written; and so far from degrading Mr. Eyre's press (Warrington), I sincerely believe it has never been employed about so really useful a work; all its metaphysics, divinity, philosophy, and even poetry, not excepted." Children's books were almost unknown before Mrs. Trimmer and Mrs. Barbauld gave theirs to the world. Terror and improbability seem to have been the basis of all tales by which young minds had previously been nurtured and amused. Miss More, in alluding to the change in this style of literature, and the efforts of these two writers to improve the state of children's reading, giving simple, natural incidents, instead of tales of monsters and extraordinary, impossible adventures, and endeavoring to convey some ideas of real value in their books, thereby implanting observation, thought, and love of nature and of goodness, says: "In my early youth there was scarcely anything between 'Cinderella' and the 'Spectator' for young persons." Fairy tales certainly have their value and beauty, but a young child needs something more, and they alone do not suffice for real improvement and study.

To Dr. Aikin.

1776.

Your kind and acceptable letter would have met with an earlier answer, if we could, either of us, have commanded time to write. The manner in which you receive our proposal gives us great pleasure. My dear, tender Patty! I wonder not that your softness takes alarm at the idea of parting with any of your sweet blossoms. All I can say is, that, the greater the sacrifice, the more we shall think ourselves obliged to you, and the stronger ties we shall think ourselves under to supply, as far as possible, to the child of our adoption, the tenderness and care of the parents we take it from. Though we should be content with either, yet of the two we shall like better Charles, if you determine to give him us, than the unborn; perhaps, however, by this time I am wrong in calling him so: but if he was fixed upon, it would be longer before the scheme could take effect, and more uncertain whether he would live and thrive. This, however, is a point you must determine for us: we shall acquiesce in either.

You are very favorable to my fragments; fragments, however, they are like to continue, unless I had a little more time. I want much to see your Essays; how do you proceed with them? To attack Shakespeare! heresy, indeed!

I will desire Mr. Montague to chastise you, except by way of penance you finish the ode you once began in his praise. I am of your opinion, however, that we idolize Shakespeare rather too much for a Christian country. That inconsistencies may be found in his characters is certain : yet, notwithstanding that, character is his distinguishing excellence ; and though he had not the learning of the schools in his head, he had the theatre of the world before him, and could make reflections on what he saw. An equal vein of poetry runs through the works of some of his contemporaries ; but his writings are most peculiarly marked by good sense and striking characters ; so that I think you do him not justice if you call him only a poet.

Mrs. Barbauld's "Lessons for Children" were translated into the French, and made one of an excellent series of English books considered worthy of being used in that way. In the preceding letter to her brother she mentions the interest taken in her fragments. Among these, probably, was the poem of which Horace Walpole, in writing to his friend, the Rev. William Mason, himself a poet, known as the author of the "Garden" and some tragedies, says : "Mrs. Barbauld's 'fragment' was excellent." This fragment is the poem on "Autumn," and will be found among her other works. The following letter to Miss Dixon contains thanks for some needlework, couched in a very pretty fable.

To Miss Dixon, afterwards Mrs. Beecroft.

Palgrave, March 17, 1777.

Arachne, my dear Miss Dixon, — so goes the story, — was unfortunate enough to incur the mortal displeasure of Minerva by too pompous a display of her skill in embroidery; and since that event very few ladies who have courted the favor of Minerva have chosen to run the hazard of provoking her by the delicacy of their needlework. Now, as I do not believe that Arachne or Minerva either (no dispraise to her goddess-ship) ever wrought anything prettier than the roses you have been so obliging as to send me, — Flora, indeed, promises to produce some very like them in a few months, — I wonder much at your being so great a favorite with the goddess as I find you are, by the story which accompanied them, and that she thinks proper to encourage you in handling both your pen and your needle in the manner you do. Indeed, my dear, I was equally surprised and flattered at the very obliging manner in which you have shown that you remember me; and though much struck with the elegance of your fancy and the skilfulness of your fingers, I am still more delighted with the proof they give me of your regard and affection.

It is generally said that at your age impressions of friendship are easily made and soon worn out; but it is not so with you; and, to say the truth, I should be mortified if it were, for I have myself too lively and pleasing a remembrance of the happy and sportive hours we enjoyed together at Thorpe, not to wish they should be equally dear to your mind. My thoughts, as well as Mr. B.'s, have often pursued you since. We have figured you as amongst your sweet companions, at once improving your heart in sensibility, accomplishing yourself in all that is elegant, and enjoying without fear or anxiety all the simple, innocent, cheerful pleasures which belong to that period of life you are now in. Enjoy and relish them while you may. You will never be again, — I do not say so happy, for I hope your happiness will ever increase, — but you will never enjoy again the same kind of happiness which you do now, nor with so little mixture of uneasiness; and the way to prolong it is to keep as late as possible that entire openness, simplicity, and ingenuousness which is the beautiful characteristic of your age.

Another of these pleasant little allegories here meets the reader, and this charming tale is in Mrs. Barbauld's peculiar style and most happy manner. That she had a remarkable talent for this kind of composition, is not to be doubted; and this is one of her best little fables, — a short prose poem, one may call it, so smooth and perfect is the language, and so full of harmony the turn of expression. The conclusion is very nicely made, in desiring for her friend leisure without ennui.

PALGRAVE, November 11.

I have long been determined to seize the first moment of leisure to write to my dear Miss Dixon; but leisure is one of those things of which I enjoy the least, so I am at length determined to write without it. By the way, do you know the pedigree and adventures of Leisure?

She was born somewhere amongst the Chaldean shepherds, where she became a favorite of Urania; and, having been instructed in her sublime philosophy, taught men to observe the course of the stars, and to mark the slow revolution of seasons. The next we hear of her is in the rural mountains and valleys of Arcadia. In this delightful abode her charms made a conquest of the god Pan, who would often sit whole days by her side, tuning his pipe of unequal reeds. By him she had two beautiful children, Love and Poetry, the darlings of the shepherds, who received them in their arms, and brought them up amidst the murmur of bees, the falls of water, the lowing of cattle, and the various rural and peaceful sounds with which that region abounded. When the Romans spread the din of arms over the globe, Leisure was frightened from her soft retreats, and from the cold Scythian to the tawny Numidian could scarcely find a corner of the world to shelter her head in. When the fierce Goth and Vandal approached, matters were still worse, and Leisure took refuge in a convent on the winding banks of the Seine, where she employed herself in making anagrams and cutting paper. Her retirement, however, did not pass without censure, for it is said she had an intrigue with the superior of the convent, and that the offspring of this amour was a daughter named Ennui.

Mademoiselle Ennui was wafted over to England in a northeast wind, and settled herself with some of the best families in the kingdom. Indeed, the mother seldom makes any long residence in a place without being intruded on by the daughter, who steals in and seats herself silently by her side.

I hope, however, my amiable friend is now enjoying the company of the mother without fear of a visit from the daughter, whom her taste and liveliness will, I am sure, ever exclude from her habitation.

The following letter to her brother, in acknowledgment of his new book, has some observations on poetry and its application to common objects which seem very just. She describes a little of her employment to him in the school, in the preparation of the play which the boys are to act; and one can fancy the "Tempest," under her able management, being presented very creditably by her juvenile performers. Dr. Aikin's keen observation of nature, and his love for natural objects, led him to study the botany and fauna of the region where he resided, and his professional rides were a source of pleasure to him, as he with them combined his favorite studies.

PALGRAVE, 1777.

You have given us too much pleasure lately not to deserve an earlier acknowledgment. I hope you will believe we were not so dilatory in reading your book * as we have been in thanking you for it. It is indeed a most elegant

* An Essay on the Application of Natural History to Poetry.

performance; your thought is very just, and has never, I believe, been pursued before. Both the defects and beauties which you have noticed are very striking, and the result of the whole work, besides the truth it conveys, is a most pleasing impression left upon the mind from the various and picturesque images brought into view. I hope your Essay will bring down our poets from their garrets, to wander about the fields and hunt squirrels. I am clearly of your opinion, that the only chance we have for novelty is by a more accurate observation of the works of nature, though I think I should not have confined the track quite so much as you have done to the animal creation, because sooner exhausted than the vegetable; and some of the lines you have quoted from Thomson show with how much advantage the latter may be made the subject of rich description. I think, too, since you put me on criticising, it would not have been amiss if you had drawn between the poet and natural historian, and shown how far, and in what cases, the one may avail himself of the knowledge of the other, — at what nice period that knowledge becomes so generally spread as to authorize the poetical describer to use it without shocking the ear by the introduction of names and properties not sufficiently familiar, and when at the same time it retains novelty enough to strike. I have seen some rich descriptions of West Indian flowers and plants, — just, I dare say, but unpleasing merely because their names were uncouth, and forms not known generally enough to be put into verse. It is not, I own, much to the credit of poets, — but it is *true, — that we do not seem disposed to take their word for* anything, and never willingly receive *information* from them.

We are wondrous busy in preparing our play, "The Tempest"; and four or five of our little ones are to come in as fairies; and I am piecing scraps from the "Midsummer Night's Dream," etc., to make a little scene instead of the mask of Ceres and Juno. We have read Gibbon lately, who is certainly a very elegant and learned writer, and a very artful one.. No other new books have we yet seen, — they come slow to Norfolk, — but the "Diaboliad," the author of which has a pretty sharp pen-knife, and cuts up very handsomely. Many are the literary matters I want to talk over with you when we meet, which I now look forward to as not a far distant pleasure.

We will come and endeavor to steal away Charles's heart, before we run away with his person. Adieu! Heaven bless you and yours!

Thanks to my dear Miss Dixon for her frank and affectionate letter. A thousand good wishes attend her; but, as I hope to breathe them soon from my lips, I shall spare my pen a task to which it is not adequate.

You have rejoiced my heart by allowing me to hope that we shall still see you at Palgrave before the important event takes place. If you had not acknowledged that you were going to be married, I should naturally have concluded it from your saying you have not time to read "Cecilia." Not time to read a novel! — that is so grave! Nay, if I had not known you, I should have supposed you had been actually married a dozen years at least. But you *must* read "Cecilia," and you must read Hayley's poem, and you may read Scott's poems if you like, and at least you must look at the plates, etc.

Mrs. Chapone, the gifted friend of Miss Elizabeth Carter, and better known, under her maiden name of Mulso, as the intimate and companion of Samuel Richardson the novelist in her early years, met Mrs. Barbauld in 1775. In a letter to a friend, Mrs. Chapone, in regretting her enforced "exile" from London and its society, says that the illness of her aunt has deprived her of the pleasure of meeting many delightful acquaintances. One only of these she names, — "Mrs. Barbauld in particular I regret, as the opportunities of cultivating her acquaintance are so scarce and valuable. I am very glad to find you improve your opportunities so well, for I entirely agree with you in your idea of her character, and think her a prize not to be neglected. I wish you would institute a correspondence with her; for, notwithstanding the cold caution which age brings upon me every day, I cannot help being strongly inclined, on the evidence before me, to give her credit for all those qualities of the heart and temper which must be joined to her great understanding to make her worthy of your friendship. I regret particularly the snug day at my brother's." *

* Mr. Mulso.

CHAPTER VI.

MRS. BARBAULD TAKES CHARGE OF SOME YOUNG SCHOLARS. — WRITES THE "PROSE HYMNS." — HER AIM IN WRITING THEM. — VISITS LONDON. — LETTERS TO DR. AIKIN. — VISITS NORWICH. — PECULIARITIES OF THE OLD TOWN. — LETTERS TO MISS MORE. — MISS MORE'S POEM ON "SENSIBILITY." — ADDRESS TO MRS. BARBAULD. — DR. AIKIN REMOVES TO YARMOUTH. — VISIT TO LONDON IN THE CHRISTMAS HOLIDAYS. — MEETS MANY FRIENDS THERE. — JOSEPH JOHNSON, HER PUBLISHER. — MISS BURNEY. — LETTERS.

MRS. BARBAULD'S success in teaching, and singular devotion to the young children under her charge, induced several gentlemen to persuade her to assume the personal care and instruction of their little boys, and she received some at the early age of four years. Among these boys was Thomas Denman, afterwards a distinguished member of the legal profession. Lord Denman was eminent for his liberal political views, sagacity and ability as a lawyer, and integrity in his professional relations. He held many high offices, being Lord Chief Justice, and created for his various services a peer of the realm. Miss Aikin, writing to Dr. Channing of Lord Denman's taking leave of Lincoln's Inn Court in consequence of his promotion to the position of the Chief Justice, mentions the speech made on this occasion by his old friend the Vice-Chancellor, and then adds, "This glorious man — by the way, his person is made for dignity — was Mrs. Barbauld's pupil at four years old. I think it must have been chiefly for him that her 'Hymns in Prose' were written. He cherishes her memory most religiously. In a great public entertainment where I met him last year, he came up to me and said, with a look of delight, 'I dreamed of Mrs. Barbauld only last night.' He has a love and taste for poetry and elegant literature worthy of her scholar, and I doubt not that she sowed the seed." This letter was written in 1832. In another of an earlier date, Miss Aikin described her own feelings on the subject of the "Prose Hymns" to the same valued friend: "Of all the products of my Aunt Barbauld's fine genius, which you have commemorated in a manner most gratifying to my feelings, there is none which during my whole life I have prized so highly as her "Hymns for Children"; by which, with the most delightful allurements of style, the infant mind is insensibly led to look up through all which it beholds, whether of animate or inanimate, physical or moral nature, to the infinitely wise and beneficent cause of all." Another of these infant pupils of Mrs. Barbauld was in after years the celebrated antiquarian and classical scholar, Sir William Gell, the distinguished explorer of the Plain of Troy and Pompeii. As Miss

Aikin states, it was for the use of this infant class that Mrs. Barbauld wrote her beautiful prose hymns.

She, herself, in the Preface, says of the Hymns and her object in writing them, it was "the peculiar design of this publication . . . . to impress devotional feelings as early as possible on the infant mind; fully convinced, as the author is, that they cannot be impressed too soon, and that a child, to feel the full force of the idea of God, ought never to remember the time when he had no such idea, — to impress them, by connecting religion with a variety of sensible objects, with all that he sees, all he hears, all that affects his young mind with wonder or delight; and thus by deep, strong, and permanent associations to lay the best foundation for practical devotion in future life." One sentence alone in the Hymns seems to be worth volumes of instruction to the thoughtless or inconsiderate who may have the care of children, — "Respect in the infant the future man. Destroy not in the man the rudiments of an angel." Too much cannot be said of the simple beauty and absolute perfection of the Hymns. Called prose by their gifted author, they abound in the most harmonious periods, and pure, elevating imagery of true poetry, and must strongly impress their claim and value upon all who read them; and each fresh reading will only strengthen the admiration and pleasure they impart. Written for the very young, they cannot fail to affect the intelligent, cultivated, and well-developed mind by their gradually elevated tone of thought, simple though it be, and the purity, devotional spirit, and charming style of expression so peculiarly adapted for the ideas and religious teachings they convey.

In Miss Aikin's sketch of her own early life, she alludes to the love of nature awakened in her mind by her observing and intelligent father, and adds: "This interest was inexpressibly exalted by Mrs. Barbauld's 'Prose Hymns,' which were taught me I know not how soon. Her 'Early Lessons' had prepared the way, for in them too there dwells the spirit of poetry; but the Hymns gave me the idea of something bright and glorious hung on high above my present reach, but not above my aspirations. They first gave me the sentiment of sublimity, and of the Author of all that is sublime. They taught me piety." These Hymns are, and will remain, unequalled for their spirit of pure, exalted devotion, deep yet simple thought, and the grandest purity of style, which renders them attractive and profoundly interesting to the mind of the little child, while that impression must also be felt by all who read them.

PALGRAVE, 1777.

I am happy that I can now tell you we are all safe at Palgrave, where we arrived last night about ten o'clock. Charles has indeed been an excellent traveller, and though, like his great ancestor, "some natural tears he shed," like him, too, "he wiped them soon." He had a long, sound sleep last night, and has been very busy to-day, hunting the puss and the chickens. And now, my dear brother and sister, let me again thank you for this precious gift, the value of which we are both more and more sensible of as we become better acquainted with his sweet disposition and winning manners. As well as a gift, it is a solemn trust, and it shall be our study to fulfil that trust. The thought of what parents we have taken him from will be a constant motive for our care, tenderness, and affection.

Remember us most affectionately to Dr. and Mrs. E—— and Betsy ——, and give a kiss for me to Arthur and George; and so you may to Betsy, now I think of it.

Everybody here asks, "Pray, is Dr. Dodd really to be executed?" as if we knew the more for having been at Warrington.

PALGRAVE, January 19, 1778.

It is real concern to me that I could not write to you from London. . . . . Let me now, then, begin with telling you that we too, Miss B——, and one of our boys, got safe to Palgrave this afternoon. And now for the first time Mr. Barbauld and I experienced the pleasure of having something to come home for, and of finding our dear Charles in perfect health and glad to see us again; though wondering a little, and rather grave the first half-hour. Well, and what have you seen, you will say, in London? Why, in the first place, Miss More's new play, which fills the house very well, and is pretty generally liked. Miss More is, I assure you, very much the ton, and moreover has got six or seven hundred pounds by her play: I wish I could produce one every two winters; we would not keep school. I cannot say, however, that I cried altogether so much at "Percy" as I laughed at "The School for Scandal," which is one of the wittiest plays I remember to have seen; and, I am sorry to add, one of the most immoral and licentious, — in principle, I mean, for in language it is very decent. Mrs. Montague, not content with being the queen of literature and elegant society, sets up for the queen of fashion and splendor. She is building a very fine house, has a very fine service of plate, dresses and visits more than ever; and I am afraid will be full as much the woman of the world as the philosopher. Pray, have you read a book to prove Falstaff no coward? I want to know what you think of it: the present age deals in paradoxes. A new play of Cumberland's and another of Home's are soon to come out. Charles's little book is very well, but my idea is not executed in it; I must therefore beg you will print one as soon as you can, on fine paper, on one side only, and more space and a clearer line for the chapters. Prefix, if you please, to that you are going to print, the following

ADVERTISEMENT.

This little publication was made for a particular child, but the public is welcome to the use of it. It was found that amidst the multitude of books professedly written for children, there is not one adapted to the comprehension of a child from two to three years old. A grave remark, or a connected story, however simple, is above his capacity, and nonsense is always below it; for folly is worse than ignorance. Another great defect is the want of *good paper, a clear and large type, and large spaces.* Those only who have actually taught young children can be sensible how necessary these assistances are. The eye of a child and of a learner cannot catch, as ours can, a small, obscure, ill-formed word amidst a number of others all equally unknown to him. To supply these deficiencies is the object of this book. The task is humble, but not mean; for to lay the first stone of a noble building, and to plant the first idea in a human mind, can be no dishonor to any hand.

In this letter to her brother, and in the advertisement, the reader will see from Mrs. Barbauld's own words that she held it no trifling responsibility to write for children well; and her sentiment on the subject is certainly noble and true. She also tells him of her visit to London and her laughter at Sheridan's new play, "The School for Scandal," and how she wept at Miss More's new tragedy, "Percy." Her letter contains a description of Mrs. Montague's new house. That lady, not being content with being the head of a literary set which she adorned by her talents and taste, aspired to greater conquests and social successes, and had built herself a new and elegant mansion, known as Montague House, in Portman Square. Until recently this house was quite as she left it externally; but the hand of change has begun its work, and already it is much altered by what are termed "modern improvements." In Mrs. Montague's own letters, she tells her friends some of her trials in getting it completed; but at last it was finished, and quite eclipsed the house in Hill Street, where she had so long gathered round her a circle of eminent people. Montague House was more magnificent than the earlier residence; but the circle was also much larger, less free from formality, and less social.

PALGRAVE, 1778.

'T is well I got a letter from Warrington when I did,—very well indeed; for I began to be in such a fury, and should have penned you such a chiding! Do you know, pray, how long it is since I heard from any of you? But, as I do sometimes offend myself, I think I will forgive you, especially as I wonder how you find time even to read, with labors so multifarious (as Johnson says) going forward. The fate of Miss B——'s letter is very remarkable. It was written as full—I am sorry to mortify you, my dear sister—as the paper would hold, folded, sealed, directed, and put *somewhere;* but when I had finished mine, and wanted it to put in the frank, it could be found *nowhere.* 'T is needless to tell you how the paper-case was cleared, the cupboard routed out, pockets searched, and everybody who had entered the room squinted at with an evil eye of suspicion. The letter has never made its appearance to this day; and, what vexes Miss B—— is, that Patty can but be in her debt, and that she was before. Now half this letter, she says, was about Charles, which may serve to excuse me, who finished in a violent hurry. I left him to the last, but was obliged to conclude abruptly. I am afraid to tell you much about him, lest you should fall in love with him again, and send somebody to kidnap him; though I think Charles would have a good many defenders in this house if you did. You will see by the enclosed I have been employing my pen again for him, and again I must employ you to get it printed.

PALGRAVE, January 20, 1779.

You are a pretty fellow to grumble, as my mother says you do, at my not writing! Do not you remember, when you sent a sheet of Charles's book, you said you did not mean the line you sent with it for a letter, but would write soon? so that by your own confession you are now in debt to me. Charles bore a part in our examination, by repeating a copy of verses on the boy who would not say A, lest he should be made to say B; and we, let me tell you, deserve great praise for our modesty and self-denial in not making a parade with his Greek, for he *could* have repeated an ode of Anacreon. But, notwithstanding this erudition, a few English books will still be very acceptable.

We are just returned from Norwich, where we have been so much engaged with dinners and suppers that, though I fully intended to write from thence, and began a letter, I really could not finish it. The heads of all the Norwich people are in a whirl, occasioned by the routs which have been introduced amongst them this winter; and such a bustle, with writing cards a month beforehand, throwing down partitions, moving beds, etc.! Do you know the different terms? There is a squeeze, a fuss, a drum, a rout, and lastly a hurricane, when the whole house is full from top to bottom. It is matter of great triumph to me that we enjoy the latter for ten months in the year.

In this letter of January, 1779, Mrs. Barbauld alludes to a visit they had just made in Norwich, then a city of considerable social and literary activity, which has long since departed, leaving it at the present time a dull, provincial place. At that time it boasted of being the birthplace and residence of several literary men, and there were many old families whose wealth and hospitality made it celebrated in the last century. The manufacturing interest also was large, and brought prosperity and affluence to the inhabitants. The names of the Taylors, Enfields, Sayerses, Smiths, Martineaus, and Mrs. Opie will give a hint of the class of cultivated, intellectual people who gave the old city its literary prominence for a time. Add to this set of literary people the fact of its being the site of a cathedral, and one can fancy the stately Church people who would bring with them an air of refinement, elegant manners, and dignity becoming their connection with one of the oldest and finest cathedrals in the kingdom. Miss Martineau, in her sketch of Mrs. Opie, describes some of the peculiarities and provincial oddities of Norwich in the latter half of the last century. She compares its literary coterie, and the conceit and pedantry of its members, to that of Lichfield, which is still remembered, and adds that "Norwich was very like Lichfield, ... only with less sentimentality, and with some additional peculiarities of its own. It had its cathedral, but neither the proverbial dulness nor the all-conquering High-Churchism of most cathedral towns: the liberality of good Bishop Bathurst prevented the latter during the long course of his episcopate; and the manufactures of Norwich preserved it from stagnation. It is true that when invasion was expected, the Church and Tory gentry set a watch upon the cathedral, lest the Dissenters should burn it for a beacon to 'Boney'; and the manufacturers who were of Liberal opinions were not accepted as volunteers, but were simply intrusted with the business of providing for the conveyance of the women and children into the interior whenever the French should land at Yarmouth or Cromer. But still, while Bishop Bathurst touched his hat to the leading Dissenters of the place, and Norwich goods were in demand for the Spanish and Portuguese markets, the old city could not stagnate like other cathedral towns. . . . . When William Taylor became eminent as almost the only German scholar in England, old Norwich was very proud, and grew, to say the truth, excessively conceited. She was (and she might be) proud of her Sayers; and Dr. Sayers *was* a scholar.

She boasted of having produced several men who had produced books of one sort or another (and to produce a book of any sort was a title to reverence in those days). She boasted of her intellectual supper-parties, where, amidst a pedantry which would now make Laughter hold both his sides, there was much that was pleasant and salutary; and finally she called herself the Athens of England." In her conclusion, this gifted daughter of old Norwich sums up its departed glories by saying, "Its bombazine manufacture has gone to Yorkshire, and its literary fame to the four winds." Mrs. Barbauld's letter tells us of these "intellectual supper-parties," and we can fancy that Mrs. Barbauld must have been well fêted by these good people, from her intimate knowledge of all their gayety.

From Mrs. Barbauld to Miss H. More.

Palgrave, November, 1783.

Dear Madam, — If any one were to ask me whether Miss More and Mrs. Barbauld correspond, I should say, "We correspond, I hope, in sentiment, in inclinations, in affections; but with the pen I really cannot say we do. Her pen is better employed, and mine, alas! is seldom employed at all but in the routine of business." I cannot, however, always repress the desire of hearing how you do, and of letting you know there is one in a corner of Norfolk whose heart preserves in their full glow the love and esteem with which you have long ago inspired it. These sentiments have received a fresh accession of strength by the sight of your "Sacred Dramas," a work I have expected with impatience ever since you favored me with a peep at "Moses." It is too late, my dear Miss More, to compliment you on the execution of your pleasing plan; but you must give me leave to mention how sensibly I was touched with pleasure on seeing the tribute you have paid to friendship, in the obliging lines which soon caught my eye in the sweet poem annexed to the Dramas. It was a sensible mortification to me that I did not meet you in London last Christmas; perhaps I shall be more fortunate this vacation. We mean to spend part of it at Bristol, at Mr. Estlin's; and if you are in Bristol then, I need not say how great an addition it will be to the happiness we hope to enjoy there.

We have lately been reading Mr. Soame Jenyns's Essays; you have seen them, no doubt. I think, too, that you will agree with me in pronouncing many of them very ingenious and very whimsical. What, for instance, do you think of the idea of coming into this world to be punished for old offences? How would it sound, think you, if people were to date, — 'In the twentieth year of my imprisonment, from my cell in such a place'? What discomfort must it be to a poor creature, whose lot is poverty and affliction here, instead of promising himself his portion of good things hereafter, to think that he is only paying off old scores! If Mr. Soame Jenyns has the gout, for instance, as many worthy people have, it must be pleasant to hear the corollaries he cannot but deduce from it.

But I run on till I am afraid I shall oblige you to try to recollect some peccadillo in your pre-existent state, for which you are troubled with this letter; therefore, that I may not lie heavy upon your conscience, as well as exercise your patience, I will bid you adieu, after delivering Mr. Barbauld's compliments and best wishes.

I am, my dear madam,

Your affectionate friend and obedient servant,

A. L. Barbauld.

This letter to Miss More is in acknowledgment of the new book just published, the "Sacred Dramas," which was sent to her by its amiable and talented author; and Mrs. Barbauld tells her how deeply she was affected by the beautiful lines addressed to herself in the poem on "Sensibility." This poetical epistle, addressed to the Hon. Mrs. Boscawen, eulogizes true friendship among women, and in it Miss More depicts the charms and character of some of the distinguished women of the period. I have already taken a few lines from her character of Mrs. Boscawen, and will now quote that part which contains a true and graceful tribute to her friend Mrs. Barbauld. After a glowing apostrophe to the modern school of poetry and art and the new beauties which they displayed, and the expression of a hope that Mrs. Boscawen will accept these unpolished lays, —

"Nor blame too much the verse you cannot praise,"

Miss More continues her address to Mrs. Boscawen:—

"Yes, still for you your gentle stars dispense
The charm of friendship and the feast of sense:
Yours is the bliss, and Heaven no dearer sends,
To call the wisest, brightest, best your friends.
And while to these I raise the votive line,
O let me grateful own these friends are mine;
With Carter trace the wit to Athens known,
Or view in Montague that wit our own:
Or mark, well pleased, Chapone's instructive page,
Intent to raise the morals of the age.
Or boast, in Walsingham, the various power
To cheer the lonely, grace the lettered hour:
Delany, too, is ours, serenely bright,
Wisdom's strong ray, and virtue's milder light:
And she who blessed the friend, and graced the lays
Of poignant Swift, still gilds our social days;
Long, long protract thy light, O star benign!
Whose setting beams with milder lustre shine.
Nor, Barbauld, shall my glowing heart refuse
Its tribute to thy virtues or thy Muse;
This humble merit shall at least be mine,
The poets' chaplet for thy brow to twine;
My verse thy talents to the world shall teach,
And praise the genius it despairs to reach.
Yet what is wit, and what the poet's art?
Can genius shield the vulnerable heart?
Ah, no! where bright imagination reigns,
The fine-wrought spirit feels acuter pains;
Where glow exalted sense and taste refined,
There keener anguish rankles in the mind;
There, feeling is diffused through every part,

Thrills in each nerve, and lives in all the heart;
And those whose generous souls each tear would keep
From others' eyes, are born themselves to weep.
Can all the boasted powers of wit and song,
Of life one pang remove, one hour prolong?
Fallacious hope! which daily truths deride;
For you, alas! have wept, and Garrick died!"

Dr. Aikin was not satisfied with his professional prospects at Warrington, and the social charms of the place had very much fallen off, as the Academy became less popular and successful. The little circle of tutors and their families, who made up the pleasant intercourse of the town, was broken by death and the removal of those connected with it. His father's death, his sister's marriage, and the changes at the Academy, all had their influence on the small group of intelligent and genial friends, and deprived the place of its superior attractions and advantages for a professional and literary man. He resolved, therefore, to remove to a better situation for professional advancement; and, being told that Yarmouth was in need of the best medical advice, he took up his abode there for a time, only to find that the opportunity for practice was smaller than he had been led to suppose. His mother, who resided with him after the death of Dr. Aikin the elder, accompanied the family on their journey. Miss Lucy Aikin, in her "Early Recollections," writes of the year 1784: "My grandmother, her maid, my little brother, and myself were packed in a post-chaise; my father accompanied us on horseback. It was Christmas week, the snow deep on the ground; the whole distance was two hundred and forty miles across the country, and we were six days in accomplishing it. The last night we spent at my aunt Mrs. Barbauld's house at Palgrave, where my grandmother remained behind; she died in a few days, of the cold and fatigue of the journey." This must have been a fresh blow to the affectionate and sensitive heart of Mrs. Barbauld, already much saddened by the death of her father. In her poetical epistle to her friend Dr. Enfield, on his revisiting Warrington in 1789, she concludes with these pathetic lines, which indicate how tenderly she cherished the memories and happiness of departed days, spent with her parents at her early home.

Were it, like thine, my lot once more to tread
Plains now but seen in distant perspective,
With that soft hue, that dubious gloom o'erspread,
That tender tint which only time can give;

How would it open every secret cell
Where cherished thought and fond remembrance sleep!
How many a tale each conscious step would tell!
How many a parted friend these eyes would weep!

But, O the chief! — If in thy feeling breast
The tender charities of life reside,
If there domestic love have built her nest,
And thy fond heart a parent's care divide;

Go, seek the turf where worth, where wisdom lies,
Wisdom and worth, ah, never to return!
There kneeling, weep my tears, and breathe my sighs,
A daughter's sorrows o'er her father's urn!

The school at Palgrave was full and prosperous, and the scholars were from the families of noblemen and gentlemen of the best class. Among these may be named Basil, Lord Daer, a favorite pupil, whom Mrs. Barbauld often mentions in her letters written long after this as one whom she knew well, and loved. Three of his brothers, one of whom was the last Earl of Selkirk, two sons of Lord Templetown, Lord More, Lord Aghrim, and the Hon. Augustus Phipps, were among the pupils. William Taylor of Norwich and Dr. Sayers of that city have already been mentioned as bright and interesting boys, who made brilliant scholars. Lord Denman and Sir William Gell also should be included in this list, which names a few only of the boys who profited by Mr. and Mrs. Barbauld's excellent care and instruction. In the school vacations at Midsummer and Christmas, Mr. and Mrs. Barbauld enjoyed many pleasant journeys, and visits to friends in various parts of England and Scotland. The summer vacation was usually passed in travelling in the country and visiting friends there, the winter holidays in lodgings in London. From her letters to her brother we learn that they were welcome guests and honored, intimate friends in many elegant and charming homes. In Mrs. Montague's fine new mansion, Montague House, they saw all of London society that was great in literature and science, — men and women whose names are still celebrated for their genius, culture, and brilliancy; and that was one only of the many houses where they were frequent visitors. Joseph Johnson, of St. Paul's Churchyard, her publisher, was a good friend of Mrs. Barbauld; and she tells her brother she is almost afraid to name the hour at which some of his agreeable and social parties end. There she met many literary people in a more simple style, and the conversation was less formal, and people mixed more easily in his rooms, than in the more magnificent residences of her West End fashionable friends. This good but rather unfortunate man was a kind-hearted though somewhat dilatory publisher. He had much taste and discrimination, and published Cowper's poems, which had been rather contemptuously rejected by some other booksellers, ignorant of their beauty and merits. Many other valuable and important books of the time issued from his press. He was Miss Edgeworth's publisher also, and when imprisoned in the King's Bench Prison, in 1799, for a publication considered treasonable, was visited by Mr. and Miss Edgeworth, who were then on a visit to London; and many of the authors in whose works he had interested himself made it a point, as the Edgeworths did, to pay him attention in his misfortune. Afterwards he was much connected and rather intimate with Godwin, Holcroft, and some others of that revolutionary and radical set, and it was rather a disadvantage and injury to be associated with him either in a social or a business way.

LONDON, January 2, 1784.

Well, my dear brother, here we are in this busy town, nothing in which (the sight of friends excepted) has given us so much pleasure as the balloon which is now exhibiting in the Pantheon. It is sixteen feet one way, and seventeen another; and when full (which it is not at present) will carry eighty-six pounds. When set loose from the weight which keeps it to the ground, it mounts to the top of that magnificent dome with such an easy motion as put me in mind of Milton's line, "rose like an exhalation." We hope to see it rise in the open air before we leave town. Next to the balloon, Miss B——* is the object of public curiosity; I had the pleasure of meeting her yesterday. She is a very unaffected, modest, sweet, and pleasing young lady: but you, now I think of it, are a Goth, and have not read "Cecilia." Read, read it, for shame! I begin to be giddy with the whirl of London, and to feel my spirits flag. There are so many drawbacks, from hair-dressers, bad weather, and fatigue, that it requires strong health greatly to enjoy being abroad. The enthusiasm for Mrs. Siddons seems something abated this winter. As the last season was spent in unbounded

* Fanny Burney.

admiration, this, I suppose, will be employed in canvassing her faults, and the third settle her in her proper degree of reputation.

In this letter Mrs. Barbauld describes their Christmas visit to London, and how much she liked Miss Burney, then the object of general interest as the author of "Evelina" and "Cecilia," books which formed a new era in light literature as evidences of the study of human nature and descriptions of people; and they amused, delighted, and surprised the public, who found themselves wildly excited over the adventures and misfortunes of the heroine, the vulgarities and oddities of the other characters. The "Braughtons" were the theme of universal discussion, and the author was the admiration of a circle which boasted such members as Dr. Johnson, Burke, Sir Joshua Reynolds, Mrs. Montague, Sheridan, and others celebrated for their talents, brilliancy, and wit. Her diary, written for the perusal of her family, gives the reader of the present day a most thorough insight into the character and description of the looks, manners, and peculiarities of the most noted men and women of her time. No one in Great Britain of as keen observation and ready powers of description, perhaps, had more advantages and opportunities of acquaintance with great and little people than "little Fanny Burney," later known as Madame D'Arblay after her marriage with a French *emigré*, an officer of distinction. Mrs. Barbauld met her at the house of a mutual friend, Mr. Barrows, by her own wish, an appointment being made by Mrs. Chapone, who introduced her there to Miss Burney; and long after Mrs. Barbauld renewed the acquaintance in a manner which Madame D'Arblay mentions in her diary as most kind and pleasant. In the letter which follows, written after her return to Palgrave, Mrs. Barbauld tells Dr. Aikin of the continual visiting they had done while in London, and of the pleasure they found in it; of all the novelties of the day, — the automaton, the newly arrived American minister, Mr. Adams, and the members of the American Congress, then just landed in England at the conclusion of the long war between Great Britain and her colonies.

PALGRAVE, January 21, 1784.

MY DEAR BROTHER, — We arrived at Palgrave yesterday. I much wished to have written again from London; but I could not get further than half a letter, which was therefore committed to the flames. Bating the circumstance of being greatly hurried, we spent our time very pleasantly in London, and had a great deal of most agreeable society. Our evenings, particularly at Johnson's, were so truly social and lively that we protracted them sometimes till — But I am not telling tales. Ask —— at what time we used to separate. Our time, indeed, in London was chiefly spent in seeing people; for, as to seeing sights, constant visiting and the very bad weather left us little opportunity for anything of that kind. There is a curious automaton which plays at chess. His countenance, they say, is very grave and full of thought, and you can hardly help imagining he meditates upon every move. He is wound up, however, at every two or three moves. The same man has made another figure, which speaks; but as his native tongue is French, he stays at home at present to learn English. The voice is like that of a young child.

We spent two very agreeable days at Mr. ——'s. We saw there many Americans, members of the Congress, and plenipos. We were often amused with the different sentiments of the several parties in which we passed the day. At Mr. Brand Hollis's, the nation was ruined; notwithstanding which we ate our turkey and drank our wine as if nothing had happened. In the evening party there was nobody to be pitied but the poor king; and we criticised none but Mrs. Siddons. It is impossible, however, not to be kept awake by curiosity at learning the extraordinary manœuvres and rapid changes that have happened lately. Do you know that at two o'clock on the day the Parliament met, Mr. Pitt had not received his return? so that Mr. Fox had almost begun the debates before Pitt knew he was even a member!

In the letter which follows, Mrs. Barbauld describes the mode of soliciting votes then in fashion, with natural indignation and disgust at the vulgarity and freedom of the high-born titled ladies who disgraced their sex and station by canvassing in such a manner. The beautiful Georgiana, Duchess of Devonshire, was one of the ladies notorious in this election, and her name easily supplies the blank left in the letter, as she was often in Covent Garden wearing the colors of Charles James Fox, her relation; and the report that she had won the vote of a hesitating butcher with a kiss was commemorated in gross caricatures and libels.

PALGRAVE, May, 1784.

Let me begin with telling you, what you have some reason to complain of me for not having told you before, that we are very well. Mr. B—— has begun to eat his dinners; and we smile upon the year, as the year begins to smile upon us. We propose going to Birmingham this vacation, and we understand Oxford and Daventry are in the way; so that we hope a great deal lies before us to please the eye and touch the soul of friendship: but busy must we be before we have earned our vacation.

What do you think of the behavior of our great ladies on the present election? I thought the newspapers had exaggerated; but Mr. —— says he himself saw the two Lady ——s and Miss —— go into a low alehouse to canvass, where they stayed half an hour; and then, with the mob at their heels offering them a thousand indignities, proceeded to another. These he mentioned as unmarried ladies, and therefore less privileged. The Duchess of ——, Mrs. ——, and many others, equally expose their charms for the good of the public.

Have you got Hoole's "Ariosto"? We are reading it; but think the translation, except in a few passages, wonderfully flat and prosaic: the adventures are entertaining, however.

CHAPTER VII.

MR. AND MRS. BARBAULD RELINQUISH THEIR SCHOOL.—THEY MAKE A CONTINENTAL JOURNEY.—LETTERS WRITTEN TO THE FAMILY AND FRIENDS ON THIS JOURNEY.—PERSONS WHOSE ACQUAINTANCE THEY MAKE.—THEY MEET JOHN HOWARD.—MAGNETISM.—MANNERS AND CUSTOMS.—MODE OF TRAVELLING.

IN the year 1785, Mr. and Mrs. Barbauld found that their arduous cares and engrossing life of instruction, though occasionally relieved by vacations and pleasant excursions, were too exhausting, and that an entire change of scene and relief from continuous duties was an absolute necessity. They therefore gave up their school at Palgrave, and Mr. Barbauld resigned his pastoral charge, which released them from longer residence there, and they made arrangements for a Continental tour which was prolonged for several months, and was productive of much benefit and enjoyment to them. After leaving Palgrave, they made a visit to Dr. Aikin at Yarmouth, and then went to Dover, to sail for France. They left England the 17th of September, 1785, and were absent until the following June, during which interval they travelled in France and passed some time in Switzerland.

To MRS. J. TAYLOR.

YARMOUTH, September 1, 1785.

DEAR MADAM, — Though I have had the pleasure (it was a very real one) of a glimpse of Mr. Taylor, yet I cannot prevail on myself to intrust either him or Mr. Barbauld with those affectionate wishes and grateful acknowledgments of your friendship which, before I leave England, I wish to convey to you with my own hand. Mr. Barbauld will tell you our route. Now it comes to the point, I cannot help feeling it a solemn thing to leave England, and all our dear connections in it, for so many months. Often will they be in our minds; and when we recollect those who hold the highest places in our esteem and affection, Mrs. Taylor will always be presented to our thoughts. Allow me, dear madam, again to thank you for your kindness to us at Norwich, and the pleasure we enjoyed in that short but delightful intercourse with you and your family. On that family may health and every blessing ever rest!

By the time we return, I think I shall have had a sufficient draught of idleness, and be very ready to engage again in some active pursuit; but at present, Avaunt care! and *Vive la bagatelle!* for we are bound for France.

The following letter, the first written on her journey, gives her brother their experiences as far as Dover, where they were then waiting for the packet to sail.

DOVER, September 17, 1785, 8 o'clock.

Fair stood the wind for France, —
When we our sails advance;
Nor now to trust our chance
Longer would tarry.

It is not very fair either, for there is scarcely wind enough; but what there is, is in our favor. We are just got here, and a packet sails to-night, so I suppose we shall go in a few hours; for the night is the most beautiful, the most brilliant, that ever rivalled day. The moon, which is nearly full, illuminates the majestic chalky cliffs, the stately castle, and the element we are going to trust ourselves to. The views about Dover are very bold and very beautiful. But let me give a regular account of ourselves. From London we had the good fortune to take part of a chaise to Dover with Dr. Osborn. He is a most entertaining, agreeable companion; and we never had a more agreeable journey, especially to-day, for yesterday it was rainy, and we did not get into Rochester till nine at night; consequently lost in a great measure the windings of the silver Medway. But to-day was uniformly fine; and greatly delighted we were with the view of Chatham, Stroud, and Rochester, from a hill just above the town, which we walked up. The Medway makes a fine bend here. The hop-pickers were at work as we went along, but not with their usual alacrity; for the late storm has blasted the hops to such a degree that twenty thousand pounds' worth of damage, they say, is done. The country is beautifully variegated all the way, and has many fine seats; among which Sir Horace Mann's was pointed out.

From this rich, enclosed country you come to the open downs, more grand and striking. The first view of Dover Castle is noble; and still more finished that of the town, which we saw from Dr. O——'s house, where we dined. It has the castle on one side, hills on the other, a valley between (in which is the town), and the sea beyond. I think we shall hardly see more beautiful scenes in France. We here took leave of our last English friends. I forgot to say we took a hasty peep at the venerable cathedral of Canterbury, to which I would at any time willingly go a pilgrimage, though not barefoot.

Dr. Aikin, after his sister's departure, in writing her says: "How I long to be with you to quaff the pendent vintage as it grows; to see the gay people in their gayest mood, and lead the dance with a sunburnt Champenoise on the green turf! Here, different employ! We are fitting out fishing-boats, preparing nets and cordage, launching to sea, and out for the mighty shoals of herrings in their annual migration. Already some are brought in, and carts loaded with them are driving by. Here is industry, and here are the sources of wealth; but where are pleasure and elegance and vivacity? If employments must give a tincture and flavor to those occupied in them, surely one would prefer the perfume of the grape to the stench of a herring." His biographer speaks of the inspiring influence of his sister's letters, describing alternately the gay and sublime scenes, the new and varied experiences of travel, which unfolded themselves before her astonished and admiring eyes, — and says that they animated his fancy and roused his vivid imagination to the composition of a poetical epistle, part of which I quote. In this he very charmingly follows in imagination the travels of his sister through the novel and beautiful scenery which she beholds; his fancy, after a rapid chase, joins her in her journey through the South of France, and he begins his imaginary travels in Burgundy.

> "O'er land, o'er sea, freed fancy speeds her flight,
> Waves the light wing, and towers her airy flight;
> And now the chalky cliffs behind her fly,
> And Gallia's realms in brilliant prospect lie."

He desires the lovely country and climate to exert their soothing influence on the tired and toil-worn travellers: —

> "Fair land! by nature decked, and graced by art;
> Alike to cheer the eye and glad the heart,
> Pour thy soft influence through Lætitia's breast,
> And lull each swelling wave of care to rest;
> Heal with sweet balm the wounds of pain and toil,
> Bid anxious, busy years restore their spoil;
> The spirit light, the vigorous soul infuse,
> And, to requite thy gifts, bring back the Muse."

Mrs. Barbauld's own letters to her brother and

friends fully describe her first fresh impressions of the lovely scenes and odd manners and customs of the people whose countries she saw on her journey. She speaks of the advantages and disadvantages of travel after they had been for some time on their journey, and contrasts home favorably with all the beauties of climate and the novelties which continually met their eyes. They went as far south as Marseilles, and thence pursued their way to Geneva; where Mr. Barbauld found he had some relations, on his mother's side, whose acquaintance he made. Mrs. Barbauld mentions the society in that city as being extremely cultivated and agreeable. She described a Sunday in Geneva to her friend Mrs. Kenrick, and was evidently much struck by the peculiar mode of conducting the Protestant services. Those who have had the opportunity of attending a Swiss Protestant service can fancy her sensations at seeing the minister put on his hat after naming the text of his sermon, and the congregation follow this custom if they choose. This practice is still observed, and the modern traveller may see it and be as much amazed as she was at first noticing it. She tells Mrs. Kenrick that there are some things learned by travel, for she has discovered that she can eat many kinds of food distasteful to her at home "without making faces much," which strikes one as hardly a necessary lesson at her age.

BESANÇON, October 9, 1785.

DEAR BROTHER, — I wrote letters from Calais and from Troyes, the contents of which have, I hope, been communicated to you. From Troyes we proceeded to Dijon by a road so delightful that I strongly wished my sister and you could have been with me, — a wish which I cannot help forming, though a vain one, whenever any object particularly pleasant presents itself. During the greatest part of this road we had the full view of the Seine, which we traced upwards to within half a league of its source, and saw it grow less and less, untwisting, as it were, to a single thread. The valley in which it ran was narrow, of a beautiful verdure, and bounded by hills of the most gentle ascent covered with trees or herbage: cattle of all sorts, among which were several flocks of goats, were feeding in sight. The road often ran upon the ascent; and we saw the river, sometimes bordered with trees and sometimes fringed with grass or rushes, winding beneath in the most sportive meanders, — for we saw and lost it nine times from one spot. The scene was in general solitary; but, if we came to a spot particularly pleasant, it was sure to be marked by a convent, the neatness of which (generally white) added to the beauty of the scene. After we had lost the Seine, we came to the Val de Suson, a still more romantic place, and very like Middleton Dale, only that the rocks were richly covered with trees. Through the first part of this valley runs the river Suson; the rest is still narrower, and between high rocks.

At Dijon we delivered our first letter of recommendation,

which introduced us to M. De Morveau, a man of great merit, who was *avocat général*, but has quitted his profession for the sake of applying himself to philosophical studies, and chiefly chemical. He writes all the chemical articles in the "*Nouvelle Encyclopedie.*" He esteems Dr. Priestley, Dr. Black, and Mr. Kirnan, to be the chief men in England in the philosophical way. M. De Morveau was one of the first who ascended in a balloon. He showed us their Academy, which is one of the first provincial ones. The *Palais des Etats*, in Dijon, is the finest building in it; the front of it forms one side of a very handsome square, and the wings extend much beyond it. It is adorned with statues and paintings by the pupils of the drawing-school. From the tower, on which is an observatory belonging to this building, is a charming view of the country: the hills of Burgundy covered with vines; the rivers of Ouche and Suson, which encircle the town; and the town itself, which is large, though not very populous. On our way from Dijon to Dole we saw more of the vintage than we had hitherto done, — and a gay scene it is; though I must confess my disappointment at the first sight of the vines, which are very low, and nothing like so beautiful as our apple-trees. They say they have more wine this year than they can possibly find vessels to put it in; and yet the road was covered with teams of casks, empty or full, according as they were going out or returning, and drawn by oxen whose strong necks seemed to be bowed unwillingly under the yoke. Men, women, and children, were abroad: some cutting with a short sickle the bunches of grapes; some breaking them with a wooden instrument; some carrying them on their backs from the gatherers to those who pressed the juice; and, as in our harvest, the gleaners followed. From Dole we should have gone directly to Besançon, but were induced to strike out of the road to visit the *grottes stalactites* of Auxcelles; to see which we crossed in a ferry the river Doux, a fine stream with banks beautifully wooded, and got into a place most wild and solitary, through such terrible bad roads that what we thought would have been the affair of a few hours detained us there the whole night: the grotto, however, repaid our trouble. Had you been there, you would have seen it with a more philosophical eye, and have told us how the continual dropping of water through those rocks forms those beautiful petrifications, which when polished, as they sometimes are, have the lustre and transparency of crystal. But it required only eyes to be struck with the view of a vast subterranean shaft running through a whole rock, which had the appearance of a most magnificent Gothic church; tombs, images, drapery, pillars, shrines, all formed without much aid from fancy, by nature working alone for ages in these long and lofty caverns. We walked in it, I believe, about two furlongs, and it might be another to the end. Besançon is by far the best town we have seen; the streets are long and regular, the hotels of the chief inhabitants palaces for princes, and the public buildings noble. But you would have been most struck with the hospital, managed in all the internal parts by those good nuns, *Les Hospitalieres*, with such perfect neatness that, in a long chamber containing thirty-five beds, most of them full, there was not any closeness or smell to be perceived. The beds were of white cotton, and by each bed a table and chair. Some of the nuns were attending here; others in the dispensary making up medicines; others in the kitchen making broths, etc.: and all this they do without salary, and many of them are of good families.

NOYON, *October* 13. — I could not finish my letter time enough to send it from Besançon, which gives me an opportunity to tell you in brief that we are got to within a stage of Geneva, and are now sitting in a room which overlooks the delightful lake. We were too late last night for Geneva, as they shut the gates at half after six, and open them for no one. We hope to get there this morning, and to receive letters from you, which my heart longs for. I have only to tell you further that I have seen the Alps, — a sight so majestic, so totally different from anything I had seen before, that I am ready to sing *Nunc dimittis.*

Tell me in your next how long you have been sitting by a coal fire. We have had no fire but twice or three times, a little in the evening, since we set out; and in the middle of the day the heat has been very strong. I suppose, however, we shall find it colder at Geneva.

Louis Bernard Guyton de Morveau, of whom Mrs. Barbauld speaks, was a learned French chemist; and, in addition to the office she mentions, he was republican deputy to the Legislative Assembly and the Convention, member of the Committee of Public Safety and Council of Five Hundred, and in the time of Napoleon's government, one of the Administrators-General of the Mint, and director of the Polytechnic School. He was the discoverer of the means of destroying infection by acid vapors, and the author of many chemical treatises.

In the following letter to Dr. Aikin, Mrs. Barbauld acknowledges the receipt of his verses, and compliments his poetical epistle by telling him that it is not necessary that he should travel to write poetry well. Dr. Aikin was fond of poetry, and wrote several very pretty and graceful pieces. He published a small volume of his poems.

.... And so much in French; which, though it begins to be easier to me, is still to me either in writing or speaking like using the left hand; and I now want the language the most familiar to me, the most expressive, that with less injustice to my feelings I may thank you for your charming letter. It is not necessary for *you* to travel in order to write good verses; and indeed, to say truth, in the actual journey many things occur not altogether so consonant with the fine ideas one would wish to keep upon one's mind. The dirt and bustle of inns, and the various circumstances, odd or disgusting, of a French *diligence*, are not made to shine in poetry. I shall, however, keep your exhortation in mind;

and when, to complete the inspiration, I have drunk of the fountain of Vaucluse, which we are going to do, if the Muse is not favorable, you may fairly conclude I no longer possess her good graces. From Lyons we took the *diligence d'eau* down the Rhone to this place, a voyage which in summer, and in a vehicle more neat and convenient, would have been delightful. But we had incessant rain for two of the days; and the third, though bright, was very cold, with a great deal of wind; so that we did not reach Avignon till the morning of the fourth day. The Rhone is rapid all the way; but at Pont St. Esprit particularly so, insomuch that many passengers get out there: we did not. The Rhone has high banks all the way, or rather is enclosed between hills, covered in many places with vines and pasturage, in others pretty barren. Near St. Esprit begins the olive country. This was the first time we had been in a public voiture; it is a very reputable one, and yet you cannot conceive the shabbiness and *mal proprieté* of the boat.

We are now in a land of vermicelli, soup, and macaroni, — a land of onions and garlic, — a land flowing with oil and wine. Avignon is delightfully situated; the Rhone forms two branches here, and encloses a large fertile island. The Durance (another fine river, at present so overflowed that it is not passable) joins the Rhone some way below the town. The churches here are numerous, highly adorned, and have several good paintings. The streets are darkened with cowls and filled with beggars, drawn here, they say, by the strangers; for the people are no ways oppressed by the government, the revenue to the Pope hardly paying the expenses. We are not yet, however, in the climate of perpetual spring; like an enchanted island, it seems to fly from us. All along the course of the Rhone there are cold winds. Lyons is disagreeable in winter, both with fogs and cold. At Geneva everybody had fires and winter dresses before we left it; and Avignon, though much warmer, is not enough so to invite us much abroad, or permit us to dispense with fires. To-morrow we set off for Orange, and from thence shall go to Lisle, perhaps to Marseilles; but where we shall spend these next two months we have not yet determined. May you and my dear sister spend them with health and pleasure in that dear society where our hearts perpetually carry us, and to which we hope to return with increased affection!

I forgot to tell you that all the people speak *patois* to one another, though they speak French too; and when we landed, the people who came about us to carry our things had absolutely the air of demoniacs, with their violent gestures and eager looks, and their coarsest exclamations at every second word.

To Dr. Aikin.

Marseilles, December, 1785.

Health to you all — poor mortals as you are, crowding round your coal fires, shivering in your nicely closed apartments, and listening with shivering hearts to the wind and snow which beats dark December! The months here have indeed the same names, but far different are their aspects; for here I am sitting without a fire, the windows open, and breathing an air as perfectly soft and balmy as in our warmest days of May; yet the sun does not shine. On the day we arrived here, the 5th of December, it did; and with as much splendor and warmth, and the sky was as clear and of as bright a blue, as in our finest summer days. The fields are full of lavender, thyme, mint, rosemary, etc.; the young corn is above half a foot high: they have not much, indeed, in this neighborhood, but from Orange to Lisle we saw a good deal. The trees which are not evergreens have mostly lost their leaves; but one sees everywhere the pale verdure of the olives mixed with here and there a grove, or perhaps a single tree, of cypress, shooting up its graceful spire of a deeper and more lively green far above the heads of its humbler but more profitable neighbors. The markets abound with fresh and dried grapes, pomegranates, oranges with the green leaves, apples, pears, dried figs, and almonds. They reap the corn here the latter end of May or the beginning of June. The gathering of the olives is not yet finished; it yields to this country its richest harvest. There are likewise a vast number of mulberry-trees, and the road in many places is bordered with them; but they are perfectly naked at present. Marseilles is, however, not without bad weather. The *vent de bise*, they say, is penetrating; and for this last fortnight they have had prodigious rains, with the interruption of only a few days; so that the streets are very dirty and the roads broken up. But they say this is very extraordinary, and that if they pass two days without seeing a bright sun they think Nature is dealing very hardly with them. I will not, however, boast too much over you from these advantages; for I am ready to confess the account may be balanced by many inconveniences, little and great, which attend this favored country. And thus I state my account: —

Advantages of Travelling.	*Per Contra.*
A July sun and a southern breeze.	Flies, fleas, and all Pharaoh's plague of vermin.
Figs, almonds, etc., etc.	No tea, and the very name of a teakettle unknown.
Sweet scents in the fields.	Bad scents within doors.
Grapes and raisins.	No plum-pudding.
Coffee as cheap as milk.	Milk as dear as coffee.
Wine a demi-sous the bottle.	Bread three sous the halfpenny roll.
Provençal songs and laughter.	Provençal roughness and scolding.
Soup, salad, and oil.	No beef, no butter.
Arcs of triumph, fine churches, stately palaces.	Dirty inns, heavy roads, uneasy carriages.
A pleasant and varied country.	But many, many a league from those we love.

From Avignon (whence I wrote to you last) we went to Orange, where we were gratified with the sight of an arc of triumph entire, of rich architecture; and, though the delicacy of the sculpture is much defaced by time, it is easy to see what it must have been when fresh. There is likewise a noble ruin of an amphitheatre built against a rock, of which you may trace the whole extent, though the area is filled with cottages. These were the first remains of antiquity of any consequence I had seen, and they impressed me with an idea of Roman grandeur. Orange is a poor town, but the country is green and pleasant, and they have all country-houses. When the principality came under French government, it was promised that they should have no fresh taxes imposed; but *peu à peu*, say they, taxes are come. They had salt-springs which more than supplied them with that article; they are forbidden to work them. They grew tobacco; now, if any one has more than three plants in his garden, he is punished. From Orange we went to Lisle. In the way we stopped at Carpentras, where we were shown another arc of triumph, over which a cardinal, the bishop of Carpentras, built his kitchen; very wisely judging that nothing was more worthy to enter through an arc of triumph than a noble haunch of venison or an exquisite ragoo. Lisle is a small town, very pleasant in summer, because it is surrounded with water; and still more noted for its neighborhood to the source of that water, the celebrated fountain of Vaucluse.

During the few fair days we have had, the warmth and power of the sun has been equal to our summer days; it is truly delightful to feel such a sun in December; to be able to saunter by the shore of the Mediterranean, or sit on the bank and enjoy the prospect of an extensive open sea, smooth and calm as a large lake. It is likewise very pleasant to gain an hour more of daylight upon these short days. However, though the middle of the day is so warm, in the mornings and evenings a fire is acceptable, I must confess.

The Marseillians value themselves upon being a kind of

republic, and their port is free: the lower rank are bold and rude; the upper, by what I hear, very corrupt in their manners. There are thirty thousand Protestants; their place of worship is a country-house, which they have hired of the commandant himself. They meet with no molestation, and hope from the temper of the times that they shall erelong have leave to build a church. The minister is an agreeable and literary man, and is very obliging towards us; his wife has been six years in England, and speaks English well. Her family fled there from persecution; for her grandfather (who was a minister) was seized, as he came out from a church where he had been officiating, by the soldiers. His son, who had fled along with the crowd and gained an eminence at some distance, seeing they had laid hold on his father, came and offered himself in his stead; and in his stead was sent to the galleys, where he continued seven years. *L'honnête Criminel* is founded on this fact. Besides this family, we have hardly any acquaintance here, nor are like to have. We have, however, been two or three times with the Chanoines de St. Victor, who are all of the best families of France, as they must prove their nobility for one hundred and fifty years. They are very polite and hospitable, and far enough from bigots; for we were surprised to find how freely to us they censured auricular confession, the celibacy of the clergy, and laughed at some of their legendary miracles. I forgot to say that the country about Marseilles is covered with country-houses; they reckon ten thousand. They were first begun to be built on account of the plague: everybody has one. There is a fine picture of the terrible plague here at the *Consigne*, and another at the Town House. They are very exact at present in their precautions. I am sure the plague cannot be occasioned merely by want of cleanliness, for then Marseilles could not escape.

Remember that we are longing for letters, and that news from you will be more grateful to us than groves of oranges or Provençal skies.

TO MRS. KENRICK.

GENEVA, October 21, 1785.

My dear Eliza has desired me to write to her during our tour. She could not have put me upon an employment more agreeable to myself, for I am continually wishing those I love in England could share the pleasure we receive by the new scenes and objects which are continually passing before our eyes; and, though I can give you but a very inadequate idea of them, it will be without any drawback from fatigue, bad inns, dirt, and various other etc's., which may be put on the opposite side when the travelling account is balanced. We landed at Calais, September 18, and you may wonder that we have as yet only reached Geneva; but Mr. B., from kind regard to my health, and indeed the convenience of us both, thought it best to make short stages; besides which, we have stopped wherever there were churches or fine things to be seen. One very agreeable ornament of the towns abroad, which in England we are strangers to, is their fountains, the more pleasing as they connect public utility with a degree of magnificence. They excel us likewise in public walks, and in every fortified town the ramparts alone afford very fine ones.

We find ourselves very happy in Geneva; and, if the season was not so far advanced, should like to spend a month or two here: indeed, we have been singularly fortunate, for Mr. B. has found out a family of relations here, of the name of Rochemont, very amiable and respectable people; and the society here in general seems easy, sprightly, and literary. English is much understood, and very tolerably spoken by many. The town is still divided into parties, and one side will tell you that Geneva is no longer what it was, that it has lost its liberty and everything worth living for; and thus far is true, that the government is become entirely aristocratical, and is at present so strict that half a dozen people cannot have a weekly meeting at each other's houses, unless they choose to declare they keep an open tavern. The situation of Geneva, as you well know, is delightful. I am just returned from an excursion to the mountain of Saléve, within a league of the town; from whence on one side you have a view of Geneva, with its lake of the purest blue, a large plain between the chain of Mount Jura and that of the Alps, cultivated like a parterre, and full of villages, country-houses, and farms, watered by the Arve, which meanders through it in the most sportive manner, making several islands, and beyond Geneva falls into the Rhone. The vintage is not here got in, so that the vineyards are still in their beauty. On the other side Saléve, the mountains open upon you in all their grandeur. Mr. B. is gone to the Glaciers, to feast his eyes with a nearer view of these stupendous mountains; but I thought the expedition beyond my strength, and I am during his absence in a family of Genevois, who are very good kind of people.

Will you hear how they pass the Sunday at Geneva? They have service at seven in the morning, at nine, and at two; after that they assemble in parties for conversation, cards, and dancing, and finish the day at the theatre. Did not you think they had been stricter at Geneva than to have plays on the Sunday, especially as it is but two or three years since they were allowed at all? The service at their churches is seldom much more than an hour, and I believe few people go more than once a day. As soon as the text is named, the minister puts on his hat, in which he is followed by all the congregation, except those whose hats and heads have never any connection; for you well know that to put his hat upon his head is the last use a well-dressed Frenchman would think of putting it to. At proper periods of the discourse, the minister stops short, and turns his back to you, in order to blow his nose, which is a signal for all the congregation to do the same; and a glorious concert it is, for the weather is already severe, and people have got colds. I am told, too, that he takes this time to refresh his memory by peeping at his sermon, which lies behind him in the pulpit.

Nobody ought to be too old to improve; I should be

sorry if I was; and I flatter myself I have already improved considerably by my travels. First, I can swallow gruel soup, egg soup, and all manner of soups, without making faces much. Secondly, I can pretty well live without tea; they give it, however, at Geneva. Thirdly, I am less and less shocked, and hope in time I shall be quite easy, at seeing gentlemen, perhaps perfect strangers, enter my room without ceremony when I am in my bedgown. I would not have you think, however, I am in danger of losing my modesty; for if I am no longer affected at some things, I have learned to blush at others; and I will tell you, as a friend, that I believe there is but one indecency in France, which is, for a man and his wife to have the same sleeping-room. "Est ce votre chambre, madame, ou celle de M. votre époux?" said a lady to me the other day. I protest I felt quite out of countenance to think we had but one.

It is time to leave Geneva, for I see from my window the tops of Mount Jura, which are already covered with snow; and we have had a *vent de bise* so severe that I have been confined to my chamber, it is now the sixth day, with a very painful swelled face.

In her letter from Aix to Dr. Aikin, Mrs. Barbauld speaks of meeting his friend, and also her own and her husband's, the eminent philanthropist, John Howard, who was then on his second tour of examination of the lazarettos and prison-dens of the Continent. She says that he was "well and in good spirits." This excellent man had for some years devoted himself to the benevolent work for which he became so famous; and after this journey he became interested in a new inquiry into an important subject, that of the cause and cure of the terrible pestilence which ravaged the southern countries of Europe and the Levant, — the plague. On his journey through the eastern countries of Europe, which he undertook in 1789, he was seized with a malignant fever, which carried him off after a short illness on the 20th of January, 1790. In one of Mrs. Barbauld's letters to her brother, written at the time of his son's sudden insanity, which made him only an object of care and distress to his father for the remainder of his life, she tells him that young Howard was drinking tea with a friend's family, when he suddenly declared that the cup of tea just made for him by the lady was poisoned, and accused her of attempting to kill him, in a terrible rage, which showed unmistakably his mental disorder. In the letter from Aix, Mrs. Barbauld alludes to "the folly of the day" in France, — "Animal Magnetism," and tells her brother he may make a sensation by introducing the new treatment in London. Travelling in *diligences* was then in vogue on the Continent, and unless parties could procure a carriage, they were forced to take that mode of conveyance. The Barbaulds travelled part of the time in *diligences*, and for the rest in their own carriage, which was by far the most agreeable and independent manner of making a journey at that time, as they could easily procure fresh horses at the post-stations, and rapidly and pleasantly see the country.

Aix, February 9, 1786.

. . . . With regard to ourselves, we have at length quitted Marseilles, where, to confess the truth, we stayed long enough to be pretty well tired of it; for we had scarce any acquaintance, and no amusements (the play excepted) but what we could procure to ourselves by reading or walking. Some delightful walks we did take under a bright sun and a clear blue sky, which would have done honor to the fairest months in the English calendar. We sailed one fine day to the little chateau *d'If*, a league from the port. It is used as a prison for extravagant or disorderly young men, whom their parents get shut up here, — sometimes to avoid the disgrace of a more public punishment. We had a great pleasure at Marseilles in seeing your friend Mr. Howard: he was well and in good spirits. He went by the name of the English Doctor, and as such has prescribed, he told us, with tolerable success. If you have a mind to strike a good stroke in London, introduce magnetism; 't is in France the folly of the day. There is a society at Marseilles for that purpose, composed of gentlemen. They boast they can "lay asleep" when they please, and for as long as they please; and that during this sleep or trance the mind can see the operations going forward in the corporeal machine, and predict future events. One of them offered to try his skill on Mr. Barbauld;

but after a long and unpleasant operation of rubbing the temples and forehead, he was obliged to desist without success. Mr. Howard will tell you, however, they operate better at Lyons, as he saw several women at the hospital put to sleep in a minute by only passing the hand over their forehead.

At Marseilles we again bought a carriage (an English chaise), in which we hope to perform the rest of our journey; at least to Paris. The road from Marseilles to Toulon is over mountains which, though not very high, are the beginning of the Alps. They are in many parts quite naked and craggy; in others covered with forests of pines; and in many they have had the industry to make terraces one over another to the very top, on which they have planted vines, though the culture must demand prodigious labor, for they must bring all the earth. The almond-trees, which are now in full flower, scattered here and there, embellish the scene. At Toulon we saw the arsenal, which contains the *corderie*, the *salle d'armes*, the naval stores, etc. There is something horrible in the clanking of the chains of the galley-slaves, who are chained two and two, and employed in various works within the place. Three or four galleys lie in the harbor, but they are not used except for lodging the *forçats*. From Toulon we went to Hieres; and how think you did we go? On foot every step of the way, and it is nine miles at least. We went on foot because the roads are still so bad we dared not venture in a carriage. Hieres is a specimen of the Italian climate and Italian productions: to the south it is open to the sea; every other quarter is fenced with hills.

The town lies on the descent of the hill, and is surrounded with groves of orange and lemon trees, glowing in the brightest beauty, and with all the variety of color, from the palest lemon to the deep and almost blood-red species of orange. The leaves, of a vivid green, give a relief to the fruit, which is in so great an abundance that I have hardly seen apple-trees so full. It is a delicious spot, quite the garden of the Hesperides, and enjoys a constant verdure. The hedges are composed of myrtle, holm-oak, and lentisk, of the ashes of which latter they make a lye with which they preserve their raisins. They gather green peas soon after Christmas; every month brings its peculiar harvest. Besides the corn, wine, and oil, which they share in common with their neighbors, they have vast quantities of strawberries, peaches, kidney-beans, all kinds of fruit and garden stuff. Sweet waters and essences are distilled from the orange-flowers and the peel of the bergamot, the cedrat, and some other kinds valuable for their fragrance. Some of the orange-gardens are worth from twenty to twenty-six thousand livres a year. From an opposite hill there is a view of the town; above it a convent of Bernardines, and higher still the ruined walls and castle of the old town; the whole surrounded with a bright circle of green and gold, and houses of a shining white in the midst of the orange-gardens; farther, the paler green of the olives; to the south, the sea and the fishery salt-works; and opposite, the islands of Hieres, where is plenty of game. Winter is seen peeping at this little paradise from the top of a distant mountain covered with snow; and sometimes, in deed, he sends a hoar-frost, after which the oranges drop by hundreds from the trees.

To complete our expedition and vary the mode of travelling, we returned as follows: I upon the *bourrique* of a *paysanne*, between two loaded panniers, Mr. B. walking before; and the woman, a stout, sunburnt, cheerful Provençal, by the side of the ass, driving, guiding, and hallooing it onward. Bread and figs, which we put in the pannier and ate as we went along, were our breakfast. I rode thus two leagues, and walked with Mr. B. the third. And now, having touched the utmost limit of our long tour, it is with inexpressible pleasure we reflect that every step we shall for the future take will bring us nearer again to those dear friends in whose society we hope to spend the rest of our life. We propose returning by Nismes, Montpelier, and Bordeaux. Aix is a clean, pretty town; the baths and the fountains of hot water are worth seeing. It is full of clergy and men of the law. We got acquainted with two gentlemen (an officer and an ecclesiastic) who were very civil to us; but we could not help being diverted with the eagerness with which they recited their own verses (for they were both versifiers), their gestures, their compliments to each other, and their total freedom from that awkward bashfulness which hangs on us English when we have written something clever that we long to bring into notice, and do not know how to bring it about.

CARCASONNE, February 15, 1786.

If at any time, and in any place, a letter from my dear Mrs. Beecroft has always given me a sensible pleasure, she will judge how grateful it must have been to my heart to be remembered by her with so much kindness and affection, and to be informed of her welfare, when the long absence, when the tracts of land and seas between us and those most dear to our hearts, render accounts from England doubly interesting. And indeed, when I reflect that I am transported from the banks of the Waveney to the shores of the Mediterranean, I am ready to cry out with Simkin, —

"Methinks we 're a wonderful distance from home."

The scenes we have passed through gratify curiosity and fill the imagination; but you, my dear friend, in the mean time, have found yourself in situations which awaken feelings the most tender and interesting. . . . . May you experience, may you feel, all the sympathies, all the tender charities, of every relation, all of which you are so fitted to adorn!

The ladies of this country, if I may trust what their own countrymen say of them, are not fond of these domestic ties; they wish not to be mothers of a numerous offspring! and their husbands, whose claim to the honor is somewhat more dubious, are still less flattered with being fathers to them. But let me give you some account of our route. From Calais we coasted, as I may say, the rich plains of Flanders and Artois, which, however, had lost their peculiar beauty, as the harvest was got in. We passed through a part of *Haute Picardie*, and, leaving Paris on our right, advanced into

Champagne, where we first saw the production that most distinguishes the climate of France from ours, — the boasted vineyards. Having visited the venerable cathedral of Rheims, we crossed several pleasant streams, and from Troyes traced the delightful windings of the Seine to its very source. We next visited Dijon in the midst of the vine-clad hills of Burgundy, and from thence, crossing the Saone, struck into Franchecomté; and from Dole to Besançon travelled along the banks of the Doux, a fine, full stream, through a country more varied and rich with prospects than we had yet seen. From varied, the country became romantic, and from hilly, mountainous; nature preparing, as it were, for her more majestic scenes, till at length she swells into full grandeur, and from the heights of Mount Jura the Alps are discovered to the astonished traveller.

At Geneva we were greatly delighted with the society and the situation; but the winter advanced so fast upon us that we were obliged to abandon our design of visiting Switzerland. From Geneva to Lyons we were still in the midst of *les belles horreurs*, steep mountains, cascades, and lakes. At Lyons the winter was still at our heels; so down the rapid Rhone we sailed in search of the climate of perpetual spring, but like some enchanted island it seemed to fly from our pursuit. At Lyons it was the *vent du Rhone*, at Avignon *la bise*, at Marseilles the *mistral*, which opposed our wishes; till at length, in the orange-groves of Hieres, we found the most delicious temperature of air and a verdure perpetually flourishing. But long before we reached Hieres, between

Lyons and Avignon, we got amongst the olive grounds, the figs, the almonds, and pomegranates, which spread over all Provence and Languedoc. But they have not here the green pasture, the lowing herd, the hawthorn hedge, the haunt of birds, nor the various family of lofty trees which give us shade in summer and shelter in winter. As we have been chiefly at inns hitherto, I cannot say a great deal of the inhabitants in general. That they are more lively and eager in their gestures and manner than the English is evident; but, as to that great air of gayety you mention, and which one naturally expects to find in France, it has not struck us; perhaps it might if we were more intimately admitted into their families, and saw the young and the gay; but this I assure you, they are not to be found, even in Provence, singing and dancing under every green tree. We have lately visited Nismes, a place interesting by its antiquities. La Maison Carrée is the most delicate and finished piece of architecture that can be conceived; and the *amphitheatre* gives the most striking idea of Roman greatness. It is calculated to hold 18,000 people; its vast cirque cannot be beheld from a distance without astonishment, — all the other buildings sink into nothing before it. An antiquity perhaps more beautiful still than either of them is the Pont du Gard, some leagues from Nismes, constructed to convey water to the town. It looks great as if made by the hands of giants, and light as if wrought by fairies. Nismes has likewise a more modern work, of which they boast much, — the fountain, and walks belonging to it. This, as well as the Place de Perou at Montpelier, is laid out in a style which a Brown or a Shenstone would but little approve; long, straight walks, trees cut into form, water stagnating in stone basins and exactly symmetrized. All this suits but ill with what we have been taught to call taste; yet there is an air of magnificence, and even of gayety, that in its kind gives pleasure. The very exhibition of art and expense gives an air of grandeur. Its being a work made *by* men suggests the cheerful idea that it was made *for* men; whereas our more rustic scenes seem made, if not for melancholy, at least for solitary musing; and, in the last place, the exact proportion contrasts it with the surrounding country.

You know, probably, that Montpelier is famous for perfumes. One man, who has got a large fortune by them, has planted a garden with rose-trees, several thousands in number, which in summer perfume the air to a considerable distance.

I hoped to have finished this letter where I began it, at Montpelier; but not having been able to do it gives me an opportunity to tell you that we have seen at Pesenas an *échantillon* of the diversions of the Carnival. The young men of the town, with the young ladies, masked, followed by the *paysans* and *paysannes*, danced by torchlight in the streets, upon the esplanade, and all round the town, to the music of the drum and fife, followed by a number of spectators of all ranks, all enjoying the cheerful scene. Pesenas is a delightful place; the peach and apricot already are in blossom there, so is the bean; numbers of almond-trees are in full bloom; various shrubs are green with spring, and some trees begin to put out. To crown all, we found there a very lovely Englishwoman, with whom and her husband we spent two pleasant days. We are now going to Bourdeaux, and so to Orleans and Paris; after which I am sure we shall long to return home.

Mrs. Barbauld observed with natural interest and anxiety the condition of the French Protestants, and mentions in her letters that those of the sect at Marseilles were forced to hold their services in a country-house, no other edifice being allowed them; and at Nismes they could meet only in the open air, though that town was considered the centre of Protestantism in France, and the members of that church in Nismes were estimated at thirty thousand persons.

To Dr. Aikin.

Thoulouse, February 27, 1786.

I begin this letter from Thoulouse, though I shall probably not finish it before we get to Bourdeaux. We got here last night, and hoped to have walked about the town to-day, where they say there is a good deal to be seen; but we are confined to our room by a pretty heavy fall of snow, which has continued the whole day. We are at present convinced that it is a vain expectation to escape from winter by going to these southern climates; at Bengal, I suppose it may be done: but the southern provinces of France differ more in the duration than in the degree of their winter; and beyond all doubt they have more sudden and violent *changes* of weather than we have. In consequence, they dress warmer than we do. The pelisse, the muff, the fur gloves and shoes, the hussar cloak and flannel linings, are all common here, and found necessary. Yet it is also true that through a great part of the winter they enjoy the most delicious weather; and that, with regard to one or other of their productions, there is not any time of the year in which you do not meet with harvest or blossoms; for, before the gathering of olives is over, the almond-tree is in flower. Till within these four days we have had fine weather for a long time; and Lower Languedoc, through which our route has lain since we crossed the Rhone, has worn all the lovely features of spring. At Pesenas (the last place where we made any stay), the peach, apricot, and bean were beginning to blossom; the gardens were all green with various vegetables, the fields with corn, and a few trees were even in leaf. But their springs are apt to be premature. Here (in Upper Languedoc) it is colder.

Gratified as we have been by the spring of Nature, we have been no less so by the hoary ruins of Antiquity. The vast cirque of the amphitheatre at Nismes fills the mind with an amazing idea of Roman greatness. It is defaced by a number of buildings in the area; which, however, are to be demolished, and the venerable ruin kept in better repair. To *repair* a ruin carries a better sound with it than to *build* a ruin, as we do in England. *La Maison Carrée* is a *bijou;* it has all that the utmost delicacy and richness of architecture can give. But we prefer to them both the Pont du Gard.

Nismes is the very centre of the Protestants. They are computed to be thirty thousand, and the richest part of the inhabitants; for here, as the Dissenters in England, they give themselves to trade. They have no church, nor even barn; but assemble in the *desert*, as they call it, in the open air, in a place surrounded by rocks which reverberate the voice. The pulpit is movable, and there are a few seats of stone for the elders. On their great festivals, they say, the sight is very striking.

I wish you, who have a quarrel to some of our English axioms of taste in gardening, could see the public walks of Nismes and Montpelier; both (especially the latter) laid out with great magnificence, but quite in the old style of terraces, fountains, strait alleys, and exact symmetry: but the whole is great, and was to me very new. We intended to have taken the canal at Beziers, but the bad weather prevented us. From Narbonne till near Thoulouse we had on our left a long chain of mountains, the Pyrenees. I love to see those everlasting boundaries of nations. We had not, however, any wish to cross them and try the Spanish accommodations; there are difficulties enow of that kind in France. This is the height of the Carnival, and we have seen, as we came along, the dance on the green, and the masque by torchlight; but in general I am afraid there is a good deal of coarseness in the mirth of the vulgar, and of licentiousness in the gayety of the rich. From Narbonne to

Thoulouse there are a great many *châteaux*, pompous buildings with towers, but no ornamental grounds about them as in England, nor anything in the avenues, hedges, etc., that has a look of neatness. I fancy the rats hold a glorious *sabat* in some of them. I should tell you that at Montpelier we saw the anatomical theatre, where they have two hundred students, who shave and dress hair to pay their board and lodging, and attend dissections and study surgery with great application the rest of their time; and they say they make better progress than those that have money. I am sorry I cannot send you a slip of Rabelais's scarlet gown, with which sacred relique the students are invested when they take their degrees. The meaning of which I take to be this, — that laughing may cure you when physic would miss.

The situation of Thoulouse seems calculated for trade, as the noble canal of Languedoc meets there the still more noble river of the Garonne; yet it is not commercial, as the great ambition of all the rich inhabitants is directed towards gaining a seat in Parliament, which ennobles them; and then they leave trade. You may guess with what feelings we saw the seat of that parliament which condemned Calas. The spirit of the times, however, thank Heaven! is greatly altered.

BOURDEAUX, *March* 3. — We are arrived here to-day. The road from Thoulouse to this town is remarkably pleasant. It lies mostly along the banks of the Garonne, and several fine rivers which fall into it; the Tarn, the Aveyron, etc.

On the other side is a ridge of hilly ground quite sandy, covered with vines, which indeed have a most desolate appearance at this time of the year; but fancy can spread the foliage and hang the purple clusters. On the river-side are fine rich valleys covered with corn, and here and there pasture-ground: no more olives, but groves of oak; no more almond-blossoms, but hedges of hawthorn. On Shrove Tuesday (which was a remarkably fine day) every town and every village was poured out upon the road, all dressed and dancing, each lad with his lass. What I should not have supposed, they dance too on Ash Wednesday; for, though the churches were pretty full in the morning of dismal-looking figures in black hoods, who came to confess the sins of the Carnival, the greater part put the English interpretation upon a holy day, and considered it as a holiday. Though we have not yet seen much of Bourdeaux, a walk this afternoon has convinced us it is a more magnificent town than any we have yet seen in France. It happens, too, to be the fair.

. . . . The road from Tours to Orleans on the winding banks of the Loire is delightfully pleasant; but we had not fine weather enough to enjoy all its beauty; for we have had the second winter you speak of, in all its severity of snow and frost. We were particularly pleased, however, with Tours. It has one street of more complete beauty than any *street* I have yet seen, terminated at one end by a fine bridge over the Loire, at the other by one of the noblest malls in the kingdom. Blois is delightful from its situation, and interesting from the events which have taken place within its now deserted walls. Orleans is entirely a town of commerce; and it seems to flourish, for they live remarkably well there. Trade may have been despised formerly in France; but I am sure it cannot be now there are such towns as Lyons, Bourdeaux, and Orleans, where it displays its effects in all the pride of opulence. We have been now a month in Paris, and here the objects of curiosity crowd upon us. In the provinces they are scattered here and there; but in the capital, palaces, pictures, statues, public gardens, meet you at every step, and all the powers of observation and organs of perception are agreeably filled. The societies of Paris do not obtrude themselves in like manner on your notice; on the contrary, it is pretty difficult to get sufficiently into them to judge of their complexion and character. We shall have been, however, in a few of them, and shall have seen many agreeable individuals. English is very much studied here at present: there are a great many who read, and some who talk it. Everything of English fabric and workmanship is preferred here, and not without reason. They have an idea here very contrary to ours; for they say the English invent, and the French bring to perfection. They are going to enclose all Paris and its suburbs by an immense wall. It puts one in mind of hedging in the cuckoo; but it is to prevent smuggling. We have had the good fortune to get very clean lodgings: they are near the Pont Royal and the Tuileries, both which we often cross, and never without fresh admiration at the number of beautiful buildings and gay objects. I like the gardens of the Tuileries better than our St. James's Park; for, though they are somewhat disgraced by the old-fashioned parterre, yet on the whole they are more gay, more lively; the view from the terrace commands a greater variety of objects; the Tuileries is more adorned, and the various groups of all ranks — some taking lemonade, some sitting on the grass, some even reading — give an air of ease and enjoyment more than is to be seen in our Park. This is rather an unfortunate time for seeing paintings, as the king's pictures are all taken down in order to be arranged and put up in the gallery of the Louvre, which is preparing for their reception: and when that fine building is filled with so noble a collection, it will have few things in Europe superior.

One great advantage which Paris has as a town over London is its *quais*, by which means they enjoy their river and the fine buildings upon it. As to the streets, most of them are certainly narrow, but not absolutely impracticable to the poor *piëton*, as I had been taught to believe; for, when not dressed, I walk about a good deal. They say, however, a great many accidents happen, which their boasted police takes more care to stifle than to prevent; if a man is run over by a coach, they dare not put it in any public papers. The streets are full of little cabriolets, which drive very fast; they are forbidden, but people have them notwithstanding. We have been at two of their academies, that of *Sciences*, and that of *Belles Lettres*. Several *éloges* were read, well drawn up; prizes proposed, etc. They clap hands as at the playhouse, when a sentiment or expression pleases them. The theatre sinks in France as well as England; for, as Mrs. Siddons stands alone, we may well say it sinks. They are building a very fine church, St. Geneviève; and in general there is a good deal of new building as well as in London. We have yet a vast deal to see; but we shall see it as fast as we can, that we may return to those friends who will be only dearer to us from absence.

The following letter to Mrs. Taylor of Norwich contains some excellent remarks on the condition of the stage in France, and has quite an extended description of Paris as then seen by tourists.

To MRS. TAYLOR.

PARIS, June 7, 1786.

DEAR MADAM, — Though we expect now very soon to finish our long pilgrimage, I cannot quit this country without giving you a little testimonial that in it we think of those beloved English friends from whom the sea now divides us: they are often recalled to my mind by different and opposite trains of thinking, — for contrast, you know, is one source of association; and when I see the Parisian ladies covered with rouge and enslaved by fashion, cold to the claims of maternal tenderness, and covering licentiousness with the thin veil of a certain factitious decency of manners, my thoughts turn away from the scene, and delight to contemplate the charming union formed by deep affection and lasting esteem, — the mother endowed with talents and graces to draw the attention of polite circles, yet devoting her time and cares to her family and children, — English delicacy, unspoiled beauty, and unaffected sentiment, — when I think of these (and *your* friends will not be at a loss to guess where I look for them), it gives the same relief to my mind as it would to my eye, when wearied and dazzled by their sand-walks and terraces, if it could repose upon the cheerful and soft green of our lawny turf. I would not, however, have you imagine that I am out of humor with Paris, where we have enjoyed much pleasure; only it is the result of our tour, that, taking in all things, manners and government as well as climate, we like our own country best: and this is an opinion certainly favorable to our happiness, who shall probably never leave England again. The weather with us is, and has been, extremely hot. The trees are in their freshest green; but one sees that the grass will soon be burnt if we have not rain. Indeed, they are obliged every day to water the turf in all their gardens where they are solicitous about verdure. The environs of Paris are charming, yet, I think, evidently inferior to those of London. Yesterday (Whitsunday) we were gratified with a view of all the magnificence of Versailles. In compliment to the day the water-works played, and there was the brilliant procession of the *cordon bleu;* in consequence of which all Paris in a manner was poured into Versailles; and I was ready to forgive the enormous expense and ostentation of this palace, when I saw numerous people of all sorts and degrees filling the rooms and wandering in the gardens, full of admiration, and deriving both pleasure and pride from their national magnificence; and many a one, I dare say, exulted in the thought that the *grand monarque's* horses are better lodged than is the King of England himself. The grand gallery filled with Le Brun's paintings is of a striking beauty; the gardens are full of water thrown up in artificial fountains, and glittering through artificial *bosquets;* the walks are adorned with whole quarries of marble wrought into statues. In short, art and symmetry reign entirely; and I hope they will never attempt to modernize these gardens, because they are a model of magnificence in their kind, and art appears with so much imposing grandeur that she seems to have a right to reign. The *petit Trianon*, belonging to the Queen, is in another style; with cottages and green lawns and winding walks of flowering shrubs in the English mode, which indeed prevails very much at present.

There is a person here, the Abbé D'Hauy, who teaches the blind to read by means of books printed expressly for them in a relief of white. The undertaking is curious; but they are at present somewhat in the state of the blind men brought up for painters in the island of Laputa, who were not so perfect in the mixing their colors but that they sometimes mistook blue for red.

The French stage is not, I think, at present very brilliant; three of their best actors have lately left it. But at the Italian theatre they have a delightful little piece, which under the name of a comic opera draws tears from all the world. It is called Nina, or La Folle d'Amour, and Mademoiselle Du Gazon acts the part of Nina, and does it with such enchanting grace, such sweet and delicate touches of sensibility and passion, as I never saw upon any theatre. It is the *sweet bells jangled out of tune*, but not *harsh*; no raving, no disorder of dress; but every look and gesture showed an unsettled mind, and a tenderness inimitable. At the Opera they have likewise an actress full of grace, Mademoiselle St. Huberti; but there it is a grace beyond mere nature. Everybody (that is, everybody who follows the fashion) leaves Paris in the summer, which was not the case some years ago. We stay now for a fine show, — the procession on the *Fête Dieu*, in which all the tapestry of the Gobelins is exposed in the streets. We shall return by Calais and proceed immediately to London, where we shall take lodgings for some time.

Will you do me the favor to remember us with grateful affection to all our friends at Norwich? There are so many that claim our esteem, I do not attempt to enumerate them; but do not forget to give a kiss for us to each of your dear boys, and to assure Mr. Taylor of Mr. Barbauld's and my affectionate esteem.

As the travellers turned their steps homeward, Mrs. Barbauld's letters show that she felt rather impatient to return to England, and expressed much pleasure at the prospect of meeting again her family and friends. While the Barbaulds were in Paris, the termination came of the affair of the Diamond Necklace, mysterious and disgraceful in all its incidents. In this case the notorious Cardinal Rohan figured, and Marie Antoinette was personated by a girl named Leguet or D'Oliva, at the instigation of the principal in the plot, Madame Lamotte. The trial and its result are well known; Talleyrand Perigord wrote to a friend: "Attend narrowly to that miserable affair of the necklace. I should not be surprised if it overturned the throne."

To Dr. Aikin.

Paris, June 7, 1786.

. . . . The affair of Cardinal Rohan,* which has so much engrossed the talk at Paris, is at length decided; but we have not been able to see without indignation the decisions of the Parliament altered in almost every instance by the pleasure of the King; so that judicial proceedings are mere child's play in this country. A grocer has got himself into the Bastille by writing a pamphlet on this occasion; in which he insinuates that the Queen herself was in the plot, and that Madame Oliva was the cloud by means of which she played the fable of Ixion on the poor Cardinal. In short, people's conjectures are as much afloat since the decision as before. The king of Prussia is reported to have said, "Qu'il falloit que le Cardinal montrât beaucoup d'esprit pour prouver qu'il n'avait été que bête." Among the long list of titles which figure at the head of his *Mémoire*, that of *Académicien* is not found: the reason, they say, is, that

* The Diamond Necklace.

his *avocat*, at the request of the Academy (who feared they might be disgraced by the fellowship of such an associate), persuaded him to leave it out, by telling him that, for the other titles, they implied no parts; but that of *Académicien* — supposing a man of superior genius and knowledge — might hurt him in his trial, as his only defence must rest on his proving himself *un imbécille;* and so much for the Cardinal.

We were the other day at the Museum, a place lately set up, intended as a repository for works of art; likewise as a centre of communication with the learned in any part of Europe, who, by corresponding with M. de la Blancherie, may have their discoveries published or their questions answered, if possible to answer them; nay, I believe I need not have put in that restriction, for a Frenchman is never at a loss to answer any question. The plan seems good; but I was greatly diverted with the following question, published in one of their weekly papers: "Whether the societies called Clubs in England, and now imitated in Paris, might not tend to render their members morose and *taciturnes;* since by the laws of such meetings only one person must speak at a time, and that only for a certain number of minutes?" An author may read his piece at this Museum; but as the doors are not locked, it may chance that the company slip away one by one and leave him alone, as I suspect might be the case with a young novel-writer whom we in like manner escaped from there the other day. By the way, I have found out the reason why the French have so little poetry: it is because everybody makes verses.

We have been at Versailles and St. Cloud: the latter is now fitting up for the Queen. The situation is far more delightful than Versailles; but *that*, by force of expense, has a magnificence which no palace I have seen can compare with. We saw it on Whitsunday, when the waters play. The environs of Paris are now very pleasant; and they are very animated, without being, I think, quite so crowded as those of London. They do not make hay here till St. John's day (the 24th of June), which I think is later than near London; yet the weather has been very hot.

I was recommended to an English nun; and, after going to see her twice, she had the goodness to send a parcel of books to convert me: so you see there is some zeal left in the female convents at least; as to the priests and monks, I believe they have very little indeed.

CHAPTER VIII.

THE BARBAULDS RETURN TO ENGLAND. — THEY RESIDE IN LONDON FOR A FEW MONTHS. — SOCIAL LIFE THERE. — REMOVAL TO HAMPSTEAD. — HAMPSTEAD AND ITS INHABITANTS. — MRS. BARBAULD WRITES "ADDRESS TO THE OPPOSERS OF THE REPEAL OF THE CORPORATION AND TEST ACTS." — CAUSE OF THE ACT AND OCCASION FOR THE REPEAL. — FINAL SUCCESS OF THE ADVOCATES OF THE MEASURES.

IN the following letter from London, written immediately after their return, Mrs. Barbauld describes to Dr. Aikin their last foreign sight-seeing at Chantilly, and gives the pretty inscription held by a Cupid on the Isle d'Amour. Home, to the traveller of true feeling and heart, is always the happiest part of his or her journey, and Mrs. Barbauld speaks of the "pleasing emotion" with which she again viewed the shores and white cliffs of her native island. The travellers had a good passage from Boulogne to Dover, and landed in England much benefited by their journey, which brought with it health and rest and a pleasing variety of experiences; a change of scene, climate, and society.

LONDON, June 29, 1786.

MY DEAR BROTHER, — I am happy to write to you again from English ground. We set out from Paris on the 17th, but went no further than Chantilly, as we meant to devote the whole of the next day to seeing that noble seat of the Prince of Condé, which, both for the house and grounds, is the finest we have seen in France. The stables, which hold three hundred horses, are a most beautiful piece of architecture. There is a noble museum and armory in the palace; a fine piece of artificial water in the gardens, which are laid out partly in the English, partly in the French style, and in the best taste of both; a dairy floored and lined with marble, and in which all the utensils are of marble or fine porcelain; a *menagerie;* an *orangerie,* all the plants of which (some hundreds) being set out and in full blossom diffused the richest perfume I ever was regaled with. *L'isle d'Amour* is one of the prettiest parts of the garden, abounding with alleys and walks, some close, others gay and airy, formed by light lattice-work covered with privet and adorned with the greatest profusion of honeysuckles and roses. In the centre of the island is a statue of a Cupid without wings or quiver, holding a heart with these lines: —

> "N'offrant qu'un cœur à la beauté,
> Aussi nud que la vérité,
> Sans armes comme l'innocence,
> Sans ailes comme la constance,
> Tel fut l'Amour au siècle d'or;
> On ne le trouve plus, mais on le cherche encore."

The temple of Venus is a large saloon, in which are fountains continually throwing up water, which falls again into agate vases, leaning over which are Cupids of marble. The whole room is painted, and breathes a coolness and gayety quite enchanting. As we were walking in these gardens we had the pleasure of seeing a balloon fly over our heads; it was in full sail for England with M. Tetu, who had set off from Paris that morning. However, with our humbler mode of travelling we got to Dover first: for the lightning caught the car, and, though the aerial traveller received no damage from it, he was obliged to lie by to refit his balloon, which descended not far from Boulogne. From Boulogne we took our passage. We had intended to have gone on to Calais, but it was four posts more; and besides, we were told that the passage from Boulogne, though longer, was generally performed in less time, and was now preferred; which we found to be true: we were obliged, indeed, to wait a day for a vessel, but we got over in less than four hours. And not without a pleasing emotion did we view again the green swelling hills covered with large sheep, and the winding road bordered with the hawthorn hedge, and the English vine twisted round the tall poles, and the broad Medway covered with vessels, and at last the gentle yet majestic Thames. Nor did we find these home-scenes had lost of their power to strike or charm us by all we had seen abroad.

To Mrs. Beecroft.

London, July 7, 1786.

I feel an impatience at being again on English ground, and yet not being able to hear news of you. My imagination pictures you with a lovely burden in your arms, — whether boy or girl she is not able to determine, but a charming infant, however, that exercises your sweet sprightliness in entertaining it, and delights your sensibility by its early notice. But of this delightful circumstance I want to be certain. . . . . In the mean time let me give you some account of ourselves. After having spent so much time at Paris that we were obliged to give up our original design of visiting Flanders, we returned by way of Chantilly. . . . .

I could not help being struck with the neatness and civility of all the inns on the road from Dover to London. In neatness the English are acknowledged to excel; and though the upper rank in France may practise politeness with more ease and grace than we do, yet it is certain that the lower orders are much less respectful and more *grossier* than ours of the same class.

I do not know how it is, I think verily London is a finer town than Paris; and yet it does not appear to me since my return so magnificent as it used to do: I believe the reason is, that Paris has so much the advantage in being built of stone. Another advantage to the environs derived from that is, that they are not fumigated by the abominable brick-kilns which are so numerous near our metropolis.

There is not much new at present in French polite literature. M. Florian has published a didactic romance, "Numa Pompilius," in imitation of Telemachus, but it is heavy.

Mrs. Barbauld in her letter from Caroline Street, where they lived in lodgings while undecided as to their future plans, writes to her brother of Burns, "the Scottish ploughman," whose poems she was reading.

She mentions some other instances of uneducated poets, who lacked, however, the true genius and poetic fire of Burns, and were soon forgotten. Her comparison of the simple and unstudied but genuine and natural poetry of Burns with that of Shenstone, elegant, polished, and elaborately correct, but rather feeble and wanting strength of thought and expression, rather surprises one now when the verdict of another age has placed Burns in the foremost ranks of British poets for his genius and song. Dugald Stewart, in his sketch of Burns, says that the Collection of Songs, prepared and edited with an essay by Dr. Aikin, he put into the poet's hands, and "he read" the book "with unmixed delight, notwithstanding his former efforts in that very difficult species of writing." This mighty master of song may have owed some of his inspiration to the taste of Dr. Aikin, and been led by his classical knowledge and study, which were embodied in the essay, to more extended and elevated thought on the subject.

To Dr. Aikin.

Caroline Street, January 31, 1787.

I do not owe you a letter, 't is true; but what of that? I take it for granted you will like to hear from me; and to hear from or write to you gives me more pleasure than most things in this great city. The hive is now full; almost everybody that intends to come to town is come, and the streets rattle with carriages at all hours. Do not you remember reading in the "Spectator" of a great black tower, from which were cast nets that catched up everybody that came within a certain distance? This black tower I interpret to be this great smoky city; and I begin to be afraid we are got too much within its attraction, for the nets seem to be winding round about us; nay, we had some serious thoughts last week of setting up our tent here. . . . .

We are got into the visiting way here, which I do not consider quite as idle employment, because it leads to connections; but the hours are intolerably late. The other day at Mrs. Chapone's none of the party but ourselves was come at a quarter before eight; and the first lady that arrived said she hurried away from dinner without waiting for the coffee. There goes a story of the Duchess of D——, that she said to a tradesman, "Call on me to-morrow morning at four o'clock"; and that the honest man, not being aware of the extent of the term morning, knocked the family up some hours before daybreak. Last week we met the American bishops at Mr. V——'s, if bishops they may be called, without title, without revenue, without diocese, and without lawn sleeves. I wonder our bishops will consecrate them, for they have made very free with the Common Prayer, and have left out two creeds of the three. Indeed, as to the Athanasian Creed, the King has forbidden it in his chapel, so that will soon fall.

I have been much pleased with the poems of the Scottish ploughman, of which you have had specimens in the Review. His "Cotter's Saturday Night" has much of the same kind of merit as the "Schoolmistress" of Shenstone; and the

"Daisy" and the "Mouse," which I believe you have had in the papers, I think are charming. The endearing diminutives and the Doric rusticity of the dialect suit such subjects extremely. This is the age for self-taught genius: a subscription has been raised for a pipe-maker of Bristol, who has been discovered to have a poetic turn; and they have transplanted him to London, where they have taken him a little shop, which probably will be frequented at first and then deserted. A more extraordinary instance is that of a common carpenter at Aberdeen, who applied to the professors to be received in the lowest mathematical class: they examined him, and found he was much beyond it; then for the next, and so on, till they found he had taught himself all they could teach him; and, instead of receiving him as a student, they gave him a degree.

Miss Bowdler's Essays are read here by the graver sort with much approbation. She is the lady who betook herself to writing, upon having lost her voice; but, above all, the "Political State" for 1797 is read by everybody. The Eton boys have published a periodical paper among themselves, which they say is clever. Dr. Price has a letter from Mr. Howard, dated Amsterdam; he says the Emperor gave him a long audience. A pasquinade was fixed upon the gate of the lunatic hospital at Vienna, — "*Josephus, ubicunque secundus, hic primus.*" And now, after this idle chit-chat, good part of which I have written while my hair was dressing, let me tell you I long to hear from you, and to hear you are well; and so, with Mr. B——'s and Charles's love to all, I bid you adieu.

Among the papers of Josiah Wedgwood, of Etruria, Miss Meteyard found this little note from Mrs. Barbauld. It shows the domestic life and cares of the writer, who was evidently as good a housekeeper as she was excellent in literary pursuits.

Mrs. Barbauld's compliments to Mr. Wedgwood, begs the things she bought may be sent to No. 8 Caroline Street, Bedford Square, to-morrow morning by seven; if, however, that hour is too early, they may be sent this afternoon. They must be packed fit for Hampstead.

CAROLINE STREET, March 30, 1787.

In the year 1787, Mr. Barbauld, having received a call from the Dissenters of Hampstead to become their pastor, removed there, and this note is an indication of their change of residence from London to this pleasant village. At that time Hampstead was a wild and rural place, and Hampstead Heath was still noted as the resort of robbers and footpads, who made it exceedingly dangerous for the unwary or unarmed traveller whom they might meet. The village was beautifully situated, and its close proximity to London made it a delightful residence, without destroying its rural attractions. The lover of nature and society was equally favored by an abode there, for it was the home of many of the cultivated and literary people of the day, and finely situated near open and pleasant country. Its great height and the view to be obtained from the top of the Heath gave one a feeling of freedom and exhilaration. Akenside, writing to a friend a few years before this, dates his letter, "From Hampstead's Airy Summit." Leigh Hunt wrote several poems on this rural and picturesque suburb, now greatly changed for the visitor of to-day, who sees the famous Heath very much contracted by the buildings which have been placed close to it, and can hardly realize that the rapidly increasing town was ever so wild and rustic in its scenery. Now it is neat, and has an air of comfort, but the Heath is no longer the deserted place it once was. The following sonnet of Leigh Hunt, describing Hampstead as the Barbaulds knew it, was published in the "Foliage" in 1818, a small collection of original and translated poems by him.

"A steeple issuing from a leafy rise,
With farmy fields in front, and sloping green,
Dear Hampstead, is thy southern face serene,
Silently smiling on approaching eyes.
Within, thine ever-shifting looks surprise,
Streets, hills, and dells, trees overhead now seen,
Now down below, with smoking roofs between, —
A village revelling in varieties.
Then northward what a range, —
With heath and pond
Nature's own ground ; woods that let mansions through,
And cottaged vales, with pillowy fields beyond,
And clumps of darkening pines, and prospects blue,

And that clear path through all where daily meet
Cool cheeks, and brilliant eyes, and morn-elastic feet."

TO DR. AIKIN.

HAMPSTEAD, September 5, 1787.

I am very glad to be informed what is the proper method to engage you to write verses, and should enclose herewith an order for a score or two of lines, if I thought the command were certain to be as efficacious as the lovely Anna's.

"The generous Muse, whom harsh constraint offends,
At Anna's call with ready homage bends;
Well may she *claim*, who *gives* poetic fire,
For what her lips command, her eyes inspire."

Come va l'Italiano? I have read a volume of Goldoni's Plays; which are not all worked up to superior excellence, as you may suppose, since he wrote sixteen in a season. Two are taken from Pamela; but he has spoiled the story by making Pamela turn out to be the daughter of an attainted Scotch peer, without which salvo for family pride he did not dare to make her lover marry her. Goldoni's great aim seems to have been to introduce what he calls comedies of character, instead of the pantomime, and the continual exhibition of harlequin and his *cortége*, which was supported only by the extempore wit of the actors. There is in his *Teatro Comico* a critique which puts me much in mind of Shakespeare's instructions to the players. It abounds with good sense, — which and a desire to promote good manners seem in what I have read to be his characteristics. I find by him that the prompter repeats the whole play before the actors.

Our plot begins to thicken, as —— says. We have taken into our family for six months, and perhaps longer, a young Spaniard who comes solely to learn English. We dined with the young man, his uncle, and another Spaniard, who is secretary to the ambassador, at Mr. W——'s, where there was a great mixture of languages. The secretary, as well as French and Spanish, spoke English very well; the young man, Spanish and French; and the uncle, though he had been several years in England, only Spanish. As Mr. W—— had told us they were strict Catholics, we expressed a fear lest we should not be able to provide for the youth agreeably on fast days; but he said, "*Tout jour est jour gras pour moi*": to which the uncle learnedly added, — that it was not what went into the mouth, but what came out of it, that defileth. As far as we have yet seen (but he has been with us only two days), we find him very well behaved and easy in the family; but the great difficulty is to entertain him: he is quite a man, of one or two and twenty, and rather looks like a Dutchman than a Spaniard. Did you ever see *seguars*, — leaf-tobacco rolled up of the length of one's finger, which they light and smoke without a pipe? — he uses them. "And how does Mr. B—— bear that?" say you: O, he keeps it snug in his room. I would not advise the boys to imitate his accent in French, for he pronounces it with a deep guttural. I fancy he would speak Welsh well.

It gave me very great pleasure the other day to see my father's old friend, Dr. Pulteney, whom Dr. Garthshore brought to us. It is a strange and mixed emotion, however, which one feels at sight of a person one has not seen for twenty years or more. The alteration such a space of time makes in both parties at first gives a kind of shock; — it is your friend, but your friend disguised.

We are making a catalogue of our books; and I have left a great deal of space under the letters A and B for our future publications.

At Hampstead Mr. and Mrs. Barbauld lived on Church Row, in a quaint old house, still standing, though in a very dilapidated condition. They had a very pleasant circle of friends and neighbors there, and also visited in London. Near by, at Hackney, Dr. Priestley and Mr. Wakefield resided, the latter being one of the teachers in the Dissenting college in that town; and Dr. Priestley, who was Dr. Price's successor in the chapel at Hackney, lectured to the students as a labor of love. Dr. Aikin at this time was living in Broad Street, London, and they were able to see much of him and his family, which was mutually gratifying. The old Presbyterian Chapel, of which Mr. Barbauld was the minister from 1787 to the year 1802, is believed to have been established in the reign of Charles II. by one of the ejected nonconformist clergymen whose lives are recorded by Dr. Calamy. The chapel in which Mr. Barbauld preached is supposed to have been the second on the site it occupied, and was probably erected in the year 1736, as the first building was becoming unfit for use. A third and handsome edifice is now placed there, and occupied by the present congregation, under the able and devoted pastoral care and preaching of Dr. Sadler, the present minister. He is well known in the literary world by several excellent works, and as the careful biographer and judicious editor of the Diaries of Henry Crabb Robinson, whose reminiscences have given the world so much that is personal and valuable concerning many interesting and eminent men and women. The congregation of the chapel became Unitarian at the time of the religious change which carried many Presbyterians into that sect, and its members are now of that belief.

From Mrs. Barbauld's letter describing her first impressions about a "seguar," evidently then a novelty, we learn that they soon had applications for scholars, and Mr. Barbauld took some young men as pupils into his family. Mrs. Barbauld also gave daily instruction to a young lady, whose mother moved to Hampstead that she might be near this excellent and accomplished teacher. Some years later she taught another pupil on the same plan.

HAMPSTEAD, February, 1788.

We are waiting with great impatience for two things, your book and my sister, — your child and your wife, that is to say. . . . .

I have been reading an old book, which has given me a vast deal of entertainment, — Father Herodotus, the father of history, and the father of lies too, his enemies might say. I take it for granted the original has many more beauties than Littlebury's humble translation, which I have been perusing; but, at any rate, a translation of an original author gives you an idea of the times totally different from what one gains by a modern compilation. I am much entertained in observing the traces of truth in many of his wildest fables; as where he says it was impossible to proceed far in Scythia on account of vast quantities of feathers which fell from heaven and covered all the country.

We are reading, too, Sir T. More's "Utopia." He says many good things; but it wants a certain salt, which Swift and others have put into their works of the same nature. One is surprised to see how old certain complaints are. Of the frequent executions, for instance: twenty men, he says, being hung upon one gibbet at a time; of arable land turned to pasture, and deserted villages in consequence.

I hope the exertions which are now making for the abolition of the slave-trade will not prove all in vain. They will not, if the pleadings of eloquence or the cry of duty can be heard. Many of the most respectable and truly distinguished characters are really busy about it, and the press and the pulpit are both employed; so I hope something must be done. I expect to be highly gratified in hearing Mr. Hastings' trial, for which we are to have tickets some day. This impeachment has been the occasion of much pomp, much eloquence, and much expense; and there, I suppose, it will end. As somebody said, It must be put off for the judges to go their circuit, resumed late, and so it will fall into the summer amusements.

In the preceding letter to Dr. Aikin, the first expression of strong feeling and protest against the slave-trade was uttered by Mrs. Barbauld, and the great horror she felt against it later induced her to write her spirited poem to Mr. Wilberforce, the champion of freedom for the oppressed blacks. She alludes to the trial of Warren Hastings, that famous trial which drew forth the eloquence of the greatest orators of the age, who were inferior probably to none of any age, ancient or modern. This memorable trial, which lasted from 1788 to 1795, was conducted by England's ablest statesmen and pleaders; and unquestionably the eloquence of Burke, who headed the prosecution, was founded on truth and outraged justice, which cried out for redress at the monstrous cruelty and rapacity shown by Hastings in his government to the Begums of Oude. This famous impeachment, which began the trial, was moved by Burke the 4th of April, 1786; and the trial which called forth so much of power and eloquence, which drew crowds to Westminster Hall during the time when, according to Macaulay, "the high court of Parliament was to sit, according to forms handed down from the days of the Plantagenets, on an Englishman accused of exercising tyranny over the lord of the holy city of Benares and the ladies of the princely house of Oude," was opened the 17th of February, 1788. All London was excited over it for a time; but the protracted length of the trial rather wore out the interest of all but those immediately concerned in the prosecution and defence.

HAMPSTEAD, May, 1789.*

I often please my mind with the sweet scenes of domestic happiness which you must enjoy: yourself in the arms of Mr. and Mrs. Dixon, and your children in yours. Apropos of the sweet children, I should not be at all alarmed at their speaking Norfolk; depend upon it, it will be only temporary where the parent does not speak it: and, after all, they should know the language of the country. I remember when I was in Lancashire being reproved for my affectation in not speaking as the country folks did, when in truth it was beyond my abilities.

London is extremely full now: the trial, the parliamentary business, and *fêtes* and illuminations, and the Shakespeare Gallery have all contributed to fill the great hive. But, among these various objects, none is surely so interesting as the noble effort making for the abolition of the slave-trade. Nothing, I think, for centuries past, has done the nation so much honor; because it must have proceeded from the most liberal motives, — the purest love of humanity and justice. The voice of the negroes could not have made itself heard

* To Mrs. Beecroft. — ED.

but by the ear of pity; they might have been oppressed for ages more with impunity, if we had so pleased.

HAMPSTEAD, August, 1789.*

.... I do not doubt but your attention, as well as that of every one else, has been engaged lately by the affairs in France. We were much gratified a fortnight ago by seeing Lord Daer, who had been at Paris at the beginning of the commotions, and had seen the demolition of the Bastille, and with hundreds more ranged through that till now impregnable castle of Giant Despair. He told us, that after all the prisoners in the common apartments had been liberated, they heard for a long time the groans of a man in one of the dungeons, to which they could not get access, and were at length obliged to take him out by making a breach in the wall, through which they drew him out after he had been forty-eight hours without food; and they could not at last find the aperture by which he was put into the dungeon.

Every subject of public interest, and all efforts in behalf of humanity and progress, met with the most genuine enthusiasm and a disinterested participation from Mrs. Barbauld. A firm believer in the march of intellect, the growth of liberal political and religious views, the progress and improvement of humanity everywhere, she never hesitated to speak for the oppressed and unfortunate, and make known her sympathies and convictions at the risk of uttering unpopular sentiments. The thrilling events of the open-

* To Mrs. Beecroft. — ED.

ing of the French Revolution were hailed by her as well as many others, who, prompted by their love of liberty and desire of freedom, thought they discerned in the beginning of the demands for representation and less taxation, and the royal concessions, a chance for better government and happier times in France, not dreaming of the license and the horrors of the demagogues who committed such crimes in the name of freedom. Mrs. Barbauld's poem on "The General Rising of the French Nation," expected in 1792, shows her hope and anticipation of freedom and peace for this unhappy nation, destined, alas! to so many struggles, and never long at rest since that period, — its share of the world's history for the last century being a bloody and unfortunate record. After exhorting the nation to rise and crush the despotic powers from without who attempt its destruction and inthralment, and painting the swift termination to the strife if the country will unite, and —

"Briareus-like extend thy hands,
In millions pour thy generous bands,
That every hand may crush a foe;
And end a warfare by a blow."

Mrs. Barbauld concludes with the following fine lines: —

"Then wash with sad repentant tears
Each deed that clouds thy glory's page;
Each frenzied start impelled by fear,
Each transient burst of headlong rage.

"Then fold in thy relenting arms
Thy wretched outcasts where they roam;
From pining want and war's alarms,
O call the child of misery home!

"Then build the tomb, — O not alone
Of him who bled in Freedom's cause;
With equal eye the martyr own
Of faith revered and ancient laws.

"Then be thy tide of glory staid;
Then be thy conquering banners furled;
Obey the laws thyself hast made,
And rise the model of the world!"

Dr. Aikin himself was extremely industrious, and felt anxious to see his sister using her fine talents and keen imagination constantly. He regretted that she did not more frequently favor the world with some works worthy of her reputation for genius and brilliancy of thought. In the year 1790, he very warmly expressed himself to this effect, in the following sonnet to his sister:—

"Thus speaks the Muse, and bends her brows severe:—
Did I, Lætitia, lend my choicest lays,
And crown thy youthful head with freshest bays,
That all the expectance of thy full-grown year
Should lie inert and fruitless? O revere
Those sacred gifts whose meed is deathless praise,
Whose potent charms the enraptured soul can raise
Far from the vapours of this earthly sphere!
Seize, seize the lyre! resume the lofty strain!

'T is time, 't is time ! hark how the nations round
With jocund notes of liberty resound, —
And thy own Corsica has burst her chain !
O let the song to Britain's shores rebound,
Where Freedom's once-loved voice is heard, alas ! in vain."

September, 1790.

MY DEAR MRS. BEECROFT, — It is but lately that I heard you were returned from your delightful expedition, or I should have written sooner; for I am sure so kind and charming a letter as yours demanded an early acknowledgment. I do not say I envy you your party and your tour, because I have in some measure enjoyed it along with you. I have tracked you to the top of Skiddaw, seen you impress the mountains with your light and nymph-like step, and skim over the lakes with a rapid and smooth motion, like a bird that just touches them with her wing without dipping it. I have contemplated the effect such scenes must produce on minds so turned to admire the beauties of nature as yours and your poetical companions'; and I have watched till imagination has kindled, and beauty has swelled into sublimity. Indeed, independently of scenes so wildly picturesque, a journey is the most favorable thing in the world for the imagination; which, like a wheel, kindles with the motion: I shall therefore certainly expect it to produce some fruit.

I suppose you are now returned to your course of instructive reading, and your sweet employment of instructing your little charge. Pray, have you seen Sacontala, an Indian drama translated by Sir William Jones? You will be much pleased with it. There is much fancy and much sentiment in it, — much poetry too, and mythology: but these, though full of beauties, are often uncouth and harsh to the European ear. The language of nature and the passions is of all countries. The hero of the piece is as delicate and tender a lover as any that can be met with in the pages of a modern romance; for I hope you can pardon him a little circumstance relative to the *costume* of the country, which is just hinted at in the poem: I mean the having a hundred wives besides the mistress of his heart. So much for works of entertainment! There is a publication of higher merit set on foot in France by Rabaut St. Etienne and some others, — *La Feuille Villageoise*, of which I have seen the first number. The respectable object of it is to instruct the country people (who are there remarkably ignorant) in morals, in the new laws and constitution of their country, in the state of the arts and new discoveries as far as can be of practical use to them, and, in short, to open their minds and make them love their duties. M. Berquin is engaged in something similar; but this is more extensive. There is room for all true patriots to exert themselves in every way in France, for their situation seems still but too precarious.

Mrs. Barbauld was sensibly affected by the animated sonnet of Dr. Aikin, and also much excited to thought and composition by the inspiring events of the period, — soon, unfortunately, to be turned into scenes of carnage, domestic strife, and war involving all Europe in its general results. Hope, roused by the spirit of freedom, which appeared to animate the French in the beginning of the struggle for liberty, was soon destroyed by the horrible events of the Revolution, and the crimes committed in the name of liberty made it almost worse than tyranny in its manifestations. In the year 1790, the rejection of the bill for the repeal of the Corporation and Test Acts produced her indignantly eloquent and impressive Address to the opposers of the repeal. This Act was one made in the reign of Charles II., and by one clause of it all persons before admission into any office in corporations, or the acceptance of any position, civil or military, under the crown, were obliged to receive the sacrament of the Lord's Supper according to the forms and custom of the Church of England. Already the movement for a repeal had been agitated by the Dissenters in the year 1730, but the Whig leaders, fearing it would break their party, managed by the adroitness of Sir Robert Walpole to avert the attempt, though Dr. Hoadly, Bishop of Salisbury, said he had so often given his opinion as to "the unreasonableness of these laws in a social light, and the profaneness of them theologically considered," that he must support the repeal of them if the measure was introduced. In this feeling many churchmen joined him; but, according to Lord Hervey's "Memoirs," the queen was persuaded to send for the Bishop, and use her influence to quiet his conscientious scruples by telling him that "all times were not proper to do proper things." That time the measure was avoided, though with some murmurings from the Dissenters. Again they moved to have the unjust laws abolished in 1789, and again it was rejected, being felt by many of the most liberal of the Whig party to be revolutionary and dangerous, as the tendency of the French Revolution had been to introduce violence and agitation in English affairs. Fox proposed the abolition of these religious tests; Pitt opposed the motion; and Edmund Burke stated that, had the repeal been moved for ten years before that time, he should probably have supported Mr. Fox in his position, but he had many strong reasons for believing that many of the persons calling themselves Dissenters were men of factious and revolutionary dispositions, and unmoved by any motives of religion or conscience. The bill was rejected by a very large majority, and not until 1828 did the measure pass, being then opposed, says Sir Robert Peel in his "Memoirs," "with all the influence and authority of the government recently appointed." Lord Eldon vainly described this bill to be "as bad, as mischievous, and as revolutionary as the most captious Dissenter could wish it to be." It was followed by similar concessions to the Roman Catholics in ensuing years.

CHAPTER IX.

MRS. BARBAULD'S "POETICAL EPISTLE" TO WILLIAM WILBERFORCE. — HORACE WALPOLE'S REMARKS ON MRS. BARBAULD. — LETTERS. — DR. JOHNSON'S CHARACTER. — MRS. BARBAULD'S "REPLY" TO MR. WAKEFIELD'S PAMPHLET ON WORSHIP. — SHE VISITS SCOTLAND. — VARIOUS IMPRESSIONS OF THE HIGHLANDS. — MRS. BARBAULD WRITES ESSAYS ON AKENSIDE'S "PLEASURES OF THE IMAGINATION," AND ON COLLINS'S ODES. — MEETS GENERAL PAOLI. — LETTERS.

THE "Poetical Epistle to William Wilberforce on the Rejection of the Bill for Abolishing the Slave-Trade" appeared in 1791. It was true, too true, in its descriptions of the horrors of slavery, and of course roused the fury of those who upheld the iniquitous trade. Mrs. Barbauld begins her poem, —

"Cease, Wilberforce, to urge thy generous aim !
Thy Country knows the sin, and stands the shame !
The Preacher, Poet, Senator in vain
Has rattled in her sight the Negro's chain ;
With his deep groans assailed her startled ear,
And rent the veil that hid his constant tear ;
Forced her averted eyes his stripes to scan,
Beneath the bloody scourge laid bare the man,
Claimed Pity's tear, urged Conscience' strong control,
And flashed conviction on her shrinking soul."

The influence of the best and wisest sons and daughters of Great Britain had been used by them to excite the interest and move the sympathy of the nation about the sufferings of the blacks; but the time was not come for the abolition of this terrible traffic, which has involved so many souls in crime and produced such misery for humanity.

"In vain, to thy white standard gathering round,
Wit, Worth, and Parts and Eloquence are found:
In vain, to push to birth thy great design,
Contending chiefs, and hostile virtues join;
All, from conflicting ranks, of power possest —
To rouse, to melt, or to inform the breast.
When seasoned tools of Avarice prevail,
A Nation's eloquence, combined, must fail:
Each flimsy sophistry by turns they try;
The plausive argument, the daring lie,
The artful gloss, that moral sense confounds,
Th' acknowledged thirst of gain that honor wounds;
Bane of ingenuous minds! — the 'unfeeling sneer,
Which sudden turns to stone the falling tear:
They search assiduous, with inverted skill,
For forms of wrong, and precedents of ill;
With impious mockery wrest the sacred page,
And glean up crimes from each remoter age."

Mrs. Barbauld then describes the baleful effects of slavery on its votaries, and how, —

"Injured Afric, by herself redrest,
Darts her own serpents at her tyrant's breast.

Each vice, to minds depraved by bondage known,
With sure contagion fastens on his own;
In sickly languors melts his nerveless frame,
And blows to rage impetuous Passion's flame."

She paints a picture of the domestic tyranny which is known to have been common in West Indian households, —

"Lo! where reclined, pale Beauty courts the breeze,
Diffused on sofas of voluptuous ease,
With anxious awe her menial train around
Catch her faint whispers of half-uttered sound:
See her, in monstrous fellowship, unite
At once the Scythian and the Sybarite! —
See her, with indolence to fierceness joined,
Of body delicate, infirm of mind,
With languid tones imperious mandates urge;
With arm recumbent wield the household scourge;
And with unruffled mien, and placid sounds,
Contriving torture, and inflicting wounds."

A trustworthy writer, an eyewitness of some of these terrible scenes, describes one where a fair and delicate lady was reclining at her ease, while her favorite handmaidens unpacked a trunk of new and beautiful costumes, just arrived by a ship from England; a nail which unseen protruded from the edge caught and tore one of the frail and gauzy fabrics worn in that sultry country, the product of some Indian loom. The indignant and furious mistress, not of her temper, but of the unfortunate slave, — instantly had her severely whipped for her carelessness. The cruel treatment of these masters and mistresses brought at last a terrible retribution, when the slaves rose and in their turn inflicted tortures and death, which they thought only a just return for long years of suffering.

In vain, the poet says, are all the humane arguments and efforts for the cause of the negro, and youth and beauty lose their softness and tender humanity under the hardening influence of slavery.

> "And anxious Freedom eyes her drooping fires ;
> By foreign wealth are British morals changed,
> And Afric's sons, and India's, smile avenged.
>
> "For you, whose tempered ardor long has borne
> Untired the labor, and unmoved the scorn ;
> In Virtue's fasti be inscribed your fame,
> And uttered yours with Howard's honored name ;
> Friends of the friendless — Hail, ye generous band !
> Whose efforts yet arrest Heaven's lifted hand,
> Around whose steady brows, in union bright,
> The civic wreath and Christian's palm unite :
> Your merit stands, no greater and no less,
> Without or with the varnish of success :
> But seek no more to break a nation's fall,
> For ye have saved yourselves, — and that is all.
> Succeeding times your struggles, and their fate,
> With mingled shame and triumph shall relate ;
> While faithful History, in her various page,
> Marking the features of this motley age,
> To shed a glory, and to fix a stain,
> Tells how you strove, and that you strove in vain."

Horace Walpole, the connoisseur, collector, and patron of letters, the holder of several sinecure places of value under government, the cynical and bitter writer of letters which are full of severe comments on society and his acquaintances, inveighs violently against Mrs. Barbauld. We see in him, as a representative of the government party, something of the spirit which was felt in their ranks against the outspoken sentiments of liberal thought. He wrote, in 1791, to one friend: "Not a jot on *Deborah* . . . . (Mrs. Barbauld), whom you admire: I have neither read her verses, nor will, as I have not your aspen conscience. I cannot forgive the heart of a woman that is party *per pale* blood and tenderness, that curses our clergy and feels for negroes." In writing Miss Hannah More in the same year, he alludes again to the "Epistle" to Wilberforce, and tells Miss More that her poem on slavery, then lately published, differs widely from that of her friend, to whom he evidently felt the very strongest dislike as one of the opposition party. "Deborah may cant rhymes of compassion, — she is a hypocrite; and you shall not make me read, nor with all your sympathy and candor can you esteem her. *Your* compassion for the blacks is genuine, sincere from your soul, most amiable: hers, a measure of faction."

In a letter to Miss Berry, in 1791, Walpole tells her of a meeting which was held at the Crown and Anchor

Tavern in the Strand, for the purpose of celebrating the anniversary of the French Revolution. He uses much abusive and ungentlemanly language about the people who were expected to meet there, and speaks of Mrs. Barbauld and Miss Helen Maria Williams as Deborah and Jael, and of the rioters arrested for some offensive demonstrations elsewhere says, "Eleven of these disciples of Paine are in custody, and Mr. Merry, Mrs. Barbauld, and Helen Williams will probably have subjects for elegies. Deborah and Jael, I believe, were invited to the Crown and Anchor, and had let their nails grow accordingly; but somehow or other no *poissonnieres* were there, and the prophetesses had no opportunity that day of exercising their talents or talons." In a letter in the previous year, after Mrs. Barbauld's pamphlet containing the address to the opposers of the Corporation and Test Acts had appeared, he wrote to Miss Berry, then on the Continent, and in mentioning to her Burke's new book, just then published, "Reflections on the French Revolution," adds, "His foes show how deeply they are wounded by their abusive pamphlets." He numbers among the opponents of Burke, Mrs. Macaulay "and the virago Barbaûld, whom Mr. Burke calls our *Poissardes,* who "spit their rage at eighteen-pence a head." Walpole's virulence and malice were so evident in his letters, that even the testimony of Miss Berry, who combated the opinion of

Lord Macaulay as one well acquainted with the best facts of his character, — knowledge, she says, which was "acquired by long intimacy," — was powerless to remove the impression caused by his own words, which were commented on by Macaulay as showing the cynical and bitter nature of the man. These expressions of party feeling, however, show plainly that, though Mrs. Barbauld may have been disliked as one who held and expressed liberal, perhaps radical, opinions, she was yet dreaded as a powerful and influential champion of freedom of thought, of progress, and of humanity. The talents and brilliancy which they would have welcomed to their own cause as a great acquisition of strength and power, the Tories and more conservative members of the opposition dreaded, and would fain have despised.

TO DR. AIKEN.

HAMPSTEAD, May, 1791.

What do you say to Pitt and Fox agreeing so well about the affair of libels? Is there anything behind the curtain? I hope not; for I own I have felt myself much interested for Fox since his noble and manly behavior, mixed with so much sensibility and tempered with so much forbearance towards Burke. It puts one in mind of the quarrel between Brutus and Cassius.

I am reading with a great deal of interest Ramsay's "History of the American Revolution"; and I do not wonder that the old story of Greece and Rome grows, as you say, flat, when we have events of such importance passing before our eyes, and from thence acquiring a warmth of color and authenticity which it is in vain to seek for in histories that have passed from hand to hand through a series of ages. How uniformly great was Congress, and what a spotless character Washington! All their public acts, etc., are remarkably well drawn up. We are reading in idle moments, or rather dipping into, a very different work, Boswell's long-expected "Life of Johnson." It is like going to Ranelagh; you meet all your acquaintance: but it is a base and mean thing to bring thus every idle word into judgment, — the judgment of the public. Johnson, I think, was far from a great character; he was continually sinning against his conscience, and then afraid of going to hell for it. A Christian and a man of the town, a philosopher and a bigot, acknowledging life to be miserable, and making it more miserable through fear of death; professing great distaste to the country, and neglecting the urbanity of towns; a Jacobite, and pensioned; acknowledged to be a giant in literature, and yet we do not trace him, as we do Locke, or Rousseau, or Voltaire, in his influence on the opinions of the times. We cannot say Johnson first opened this vein of thought, led the way to this discovery or this turn of thinking. In his style he is original, and there we can track his imitators. In short, he seems to me to be one of those who have shone in the *belles lettres*, rather than, what he is held out by many to be, an original and deep genius in investigation.

In this letter Mrs. Barbauld, commenting on the

"Life of Johnson" just then published, blames that newsmonger and gossip, Boswell, not unreasonably, for the ill-judged personalities and trivial scraps of talk with which he crowded the biography of his friend, otherwise a valuable and extraordinary piece of work. Dr. Aikin, in alluding to Dr. Johnson at this time, when the Life had caused his character and peculiarities to be much discussed, wrote of him as follows: "He had not, indeed, a grain of the noble enthusiasm, the calm simplicity, the elevated purpose, of a great man. His temper, habits, and system equally disqualified him from attaining that character. He was able with great accuracy to compare every literary and moral idea with the standards in his own mind, and to detect all false pretensions within his own compass. But there were heights in both to which he could not ascend. His *life* fell far short of his writings, and his faults and asperities were rather aggravated than softened by age." Dr. Aikin evidently had a strong desire to reduce some of the blind admiration for Dr. Johnson which was felt in a certain circle before the Life appeared, and so expressed himself frequently. In the following letter to her friend Mrs. Beecroft, Mrs. Barbauld contrasts the life of Mirabeau, whose *éloge* she had been reading, and that of Dr. Price, minister of the Dissenting Chapel at Newington Green, a man noted for his Christian virtues and fine character. Dr. Priestley, who succeeded him in the chapel at Hackney, preached his funeral discourse. Mr. Barbauld a few years later was called to fill Dr. Price's place at Newington.

HAMPSTEAD, May 7, 1791.

. . . . You ought, I think, to come to London every spring, to peep into the Exhibition and Shakespeare Gallery, and to see our proud metropolis when she adorns her head with wreaths of early roses, and perfumes her crowded streets with all the first scents of the spring. So uncommonly fine has the weather been this year, thatin March, if you were in a flower-shop, you might have imagined it the glowing month of June.

I last Sunday attended with melancholy satisfaction the funeral sermon of good Dr. Price, preached by Dr. Priestley, who, as he told us, had been thirty years his acquaintance, and twenty years his intimate friend. He well delineated the character he so well knew. I had just been reading an *éloge* of Mirabeau, and I could not help in my own mind comparing both the men and the tributes paid to their memories. The one died when a reputation raised suddenly by extraordinary emergencies was at its height, and very possibly might have ebbed again had he lived longer: the other enjoyed an esteem, the fruit of a course of labors uniformly directed through a long life to the advancement of knowledge and virtue, a reputation slowly raised, without and independent of popular talents. The panegyrist of the one was obliged to sink his private life, and to cover with the splendid mantle of public merit the crimes and failings of the man: the private character of the other was able to bear the severest scrutiny; neither slander, nor envy, nor party prejudice, ever pretended to find a spot in it. The one was followed even by those who did not trust him: the other was confided in and trusted even by those who reprobated his principles. In pronouncing the *éloge* on Mirabeau, the author scarcely dares to insinuate a vague and uncertain hope that his spirit may hover somewhere in the void space of immensity, be re-joined to the first principles of nature; and attempts to soothe his shade with a cold and barren immortality in the remembrance of posterity. Dr. Priestley parts with his intimate friend with all the cheerfulness which an assured hope of meeting him soon again could give, and at once dries the tear he excites.

TO DR. AIKIN.

HAMPSTEAD, 1791.

.... I do not know whether I said so before, but I cannot help thinking that the Revolution in France will introduce there an entire revolution in education, and particularly be the ruin of classical learning, the importance of which must be lessening every day; while other sciences, particularly that of politics and government, must rise in value, afford an immediate introduction to active life, and be necessary in some degree to everybody. All the kindred studies of the cloister must sink, and we shall live no longer on the lean relics of antiquity.

Apropos of France, Mrs. Montague, who entertains all the

aristocrats, had invited a marchioness of Boufflers and her daughter to dinner. After making her wait till six, the marchioness came, and made an apology for her daughter, that just as she was going to dress she was seized with a *dégoût momentanée du monde*, and could not wait on her.

There is a little Frenchman here at Hampstead who is learning the language, and he told us he had been making an attempt at some English verses. "I have made," says he, "four couplets in masculine and feminine rimes." "O sir," says I, "you have given yourself needless trouble; we do not use them." "Why, how so?" says he; "have you no rules, then, for your verse?" "Yes, sir; but we do not use masculine and feminine rimes." Well, I could not make him comprehend there could be any regular poetry without these rimes.

Mr. Brand Hollis has sent me an American poem, "The Conquest of Canaan," — a regular epic in twelve books; but I hope I need not read it. Not that the poetry is bad, if the subject were more interesting. What had he to do to make Joshua his hero, when he had Washington of his own growth?

We are at present reading Anacharsis, and are much pleased with it. There is nothing of adventure, nothing like a novel; but the various circumstances relating to the Greeks are classed and thrown together in such a manner as to dwell on the mind. It has just the effect which it would have if in the Museum, instead of being shown separately the arms and dresses of different nations, you had figures dressed up and accoutred in them: the Otaheitan mourner walking to a *morai;* the warrior full armed in the attitude of attack; and the priest with all the various instruments of sacrifice before the altar. Thus they become grouped in the mind.

I want you to propose a metaphysical question to your society, which Mr. B—— and I have had great debates upon; and I want to know your opinion and my sister's. It is this: If you were now told that in a future state of existence you should be entirely deprived of your consciousness, so as not to be sensible you were the same being who existed here, — should you or should you not be now interested in your future happiness or misery? or, in other words, Is continued consciousness the essence of identity?

In the year 1792 appeared Mrs. Barbauld's "Remarks on Mr. Gilbert Wakefield's Inquiry into the Expediency and Propriety of Public or Social Worship." This pamphlet of Mrs. Barbauld's was designed to correct what she and many others thought a dangerous and irreligious view of worship. His "Inquiry" was answered chiefly by Dissenters, and it startled many of his warmest admirers. It was a serious injury to himself, for Dr. Aikin states that the sentiments he expressed therein caused him to lose one of his two pupils, — a loss he could ill afford. Miss Aikin, in a letter written many years after the "Reply," mentions her aunt's criticism on Mr. Wakefield's "Inquiry," and says that she thinks that Mrs. Barbauld misunderstood the views of the writer of the "Inquiry," and her "Reply" was made under a mistaken idea of Mr. Wakefield's sentiments. There is not much question as to Mrs. Barbauld's comprehension of what Mr. Wakefield said. In common with many others, she was surprised and distressed by his "Inquiry"; and her "Reply," which was characterized by her usual strength of thought and beauty of language, was made to his expression of radical and startling sentiments. She answered what he said, not with a critical spirit, but feeling a natural desire to correct some of his statements.

Her Discourse for the Fast, entitled "Sins of the Government, Sins of the Nation," was published in 1793.

At this time Mrs. Barbauld contributed some of the stories and allegories which formed a part of Dr. Aikin's book, "Evenings at Home," which appeared in 1792. This work was, as previously stated, for the most part from the hand of Dr. Aikin, but his sister's share consisted of several charming tales and other pieces. Of the ninety-nine pieces which make up the work, fourteen were her productions. In the following letter to Mrs. Beecroft, she thanks her for her kind invitation to Mr. Barbauld, while she was away in Scotland, and she then describes to her friend her visit to the

"Land of brown heath and shaggy wood;
Land of the mountain and the flood."

Mrs. Barbauld's poetic eye and taste for the wild and picturesque was much gratified by her visit to Scotland. Of it she writes, "It is a country strongly marked with character. Its rocks, its woods, its water, its castles, its towns, are all picturesque, generally grand." One Captain Bent was among the first Englishmen to explore the Highlands of Scotland, and he wrote an account of his wanderings, in which he pronounced the mountains hideous with their gloomy masses of brown and dirty purple heather. A taste for the wild and picturesque was not then cultivated. He contrasts the terrible gloom and deformity which he considers are the chief features of the country with the beauty of Richmond Hill; tame and insipid we should now judge it to be in comparison.

Another traveller, a man who should have seen beauties where ordinary minds might fail to observe them, — Oliver Goldsmith, — explored the wild and almost unknown scenery of the Highlands in 1753. In a letter to Bryanton, Edinburgh, September 26, he writes: "Shall I tire you with a description of this unfruitful country, where I must lead you over their hills all brown with heath, or their valleys scarce able to feed a rabbit? .... Every part of the country presents the same dismal landscape. No grove or brook lend their [*sic*] music to cheer the stranger." One can hardly credit the fact that the author of the "Traveller" and the "Deserted Village" should have shown so little taste and sensibility; but in a letter written a little later on his journey to his uncle, the Rev. Thomas Contarine, from Leyden, he says of Holland: "I was wholly taken up observing the face of the country. Nothing can equal its beauty. Wherever I turn my eye, fine houses, elegant gardens, grottos, vistas, presented themselves. Scotland and this country bear the highest contrast: there, hills and rocks intercept every prospect; here it is all a continued plain." Sixty years had not greatly changed impressions gained about the Highlands which were expressed by R. Frank Philanthropus, in the "Northern Memoirs," printed in 1694. He wrote, "It is a part of the creation left undressed; rubbish thrown aside when the magnificent fabric of the world was created; as void of form as the natives are indigent of morals and good manners." When Mrs. Barbauld visited the Highlands, a great improvement had taken place in the habits and manners of the natives. No longer the puppets of faction and moved at will by the hand of adventurers and then abandoned to their unhappy fate as rebels, the people were becoming industrious and honest. Travelling was no longer dangerous, for roads had been cut, streams bridged, and inns had been placed in pleasant situations. The dens of robbers had been abandoned by their inmates for honest occupations and homes.

It is believed that on this occasion Mrs. Barbauld carried with her, and read to Dugald Stewart, the version of Bürger's "Lenora," by William Taylor of Norwich, her scholar in early life. Of this poem, Miss Aikin says that it made Sir Walter Scott a poet. In writing to Mr. Murch of Bath, in 1841, she says of Mr. Taylor, "A remarkable anecdote belongs to his incomparable version of Bürger's 'Lenora,' which I heard from the lips of Sir Walter Scott himself, as he was relating it to Mrs. Barbauld. After reminding her that long before the ballad was printed she had carried it with her to Edinburgh and read it to Mr. Dugald Stewart, 'He,' said Scott, 'repeated all he could remember of it to me, and this, madam, was what made me a poet. I had several times attempted the more regular kinds of poetry, but here was something that I thought I could do.'"

BUXTON, October, 1794.

MY DEAR MRS. BEECROFT, — Is it permitted me to renew a correspondence which has been too long interrupted, though our friendship, I trust, never has? Strange indeed would it be, if the esteem and affection I owe you could ever subside, or if I could ever forget the marks of kindness and attention I have always received from you. How good it was of you to invite Mr. Barbauld while I have been rambling! I should have been more satisfied with being away if he had accepted your offer; for I should have known then that he would have no occasion to regret any of the beautiful scenes

I have enjoyed without him. I have been much pleased with Scotland. I do not know whether you ever extended your tour so far: if you have not seen it, let me beg that you will; for I do not think that in any equal part of England so many interesting objects are to be met with as occur in what is called the little tour, — from Edinburgh to Sterling, Perth, and Blair, along the pleasant windings of the Forth and Tay; then by the lakes, ending with Loch Lomond, the last and greatest, and so to Glasgow; then to the Falls of the Clyde, and back by Dumfries; which last, however, we did not do, for we returned to Edinburgh. Scotland is a country strongly marked with character. Its rocks, its woods, its waters, its castles, its towns, are all picturesque, generally grand. Some of the views are wild and savage, but none of them insipid, if you except the bleak, flat, extended moor. The entrance into the Highlands by Dunkeld is striking; it is a kind of gate. I thought it would be a good place for hanging up an inscription similar to that of Dante, "*Per me si va* . . . ."

Edinburgh is so commanding a situation for a capital, I almost regretted it was not one, and that the fine rooms at Holyrood House are falling into ruins. The old and the new town make the finest contrast in the world; but, beautiful as the new town is, I was convinced, after being some days in it, that its perfect regularity tends towards insipidity, and that a gentle waving line in a street, provided it is without affectation, and has the advantage of some inequality of ground, is more agreeable than streets that cut one another at right angles.

We were much struck with the Falls of the Clyde and its steep banks richly wooded. Indeed, wherever the country is wooded it is beautiful, and it is everywhere improving in that respect: millions of trees are planted every year; but it is some time before planted trees form a feature of the country. A belt of wood, dotted clumps, a circlet of firs on a hill, have not the easy and natural appearance of a wood that fills the hollow of a valley, and shapes itself to the bendings and risings of the ground. And now let me whisper in your ear that I long very much to be at home again: the limits which I had set myself not to exceed are expired; and besides, I do not like this country, which has all the dreariness without the grandeur of scenery of that which we have left. The Crescent, however, has a beautiful appearance in a deep hollow surrounded by hills. It looks like a jewel at the bottom of an earthen cup.

In the year 1795 appeared Mrs. Barbauld's essay which was prefixed to the illustrated edition of Akenside's "Pleasures of the Imagination," and in 1797 she also wrote another critical essay in a similar style, which was the introduction to an illustrated edition of Collins's "Odes." The essays are written ably and with discrimination, and display poetic knowledge, taste, and judgment, but in the opinion of Miss Aikin are "less marked with the peculiar features of her style than any other of her prose works." The next letter feelingly mentions the French emigrants who were driven to the friendly asylum of England by the horrors of the Revolution, and received there kind treatment; though many of them, who were too proud to make their wants known, suffered terrible privations. The adventures of these poor people in reaching England were most extraordinary, and some of them read like fiction, so strange and wonderful was their escape from death at the hands of the infuriated demagogues in power, some of them drowning in their passage in little boats across the stormy channel.

To Mrs. Beecroft.

September 2, 1795.

. . . . Your emigrants are very interesting people. I think the English character has never appeared in a more amiable light than in the kind and hospitable attentions which have been pretty generally shown to these unfortunate people. I was much amused with Louvet, and interested; though I confess the interest was somewhat weakened by the reflection that he was by profession a bookseller and a writer of romances; and I think one may discover a few *traits de plume* in the high coloring he gives to the attachment between himself and his wife. What has still more interested me, — because I have a higher opinion of her character, and greater confidence in her sincerity, — is *L'Appel de Madame Roland.* What talents! what energy of character! what powers of description! But have you seen the Second Part, which has not been printed here, and which contains memoirs of her life from the earliest period to the death of her mother, when she was one-and-twenty? It is surely the most singular book that has appeared since the "Confessions of Rousseau"; a book that none but a French woman *could* write, and wonderfully entertaining. I began it with a certain fear upon my mind, — What is this woman going to tell me? Will it be anything but what will lessen my esteem for her? If, however, we were to judge of the female and male mind by contrasting these confessions with those I just now mentioned, the advantage in purity, *comme de raison*, will be greatly on the side of our sex.

In the following letter to Mrs. Beecroft, Mrs. Barbauld tells her of her meeting with General Paoli, whom, the reader will remember, she had warmly eulogized in her "Address to the Corsicans," published in the year 1773, in her "Collected Poems." One can fancy the feeling of interest and emotion with which she met the hero, though it was "thirty years" after the poem was written.

To MRS. BEECROFT.

HAMPSTEAD, July 25, 1796.

. . . . I do not know the present course of your reading, but I imagine that two works, at least, have employed the leisure of both of us, — Roscoe's "Lorenzo" and Mrs. D'Arblay's "Camilla." The former is a very capital work: I only wish that, instead of making Lorenzo the Magnificent the centre round which everything revolves, he had made the history of literature itself the professed subject of his work, and taken the Medici only in connection with that. And how do you like "Camilla"? Not so well, I am afraid, as the former publications from the same hand. I like, however, the story of Eugenia, where the distress is new, and the character of that amiable *imbécille* the uncle; and Mrs. Arlberry's character is very well drawn. I was struck, on reading the work, with the persuasion that no *second* work of an author, who has written the first after being in possession of his powers, can help falling off, and for this reason, — every one has a manner of his own, a vein of thinking peculiar to himself; and on the second publication, though the incidents may be all new, the novelty resulting from this originality is gone forever. I think Gibbon says, in his very entertaining Memoirs, that nothing can renew the pleasure with which a favorite author and the public meet one another for the first time.

I am just now reduced to regret, my dear friend, that I have taken such small paper. It cuts short what I was going to tell you of General Paoli, whom I met the other day. Had it been thirty years ago, it would have made my heart beat stronger. He told us a good deal about his godson and aid-de-camp, Buonaparte, who was going to write Paoli's annals, when he was called upon to give ample matter for his own annals.

The next letter was written to her friend Mrs. Carr, of Hampstead, while the Barbaulds were making one of their little trips for health and relaxation. Mrs.

Barbauld always seems to have found enjoyment and attraction in the country, and her love of nature was a constant source of the simplest and purest pleasure.

To Mrs. Carr.

Pit Cot, near Bridgend, July 18, 1797.

. . . We flattered ourselves with seeing some of the beauties of South Wales in coming hither, but we were completely disappointed by the state of the weather. This country is bleak and bare, with fine views of the sea, and a bold rocky coast, with a beach of fine hard sand. We have been much pleased with watching the coming in of the tide among the rocks, against which it dashes, forming columns of spray twenty and thirty foot high, accompanied with rainbows, and with a roar like distant cannon. There are fine caverns and recesses amongst the rocks; one particularly, which we took the opportunity of visiting yesterday, as it can only be entered at the ebb of the spring-tides. It is very spacious, beautifully arched, and composed of granite rocks finely veined with alabaster, which the imagination may easily form into are semblance of a female figure, and is, of course, the Nereid of the grotto. We wished to have stayed longer, but our friend hurried us away, lest the tide should rush in, which it is supposed to do from subterraneous caverns, as it fills before the tide covers the sand of the adjacent beach. I was particularly affected with the fate of two lovers (a young gentleman and lady from Clifton), whose friends were here for the sake of sea-bathing. They stole out early one morning by themselves, and strolled along the beach till they came to this grotto, which, being then empty, they entered. They admired the strata of rock leaning in different directions. They admired the incrustation which covers part of the sides, exactly resembling honeycomb; various shells imbedded in the rock; the sea-anemone spreading its purple fringe, — an animal flower clinging to the rocks. They admired the first efforts of vegetation in the purple and green tints occasioned by the lichens and other mosses creeping over the bare stone. They admired these together; they loved each other the more for having the same tastes; and they taught the echoes of the cavern to repeat the vows which they made of eternal constancy. In the mean time the tide was coming in: of this they were aware, as they now and then glanced their eye on the waves, which they saw advancing at a distance; but, not knowing the peculiar nature of the cavern, they thought themselves safe; when on a sudden, as they were in the furthest part of it, the waters rushed in from fissures in the rock with terrible roaring. They climbed from ledge to ledge of the rocks, — but in vain; the waters rose impetuously, and at length filled the whole grotto. Their bodies were found the next day, when the tide was out, reclining on a shelf of rock; he in the tender attitude of supporting her in the very highest accessible part, and leaning his own head in her lap, — so that he must have died first. Poor lovers! If, however, you should be too much grieved for them, you may impute the whole, if you please, to a waking *dream* which I had in the grotto.

CHAPTER X.

THE BARBAULDS VISIT BRISTOL. — THEY MEET DR. BEDDOES. — HIS CHARACTER. — THEY VISIT DORKING. — CALL ON MADAME D'ARBLAY. — HER ACCOUNT OF THE VISIT, AND IMPRESSION OF MR. AND MRS. BARBAULD. — MR. ROGERS'S ANECDOTE OF A POEM OF MRS. BARBAULD. — LETTER FROM MRS. BARBAULD TO MISS MORE. — SHE FORMS A FRIENDSHIP WITH THE EDGEWORTHS. — MISS EDGEWORTH'S ACCOUNT OF IT. — MRS. EDGEWORTH'S DESCRIPTION OF MR. AND MRS. BARBAULD. — SUGAR NOT USED BY THE OPPONENTS OF THE SLAVE-TRADE. — CHARACTER OF DR. PRIESTLEY BY MRS. BARBAULD. — ADDRESS TO HIM BY HER. — JOANNA BAILLIE. — HER TRAGEDIES. — DR. AIKIN'S DESCRIPTION OF HIS VISIT TO KIBWORTH.

IN Mrs. Barbauld's letter from Bristol, where they were making one of their visits at the house of Dr. and Mrs. Estlin, she writes to Mrs. Carr of meeting in that city Dr. Beddoes. He was celebrated for his endeavors to introduce the use of gases in the cure of certain diseases, and with various friends he spent much time and money in the pursuit of his investigations. He had a few years before married Anna, one of the daughters of Richard Lovell Edgeworth, and own sister of Maria Edgeworth. He was the friend of Dr. Darwin the author of the "Botanic Garden," and the patron of Sir Humphry Davy, who characterized him as "a truly remarkable man, but more admirably fitted to promote inquiry than to conduct it." Dr. Beddoes had a marked and extraordinary love of investigation and an enthusiasm for his chosen researches. He attempted the cure of pulmonary complaints by prescribing and administering gases through inhalation. In the "Life of the Wedgwoods" one reads of the experiments made, and finds that Thomas Wedgwood, who was suffering from a pulmonary complaint, passed several months at the house of Dr. Beddoes, and also assisted him with money for continuing his institution where the treatment of poor patients was pursued gratuitously. Mr. Wedgwood hoped to be benefited by the medicated airs which he inhaled, but he does not appear to have gained any relief therefrom. Dr. Beddoes seems to have had many odd fancies, one of which Mrs. Barbauld speaks of in her letter. Dr. and Mrs. Estlin had a large boarding-school in Bristol. Sir Henry Holland, in his Reminiscences, mentions their school with pleasure, and affectionately reverts to the memories of days passed there.

During this visit to the Estlins, Mr. and Mrs. Barbauld also visited Miss Hannah More at her cottage, Cowslip Green, passing with her and her sisters, a delightful day.

To MRS. CARR.

BRISTOL, August, 1797.

We are here very comfortably with our friend Mr. Estlin, who, like some other persons that I know, has the happy art of making his friends feel entirely at home with him: — he and Mrs. E. follow their occupations in the morning, and we our inclinations. The walks here on both sides the river are delightful; and the scenery at St. Vincent's rocks, whether viewed from above or below, is far superior, in my opinion, even to the beautifully dressed scenes that border the Thames, though these exceed it in fine trees. . . . .

I have seen Dr. Beddoes, who is a very pleasant man; his favorite prescription at present to ladies is, the inhaling the breath of cows; and as he does not, like the German doctors, send the ladies to the cow-house, the cows are to be brought into the lady's chamber, where they are to stand all night with their heads within the curtains. Mrs. ——, who has a good deal of humor, says the benefit cannot be mutual; and she is afraid, if the fashion takes, we shall eat diseased beef. It is a fact, however, that a family have been turned out of their lodgings, because the people of the house would not admit the cows: they said they had not built and furnished their rooms for the hoofs of cattle.

In the same year Dr. Aikin, who was quite ill, found the necessity of change of air and scene. He therefore passed four months at Dorking in Surrey. There he was cheered by the society of Mr. and Mrs. Barbauld, who made him a visit. In the "Monthly

Magazine" of that year there appeared an animated and appreciative description of the beauties of the natural objects and landscape gardening in that part of Surrey, from the pen of Dr. Aikin. In the Diary of Madame D'Arblay, there is the following description of a call made her by Mr. and Mrs. Barbauld, then with Dr. Aikin. In a letter to her father dated Bookham, 1797, she writes: "Imagine my surprise the other day, my dearest *padre*, at receiving a visit from Mr. and Mrs. Barbauld! We had never visited, and only met one evening at Mr. Burrow's by appointment, whither I was carried to meet her by Mrs. Chapone. They are at Dorking on a visit to Dr. Aikin, her brother, who is there at a lodging for his health. I received them with great pleasure, for I think highly both of her talents and her character, and he seems a very gentle, good sort of a man."

The next year, Madame D'Arblay, in writing to her sister, Mrs. Phillips, from West Hamble, Dorking, says:—

"I was extremely surprised to be told by the maid a gentleman and lady had called at the door, who sent in a card and begged to know if I could admit them, and to see the names on the card were Mr. and Mrs. Barbauld. I had never seen them more than twice: the first time, by their own desire, Mrs. Chapone carried me to meet them at Mr. Burrow's; the other time, I think, was at Mrs. Chapone's.

You must be sure I could not hesitate to receive with thankfulness this civility from the authoress of the most useful books, next to Mrs. Trimmer's, that have been yet written for children; though this with the world is probably her very secondary merit, her many pretty poems, and particularly songs, being generally esteemed. But many more have written those as well, and not a few better; for children's books she began the new walk which has since been so well cultivated, to the great information as well as utility of parents.

"Mr. Barbauld is a Dissenting minister, — an author also, but I am unacquainted with his works. They were in our little dining-parlor, — the only room that has any chairs in it, — and began apologies for the visit; but I interrupted, and finished them with my thanks." (Madame D'Arblay had just moved into her new cottage, named by her, after her last novel, Camilla Cottage; and it was in much disorder, for her marriage with M. D'Arblay had been one of affection, hardly of prudence, and they were very much straitened in their income.) "She is much altered, but not for the worse to me, though she is for herself, since the flight of her youth, which is evident, has also taken with it a great portion of an almost set smile, which had an air of determined complacence and prepared acquiescence that seemed to result from a sweetness which never risked being off guard. I remember Mrs. Chapone's saying to me, after our interview, 'She is a very good young women, as well as replete with talents; but why must one always smile so? It makes my poor jaws ache to look at her.' We talked, of course, of that excellent lady; and you will believe I did not quote her notions of smiling. . . . . Her brother, Dr. Aikin, with his family, were passing the summer at Dorking on account of his ill health, the air of that town having been recommended for his complaint. The Barbaulds were come to spend some time with him, and would not be so near without renewing their acquaintance. They had been walking in Norbury Park, which they admired very much; and Mrs. Barbauld very elegantly said, 'If there was such a public officer as a legislator of taste, Mr. Lock ought to be chosen for it.' They inquired much about M. D'Arblay, who was working in his garden, and would not be at the trouble of dressing to appear. They desired to see Alex" (her son), "and I produced him; and his orthographical feats were very well timed here, for, as soon as Mrs. Barbauld said, 'What is your name, you pretty creature?' he sturdily answered, 'B O Y.'

"Almost all our discourse was upon the Irish rebellion. Mr. Barbauld is a very little, diminutive figure, but well-bred and sensible. I borrowed her poems afterwards, of Mr. Daniel, who chanced to have them, and have read them with much esteem of the piety and worth they exhibit, and real admiration of the last amongst them, which is an epistle to Mr. Wilberforce in favor of the demolition of the slave-trade, in which her energy seems to spring from the real spirit of virtue, suffering at the luxurious depravity which can tolerate, in a free land, so unjust, cruel, and abominable a traffic.

"We returned their visit together in a few days, at Dr. Aikin's lodgings at Dorking, where, as she permitted M.

D'Arblay to speak French, they had a very animated discourse upon buildings, French and English, each supporting those of their own country with great spirit, but my monsieur, to own the truth, having greatly the advantage both in manner and argument. He was in spirits, and came forth with his best exertions. Dr. Aikin looks very sickly, but is said to be better; he had a good countenance."

In Rogers's "Table-Talk" there is an anecdote related by him of Madame D'Arblay in her old age, which is not out of place here. He says: "I know few lines finer than the concluding stanza of 'Life' by Mrs. Barbauld, who composed it when she was very old.

'Life! we've been long together,
Through pleasant and through cloudy weather;
'T is hard to part when friends are dear;
Perhaps 't will cost a sigh, a tear;
Then steal away, give little warning,
Choose thine own time;
Say not Good Night, — but in some brighter clime
Bid me Good Morning.'

Sitting with Madame D'Arblay some weeks before she died, I said to her, 'Do you remember those lines of Mrs. Barbauld's "Life" which I once repeated to you?' 'Remember them!' she replied; 'I repeat them to myself every night before I go to sleep.'"

Mr. Henry Crabb Robinson alludes to a conversation with Mr. Rogers, who repeated to him this anecdote in

1837, and also spoke of Mrs. Barbauld, as he always did when she was mentioned, with great affection and regard.

FROM MRS. BARBAULD TO MISS H. MORE.

HAMPSTEAD, 1799.

DEAR MADAM, —You have done me both honor and pleasure in the gratification you have indulged me with, of receiving, from the respected hand of the author, a treatise which every one who *reads* will *peruse*. I dare not speak to *you*, who write with so much higher views than those of fame, of the brilliancy of the style, or the merit of the work considered as a literary composition. You will be better pleased if, passing over these excellences which, though every person of taste must feel them, every person solicitous for the interests of virtue and religion must consider as subordinate ones, I express my ardent wishes that your benevolent intentions towards the rising generation, and your unwearied exertions in every path where good is to be done to your fellow-creatures, may meet with ample success. The field is large, and laborers of every complexion, and who handle their tools very differently, are all called to co-operate in the great work. May all who have the good of mankind in view preserve for each other the esteem and affectionate wishes which virtue owes to virtue, through all those smaller * differences which must ever take place between thinking beings seeing through

* The differences, however, were by no means small between Miss More's and Mrs. B——'s religious opinions.

different mediums, and subjected to the weakness and imperfection of all human reasoning. Mr. Barbauld and myself recollect with infinite pleasure the delightful and interesting day we passed under your roof the summer before last. It was only damped by your indisposition; and the accounts I have heard of your health have not been such as to favor the hope that you have been much freer from it of late. *Spare yourself*, I entreat you, for the world cannot *spare you*; and consider that, in the most indolent day you can possibly spend, you are in every drawing-room, and every closet, and every parlor window, gliding from place to place with wonderful celerity, and talking good things to hundreds and hundreds of auditors.* I do not know where you are at this moment, but if at home, I beg you will give Mr. Barbauld's and my affectionate respects to all and every one of your sisters, and accept, my dear madam, the assurance of high esteem with which

I am your obliged and affectionate

A. L. BARBAULD.

Miss Edgeworth has been named among the friends and contemporaries of Mrs. Barbauld. They met first in 1799, and till Mrs. Barbauld's death were firm and devoted friends. In the spring of the year 1799 the Barbaulds visited the Edgeworth family, who were at Clifton for the health of one of the children. In Maria's Memoir of her father, she speaks of the friendship which was then formed and the mutual

* Alluding to "Strictures on Education," by H. More, 1790.

pleasure it afforded, and says: "Among the friends he (Mr. Edgeworth) formed during this summer in England, and in consequence of the publication of his sentiments on education, was Mrs. Barbauld. Her writings he had long admired for their classic strength and elegance, for their high and true tone of moral and religious feeling, and for their practically useful tendency. She gratified him by accepting an invitation to pass some time with us at Clifton; and ever afterwards, though at a great distance from each other, her constant friendship for him was a source of great pleasure and just pride." Later on in the Memoir, Miss Edgeworth remarks that Mrs. Barbauld was the first person who made some unanswerable objections to certain parts of Mr. Edgeworth's book on "Practical Education." Miss Aikin says that one of Mrs. Barbauld's letters to Miss Edgeworth contains "some excellent criticisms on Mr. E——'s 'Practical Education.'" In the observations on "Practical Education" in the Memoir, Miss Edgeworth says that "Mrs. Barbauld was further well prepared to urge against his plan the tendency to foster aristocratic pride and perhaps ingratitude. The one-and-twenty other good reasons she said could be given, my father spared her." She objected to the mode by which he proposed to entirely separate children from all or any association with servants. In his own immense family, consisting of an almost patriarchal number of relations and children, the entire absence of domestics about the children might be secured; but in ordinary families his plan was neither practicable nor desirable.

Mrs. Edgeworth wrote of this visit of the Barbaulds in a letter to one of the family in Ireland: "We met at Clifton Mr. and Mrs. Barbauld. He was an amiable and benevolent man, so eager against the slave-trade that when he drank tea with us he always brought some East India sugar, that he might not share our wickedness in eating that made by the negro slave. Mrs. Barbauld, whose 'Evenings at Home' had so much delighted Maria and her father, was very pretty, and conversed with great ability in admirable language." Among the first measures urged by the most enthusiastic opponents of the slave-trade was that of persuading all whom they could influence to abstain from the use of sugar and other West Indian articles which were the manufacture or raised by the labor of slaves. Many conscientious persons did actually adopt this plan of abstinence from the articles of slave labor; but naturally the numbers who did not use these commodities were not great enough to prevent the demand for them, and consequent supply by slave labor. Dr. Aikin, in writing his sister at this time, tells her that he, though considering the plan an unpractical one, has at last yielded to the custom, saying, "I am at length become a practical *anti-saccharist.* I could not continue to be the only person in the family who used a luxury which grew less and less *sweet* from the reflections mingled with it. I do not in this matter look to *effects.* They are in the hands of Providence, and I neither expect nor despair about them. I resign the use of sugar merely on the conviction that, feeling as I do about the mode in which it is procured, I cannot justify the use of it to myself. It is a personal affair to me, and I neither feel a desire to make nor trouble myself about consequences. The sacrifice I find less than I expected; it is, indeed, almost too little to make to principle with the idea of merit. I know not whether mere economy might not do as much. But with respect to the young people, and even *children,* who have entirely on their own accord resigned an indulgence important to them, I triumph and admire! Nothing is to be despaired of, if *many* of the rising generation are capable of such conduct."

The preceding letter to Miss More, written in the year 1799, shows the warm feeling of friendship existing between these two eminent women. It was occasioned by the receipt of Miss More's new book, the "Strictures on Female Education," which was a powerful work, and highly valued at the time of its publication, as the state of education was extremely poor. This book was the third prose work of its gifted author, and a very able, sensible criticism of the subject. One lady said of it, showing how indifferent people were to the state of education for women, "Everybody will read her, everybody admire her, and nobody mind her."

TO DR. AND MRS. ESTLIN.

HAMPSTEAD, December 5, 1799.

MY DEAR FRIENDS, — It is now much longer than I wish it ever to be since any letter has passed between us; I wish, therefore, to hear news of you both; particularly as you are drawing near the end of a session, the fatigues of which must always more or less give some wear and tear to your health and exhaust your spirits. I hope you have not forgotten that, in order to recruit them, you proposed coming, both of you, to London this Christmas; and I hope that you have by no means forgot that it was a part of the plan to give us as much of your time at Hampstead as you can spare consistently with other engagements. Write us word, then, that you are preparing to pack off the boys and come to us; and I assure you we shall feel more enlivened by the news than by ten gallons of Dr. Beddoes's most vivifying air. How often do we recall the heartfelt pleasures we enjoyed in the daily and unrestrained intercourse of Southendown, — the philosophic discussions, the infantile mirth, the caves, the rocks, and especially the two nymphs, to whom — if they are now within your circle — we beg to be affectionately remembered! . . . .

We have been much entertained by the "Annual Anthology"; there are some charming pieces in it. To pass from poetry to divinity, have you seen a small piece, which has been much read and speculated upon here, Apeleutheros? Some attribute it to one person, some to another; but the fact is, the author has kept his secret well. It is written with great candor, but is slight, considering the importance of the subject to be discussed. It has not been published; and I cannot avoid a melancholy sensation on reflecting, that such are the times we live in, that a bookseller dares not publish a pamphlet written with perfect decency, and in which, moreover, there is not a word of politics. But we should not be better in France. How the revolutions of that country mock all calculation! I should suppose that the late events have not tended to bring newspapers into more request than they were at Southendown.

May I soon receive a favorable answer with respect to your health, spirits, and good intentions with respect to London and Hampstead! Come and brighten the chain of friendship, as the Indians say.

To Mrs. Kenrick.

Hampstead, 1800.

My dear Friend, — Whether or no I received the letter which you forgot to write, I shall not tell you; I only know that I am often reproached by my correspondents for negligence; and for the life of me I cannot think of anything that has hindered the arrival of my letters, except the cause to which you are inclined to attribute the failure of yours.

Be that as it may, I most certainly have received from you *one* letter which has given me a great deal of pleasure, and for which I will no longer defer my affectionate thanks. And what shall I tell you first? That we are well, that we have rubbed tolerably through the winter, and that we have been enjoying the sudden burst of spring, which clothed every tree and every hedge in verdure with a rapidity seldom observed in our climate. The blossoms were all pushed out at once, but unfortunately few have remained long enough to give the expectation of fruit. I fear it may be the same with your beautiful apple-orchards. We often picture to ourselves the beautiful country, and still oftener the affectionate friends and the interesting family with whom we spent so happy a fortnight last summer.

If all that has happened had not happened, or the memory of it could be washed away with Lethe, how usefully and respectably might Dr. Priestley now be placed at the head of the Royal Institution, which is so fashionable just now in London! I went a few mornings ago to hear Dr. Garnet, who is at present the only lecturer, and was much pleased to see a fashionable and very attentive audience, about one third ladies, assembled for the purposes of science and improvement. How much is taught now, and even made a part of education, which, when you and I were young, was not even discovered! It does some credit to the taste of the town, that the Institution and the Bishop of London's lectures have been the most fashionable places of resort this winter. I have received, however, great pleasure lately from the representation of De Montfort, a tragedy which you probably read a year and a half ago in a volume entitled "A Series of Plays on the Passions." I admired it then, but little dreamed I was indebted for my entertainment to a young lady of Hampstead whom I visited, and who came to Mr. Barbauld's meeting all the while with as innocent a face as if she had never written a line. The play is admirably acted by Mrs. Siddons and Kemble, and is finely written, with great purity of sentiment, beauty of diction, strength and originality of character; but it is open to criticism, — I cannot believe such a hatred natural. The affection between the brother and sister is most beautifully touched, and, as far as I know, quite new. The play is somewhat too good for our present taste.

In this letter, written to her friend Mrs. Kenrick, Mrs. Barbauld speaks of Dr. Priestley, and the unfortunate odium he had incurred by his opinions, which prevented his receiving an invitation to preside over the Royal Institution, — a position for which his great talents and information well fitted him. This Institution, then recently founded by Count Rumford, was becoming exceedingly popular, and continues, under its present able professors, to hold a very high position in the scientific world. The names of Sir Humphry Davy and Professor Faraday in the past, of Professors Tyndall and Huxley in the present, give the Institution a grand history for the past and a brilliant record for the present day. Mrs. Barbauld, in alluding to "all that has happened," referred to the treatment of Dr. Priestley at the Birmingham riots, which was caused by a popular impression against Dr. Priestley as an advocate of revolutionary and seditious opinions. The mob, after searching in a tavern where Dr. Priestley had *not* dined with some factious agitators of treasonable sentiments, hunted for him elsewhere, crying out that "they wanted to knock the powder out of Dr. Priestley's wig." Finding he was not where they supposed him to be, they proceeded to burn his chapel, and then destroyed his house, with all his valuable philosophical instruments, manuscripts, and library. He with his family barely escaped with their lives. All the great and good qualities of this justly celebrated man could not save him from suffering from the consequences of his advanced state of thought regarding politics, and his rather radical religious opinions. Though one may not accord with his political bias or articles of belief, yet it is ever to be regretted by the lovers of free inquiry and utterance that he should have been obliged to leave the country he so much loved for any other, even though that country was the site of a modern republic, and his political views must have been gratified in his American home by the observation of the earliest efforts of the founders of our present republic, which probably more nearly embodied his ideas of government than any other attempted in recent times.

Mrs. Barbauld, in her characters, has one of Dr. Aikin, which is easily known to the reader. That addressed "Happy old man!" contains the portrait of one of the trustees of the Warrington Academy. Mrs. Vaughan, mother of Mr. Benjamin Vaughan of Bristol, is portrayed in that description, —

> "Such were the dames of old heroic days,
> Which faithful story yet delights to praise."

Miss Aikin, in writing to Dr. Channing, says of it: "If you will turn to one of Mrs. Barbauld's characters (it was written, by the way, for the mother of Mr. Benjamin Vaughin, a grand-looking old lady, whose figure I still recall), you will fully understand what kind of spirit I longed to inspire into my sex." The character of Dr. Priestley is the longest of these, and really very finely touched by the hand of appreciative friendship. It begins, —

> "Champion of Truth, alike through Nature's field,
> And where in sacred leaves she shines reveal'd,—
> Alike in both, eccentric, piercing, bold,
> Like his own lightnings, which no chains can hold;
> Neglecting caution, and disdaining art,
> He seeks no armor for a naked heart."

The character is clearly drawn and not overdone, as the praise is just and discriminating.

Mrs. Barbauld addressed the following lines to Dr. Priestley some years after this.

To Dr. Priestley.

December 29, 1792.

Stirs not thy spirit, Priestley! as the train
With low obeisance, and with servile phrase,
File behind file, advance, with supple knee,
And lay their necks beneath the foot of power?
Burns not thy cheek indignant, when thy name,
On which delighted Science loved to dwell,
Becomes the bandied theme of hooting crowds?
With timid caution, or with cool reserve,
When e'en each reverend brother keeps aloof,
Eyes the struck deer, and leaves thy naked side
A mark for Power to shoot at? Let it be.
"On evil days though fallen, and evil tongues,"
To thee the slander of a passing age
Imports not. Scenes like these hold little space
In his large mind, whose ample stretch of thought
Grasps future periods. — Well canst thou afford
To give large credit for that debt of fame
Thy country owes thee. Calm thou canst consign it
To the slow payment of that distant day, —
If distant, — when thy name, to Freedom's joined,
Shall meet the thanks of a regenerate land.

In the Life of Joanna Baillie we read of the curiosity felt by the literary world as to the authorship of the "Plays of the Passions," and the many guesses hazarded about it. Mrs. Barbauld mentions Miss Baillie in her letter to Mrs. Kenrick, and tells her how much amazed she was at finding the author was not one of the already celebrated writers to whom it had been attributed, but "a young lady of Hampstead whom" she visited, "and who came to Mr. Barbauld's meeting all the while with as innocent a face as if she had never written a line." Many years later Mrs. Barbauld addressed Miss Baillie in her poem "Eighteen Hundred and Eleven,"—

> "—Then, loved Joanna, to admiring eyes,
> Thy storied groups in scenic pomp shall rise:
> Their high-souled strains and Shakespeare's noble rage
> Shall with alternate passion shake the stage."

The reader can fancy he sees Joanna and Agnes Baillie making a morning call on this eminent and respected woman whose acquaintance they had formed on moving to Hampstead. Miss Lucy Aikin, in a letter, describes the visit, and how Mrs. Barbauld praised the Plays "with all her heart." The biographer of Miss Baillie says of Mrs. Barbauld's praise, and how highly she was esteemed, that she "was an excellent woman who was raised to an unchallenged eminence in the lettered circles of her own day, as she is in danger of being undervalued in another generation." One can imagine how pleasant it must have been to the calm and reserved young woman to hear her book so highly approved of and justly commented on by a person whose judgment was so valuable and impartial. Miss Aikin says in one part of her own Recollections of Joanna Baillie, "I well remember the scene, — she and her sister arrived on a morning call at Mrs. Barbauld's; my aunt immediately introduced the topic of the anonymous tragedies, and gave utterance to her admiration with the generous delight in the manifestations of kindred genius which distinguished her." "The sudden delight" which Miss Aikin thinks must have been felt by the author of the tragedies at hearing this entirely spontaneous tribute and discriminating criticism did not move Joanna Baillie from her stern composure; and Mrs. Barbauld must have learned from others the authorship of the Plays which she alluded to in her letter, where she tells Mrs. Kenrick of witnessing the representation of one of them, De Montfort, which was then being personated in its leading characters by Mrs. Siddons and Kemble.

HAMPSTEAD, October, 1801.

MY DEAR MRS. CARR,—Though I hope the time approaches when we shall be within reach of one another again, I feel the want of our accustomed intercourse too strongly not to wish to supply it in some manner by a letter. Besides, I want to wish you joy on the peace, which came at last so unexpectedly, and almost overwhelmed us with the good news. We have hardly done illuminating and bouncing and popping upon the occasion. The spontaneous joy and mutual congratulations of all ranks show plainly what were the wishes of the people, though they dared not declare them. And now France lies like a huge loadstone on the other side the Channel, and will draw every mother's child of us to it. Those who know French are refreshing their memories, — those who do not, are learning it; and every one is planning in some way or other to get a sight of the promised land.

Our Hampstead neighbors are returning to us from the lakes, and the sea, and the ends of the earth. I have been puzzling myself to account for this universal disposition amongst us to migrate at a certain time of the year and change our way of life; and I have been fancying that we English lie under the same spell which the fairies are said to do, — by which during a month every year they are obliged to be transformed, and to wander about exposed to adventures. So some of our nymphs are turned into butterflies for the season, others into Naiads, and sport about till the sober months come, when they resume their usual appearance and occupation of notable housewives, perhaps in Cheapside or the Borough. As to you, you carry your cares with you, and therefore must be pretty much the same, except the dripping locks of the Naiad; but Sarah, I imagine, is at this moment skimming along the shore like a swallow, or walking with naked feet like a slender heron in the water, or nestling among the cliffs. Wherever she is, my love to her.

In a letter from Dr. Aikin to his sister, there is a short description of a trip he made to their birthplace and early home. It is dated July 7, 1800. "Would you have thought me, my dear sister, a likely man for such a flight of sentiment, as that, being about forty miles from Kibworth, I could not forbear to visit it? In fact, it had long been the subject of my waking and sleeping thoughts, especially of the latter, and I was resolved to give way to the impulse. So yesterday I left S——'s, mounted on his old mare, which I had tried before in a couple of short excursions, and boldly pushed on for Kettering, twenty-seven miles, that evening. This morning, starting early, I came to Harborough to breakfast, and thence, with beating heart, the five miles to Kibworth." After a long account of the changes which he observed, he adds, "I found that I had no acquaintance living at Kibworth; so, mounting again, I made a slow circuit quite through the town, which I found vastly *lessened* in my eyes; yet our old house still makes a respectable figure. It is inhabited by the widow Humphreys. The casement window and balcony remain as before. . . . .

"I made a complete tour of the churchyard, and recognized many familiar names among the tombs, but was disappointed in not meeting with that of our grandfather. Had he a monument? There were several become illegible through a coating of moss. . . . .

"Such has been my visit to my *native village.* I am not sorry I made it, though I scarcely know whether to call the impression on the whole agreeable or otherwise."

The following letter to Mrs. Carr contains a description of a trip made by the Barbaulds to the Isle of Wight, which Mrs. Barbauld says she thinks Bonaparte might like for some of his numerous family as a kingdom. At this time the English felt there was a prospect of invasion from the French, and made many preparations to meet such an attack. But the disaffected classes at home were also a cause of anxiety, as it was doubtful how they would behave in the event of such an occurrence.

SOUTHAMPTON, July 10.

MY DEAR MRS. CARR, — Have you ever seen the Isle of Wight? If not, you have not seen the prettiest place in the king's dominions. It is such a charming *little* island! In this great island, which we set foot on half an hour ago, the sea is at such a distance from the greater part of it, that you have no more acquaintance with it than if you were in the heart of Germany; and even on the coast, England appears no more an island to the eye than France does; but in this little gem of the ocean called the Isle of Wight you see and feel you are on an island every moment. The great ocean becomes quite domestic; you see it from every point of view; you have it on the right hand, you look and you have it on the left also; you see both sides of the island at once, — you look into every creek and corner of it, which produces a new and singular feeling. We have taken three different rides upon and under high cliffs, cornfields, and villages down to the water's edge, and a fine West India fleet in view, with the sails all spread, and her convoy most majestically sailing by her. We saw Lord Dysart's seat, and Sir Richard Worsley's: at the former there is a seat in the rock which shuts out every object but the shoreless ocean, for it looks towards France: at the latter there is an attempt at an English vineyard; the vines are planted on terraces one above another. Another day's excursion was to the Needles; we walked to the very point, the toe of the island; the sea-gulls were flying about the rocks like bees from a hive, and little fleets of puffins with their black heads in the water. Allum Bay looks like a wall of marble veined with different colors. The freshness of the sea-air, and the beauty of the smooth turf of the downs on which we rode or walked, was inexpressibly pleasing. The next day we visited the north side of the island, richly wooded down to the water's edge, and rode home over a high down with the sea on both sides and a rich country between, the corn beginning to acquire the tinge of harvest-time. In short, I do believe that if Buonaparte were to see the Isle of Wight, he would think it a very pretty *appanage* for some third or fourth cousin, and would make him king of it — if he could get it.

CHAPTER XI.

Removal of the Barbaulds to Stoke Newington. — Cause of it. — Lines to Mrs. Barbauld by Dr. Aikin. — History of the Chapel. — Letters. — The Annual Review. — Mrs. Barbauld edits with Essay a "Selection." — Miss Aikin's Opinion about this Essay. — Diary of Mr. Robinson, and his Introduction to Mrs. Barbauld. — Wordsworth's Admiration of "Life." — His Remarks about Mrs. Barbauld. — Sir Henry Holland's Recollections of Newington Society and Mrs. Barbauld. — She writes the "Life of Richardson." — Anecdotes about it. — Miss Aikin's Letters. — Anecdotes. — Mr. Barbauld's Death. — His Character, by Mrs. Barbauld.

IN the year 1802, Mr. Barbauld accepted the position of pastor to the society of Newington Green, which had formerly been Dr. Price's. Their reason for leaving Hampstead and the numerous friends there to whom they were warmly attached, the pleasant home and circle of literary and cultivated people who were their neighbors, was the wish which had long been felt and expressed by Mrs. Barbauld and her brother that they might live nearer each other, so that they could meet daily. Dr. Aikin having been for some little time a resident of Stoke Newington, decided them in favor of Mr. Barbauld's accepting this call, which would insure them the wished-for arrangement. Dr. Aikin suffered very much from ill health, and was finally forced to abandon the practice of his profession in London, and confine himself almost exclusively to the literary pursuits which have given him a good reputation for taste and study. For the purer air and more perfect rest he removed to Stoke Newington in 1798, and the addition to his society made by the presence of his sister and Mr. Barbauld was exceedingly gratifying to him. They had many friends around them, and amid literary pursuits and social intercourse with congenial minds found much to cheer and brighten their declining years.

In the poetical epistle addressed by Dr. Aikin to his sister at Geneva, from which some lines have already been quoted, the following are taken; they very strongly breathe the wish now fulfilled by the Barbaulds, removal to Newington. He says, —

"Yet one dear wish still struggles in my breast,
And points one darling object unpossest: —
How many years have whirled their rapid course,
Since we, sole streamlets from an honored source,
In fond affection as in blood allied,
Have wandered devious from each other's side;
Allowed to catch alone some transient view,
Scarce long enough to think the vision true!
O then, while yet some zest to life remains,
While transport yet can swell the beating veins,

While sweet remembrance keeps her wonted seat,
And fancy still retains some genial heat;
When evening bids each busy task be o'er, —
Once let us meet again to part no more!"

The village of Stoke Newington was very rural when the Barbaulds removed there, and even now, though much more populous, still retains something of its early aspect. William Howitt, in "The Northern Heights of London," says of the Green, "It is one of the oldest places of the parish, and has had ancient houses and distinguished inhabitants. It had, till of late years, a still, out-of-the-way look, surrounded in most parts by large old trees, and green lanes led to it on all sides. Population and houses have now crowded up to it on all sides." For the most part the hamlet of Stoke Newington lies in the parish of Islington, and it is rather to the north of London. Now it is a part of the great metropolis. "The Presbyterian Chapel at Newington Green, which dates from 1708, has a history of considerable interest," says Mr. Howitt. "Like most other Presbyterian Chapels in England, it found its congregation go over at a particular crisis to Unitarianism, to which it still adheres. It has had a succession of able ministers, some of whom are of world-wide notoriety." And among these celebrated names he mentions those of Dr. Price and Mr. Rochemont Barbauld. In the graveyard of the chapel are buried Dr. Price and Mr.

and Mrs. Barbauld, with other members of the society. An aged survivor of the society remembers well the face and figure of Mrs. Barbauld, and still shows her pew in the chapel, where there are two mural tablets, one commemorative of Dr. Price, the second of Mrs. Barbauld. The following letter is the first to be copied which is dated from the Barbaulds' new home. In it one traces something of the over-shadowing anxiety which the state of Mr. Barbauld's health must have caused to the affectionate heart of Mrs. Barbauld. One contemporary writer speaks of Mr. Barbauld, when in early life, as "a queer little man," and in his later years the peculiarities of his mind became extremely marked. For several years he was extremely excitable, and showed some eccentricities of conduct which increased upon him to the fatal termination of his life. Mrs. Barbauld must have exercised much self-control and firmness to have busied herself, under these trying circumstances, in various literary labors.

STOKE NEWINGTON, January 14, 1802.

MY DEAR MRS. BEECROFT, — Why have I not written to you? Ah, why indeed! I wish you would furnish me with a good reason. Long ago I should have done it, it is true. . . . . And pray when do you and the lovely —— and —— go to France? for I take it for granted that you go; and indeed you ought to go: for who would reap more amusement and information, or communicate more of it to your friends, than yourself? I met with three of the tourists lately. Mr. ——, who was formerly a Grecian, is turned Egyptian: the Egyptians are the first people in the world, the tutors of the Greeks and the inventors of all arts and sciences. Mr. —— deals in anecdotes and manners; and Mrs. —— seems to have felt most enthusiasm for the *great man*. My enthusiasm is all gone, — not for Buonaparte, for with regard to him I never had any, — but for most things. I wish there were any process, electric, galvanic, or through any other medium, by which we might recover some of the fine feelings which age is so apt to blunt: it would be the true secret of growing young. One affection, however, I hope will never die in my heart, — the dear affection of friendship.

To Mrs. Smith.

Stoke Newington, February 26, 1803.

Dear Madam, — It would have given me great pleasure to have been among those friends who crowd about you to congratulate your arrival again on English ground; but the distance first, the severity of the weather, and then indisposition consequent upon it, prevent my having that pleasure. I cannot content myself, however, without writing a line to welcome you all home. We hear you have been very much pleased with Paris, which indeed was to be expected. The canvas people and the marble people must be sufficient to make a rich voyage of it, even if the French people had not opened their mouths. . . . .

We are apt to accuse some of you travellers of bringing us

over an influenza from Paris, softened indeed in passing over the Channel, but severe enough to set us all a-coughing. We try to amuse ourselves, however, with reading; and among other things have been greatly amused and interested with Hayley's Life of Cowper, which I would much advise you to read if it comes in your way. Hayley, indeed, has very little merit in it, for it is a collection of letters with a very slender thread of biography; but many of the letters are charming, particularly to his relation, Lady Hesketh; and there is one poem to his *Mary*, absolutely the most pathetic piece that ever was written. We have also read, as I suppose you have done, Madame de Staël's *Delphine*. Her pen has more of Rousseau than any author that has appeared for a long time. I suppose you have heard it canvassed and criticised at Paris. . . . .

To Mrs. Beecroft.

July 28, 1803.

I am glad to find you have spent the spring so pleasantly. But when you say you made the excursion instead of coming to London, you forget that you might have passed the latter end of a London *winter* in town *after* enjoying the natural *spring* in the country. We have been spending a week at Richmond, in the delightful shades of Ham walks and Twickenham meadows. I never saw so many flowering limes and weeping-willows as in that neighborhood: they say, you know, that Pope's famous willow was the first in the country; and it seems to corroborate it, that there are so many in the vicinity. Under the shade of the trees we read Southey's

Amadis, which I suppose you are also reading. As all Englishmen are now to turn knights-errant and fight against the great giant and monster Buonaparte, the publication seems very seasonable. Pray, are you an alarmist? One hardly knows whether to be frightened or diverted on seeing people assembled at a dinner-table, appearing to enjoy extremely the fare and the company, and saying all the while, with a most smiling and placid countenance, that the French are to land in a fortnight, and that London is to be sacked and plundered for three days, — and then they talk of going to watering-places. I am sure we do not believe in the danger we pretend to believe in; and I am sure that none of us can even form an idea how we should feel if we were forced to believe it. I wish I could lose in the quiet walks of literature all thoughts of the present state of the political horizon.

My brother is going to publish "Letters to a Young Lady on English Poetry"; he is indefatigable. "I wish you were half as diligent!" say you. "Amen," say I. Love to Eliza and Laura, and thank the former for her note. I shall always be glad to hear from either of them. How delightful must be the soft beatings of a heart entering into the world for the first time, — every surrounding object new, fresh, and fair, all smiling within and without! Long may every sweet illusion continue, that promotes happiness, and ill befall the rough hand that would destroy them!

In 1802, Mr. Arthur Aikin, the son of Dr. John Aikin, Mrs. Barbauld's brother, undertook the care and editorship of the "Annual Review," an excellent work which unfortunately met with little encouragement, and the enterprise was abandoned in 1808. Mrs. Barbauld "reluctantly took part of the poetry and polite literature in one or two of the earliest volumes, and gave that *critique* on the 'Lay,' which the author said he had approved and admired the most," says Miss Aikin in writing to a friend and alluding to the pleasant acquaintance between Sir Walter Scott and her aunt. One writer in speaking of the queens of London society, Mrs. Montague and others, says of Mrs. Barbauld, who is named among them, that at this time she "was laying down the sceptre and consenting to be private and homely." Mrs. Barbauld never made any pretensions to rule in her sphere. To her the republic of letters was real, and she was a firm believer in the equality of man and a state of freedom. All her writings prove her reasonable hope and belief in human progress, and manifest a great degree of modesty. To have disclaimed her position in the world of letters would have been affectation, but she never claimed what was not offered her. The next letter in order describes a visit to Tunbridge Wells, to Miss Taylor of Norwich, afterwards Mrs. Reeve.

TUNBRIDGE WELLS, August 11, 1804.

I may call you dear Susan, may not I? for I can love you, if not better, yet more familiarly and at my ease, under that appellation than under the more formal one of Miss Taylor, though you have now a train to your gown, and are, I suppose, at Norwich invested with all the rights of womanhood. I have many things to thank you for: — in the first place, for a charming letter, which has both amused and delighted us. In the next place, I have to thank you for a very elegant veil, which is very beautiful in itself, and receives great additional value from being the work of your ingenious fingers. I have brought it here to parade with upon the Pantiles, being by much the smartest part of my dress. O that you were here, Susan, to exhibit upon a *donky*, — I cannot tell whether my orthography is right, but a donky is the *monture* in high fashion here; and I assure you, when covered with blue housings, and sleek, it makes no bad figure: — I mean a lady, if an elegant woman, makes no bad figure upon it, with a little boy or girl behind, who carries a switch, meant to admonish the animal from time to time that he is hired to walk on, and not to stand still. The ass is much better adapted than the horse to show off a lady; for this reason, which perhaps may not have occurred to you, that her beauty is not so likely to be eclipsed: for you must know that many philosophers, amongst whom is ——, are decidedly of opinion that a fine *horse* is a much handsomer animal than a fine woman; but I have not yet heard such a preference asserted in favor of the *ass*, — not our English asses at least, — a fine Spanish one, or a zebra, perhaps. . . . .

It is the way to *subscribe* for everything here, — to the library, etc.; and among other things we were asked on the

Pantiles to subscribe for eating fruit as we pass backwards and forwards. "How much?" "Half-a-crown." "But for how long a time?" "As long as you please." "But I should soon eat half-a-crown's-worth of fruit." "O, you are upon honor!"

There are pleasant walks on the hills here, and picturesque views of the town, which, like Bath, is seen to advantage by lying in a hollow. It bears the marks of having been long a place of resort, from the number of good and rather old-built houses, — all let for lodgings; and shady walks, and groves of old growth. The sides of many of the houses are covered with tiles; but the Pantiles, which you may suppose I saw with some interest, are now paved with freestone.

We were interested in your account of Cambridge, and glad you saw not only buildings, but men. With a mind prepared as yours is, how much pleasure have you to enjoy from seeing! That all your improvements may produce you pleasure, and all your pleasures tend to improvement, is the wish of

Your ever affectionate.

In 1804, Mrs. Barbauld was able to devote herself sufficiently to literary labors to offer a "Selection from the Spectator, Tatler, Guardian, and Freeholder," with an Essay on the genius, thoughts, and style of the writers whose papers she thus edited. This Essay added greatly to the value of the book. Though it has been regarded by many competent authorities as, perhaps, her best piece of literary labor in the critical and discriminating study of the writings and beauties of the great English authors chosen, I have not included it among the prose essays in this selection of her works, as it cannot properly be separated from the Selection to which it serves as an introduction and a study, and of which it is a masterly review. It makes the reader well acquainted with the salient points of character, the distinguishing marks of genius, and the peculiarities of style of the various authors whose works are included in the Selection.

Miss Lucy Aikin has so well represented the merit of this Essay as a critical analysis of the writers Mrs. Barbauld had studied, that her own words best convey her thoughts about her aunt's performance. She says of it: "This delightful piece may perhaps be regarded as the most successful of her efforts in literary criticism, and that it should be so is easily accounted for. There were many striking points of resemblance between her genius and that of Addison. As prose writers, both were remarkable for uniting wit of the light and sportive kind with vividness of fancy, and a style at once rich and lively, flowing and full of idiom; both of them rather avoided the pathetic; in both, the sentiments of rational and liberal devotion were blended with the speculations of philosophy and the paintings of a fine imagination; both were admirable for the splendor they diffused over a serious, the grace with which they touched a lighter, subject. . . . . The humorous delineation of manners and characters, indeed, in which Addison so conspicuously shone, was never attempted by Mrs. Barbauld; in poetry, on the other hand, she surpassed him in all the qualities of which excellence in that style is composed. Certainly this great author could not elsewhere have found a critic so capable of entering, as it were, into the soul of his writings, culling their choicest beauties, and drawing them forth for the admiration of a world by which they had begun to be neglected. Steele and the other contributors to these periodical papers are also ably, though briefly, characterized by her; and such pieces of theirs are included in the 'Selection' as could fairly claim enduring remembrance."

The Essay opens with the observation, "that it is equally true of books as of their authors, that one generation passeth away and another cometh." The mutual influence exerted by books and manners on each other is then remarked; and the silent and gradual declension from what might be called the active life of an admired and popular book to the honorable retirement of a classic is highly but impressively traced; closed by remarks on the mutations and improvements which have particularly affected the works in question.

In the Diary of Mr. H. C. Robinson, the following interesting reminiscences of his first introduction to and friendship for Mrs. Barbauld will attract the attention of the reader. In the first entry under the year 1805, after her return to England, he writes, "In December I formed a new acquaintance, of which I was reasonably proud, and in the recollection of which I still rejoice. At Hackney I saw repeatedly Miss Wakefield,* a charming girl. And one day at a party, when Mrs. Barbauld had been the subject of conversation, and I had spoken of her in enthusiastic terms, Miss Wakefield came to me, and said, 'Would you like to know Mrs. Barbauld?' I exclaimed, 'You might as well ask me whether I should like to know the Angel Gabriel!' 'Mrs. Barbauld is, however, more accessible. I will introduce you to her nephew.' She then called to Charles Aikin, whom she soon after married; and he said: 'I dine every Sunday with my uncle and aunt at Stoke Newington, and I am expected always to bring a friend with me. Two knives and forks are laid for me. Will you go with me next Sunday?' Gladly acceding to the proposal, I had the good fortune to make myself agreeable, and soon became intimate in the house.

"Mr. Barbauld had a slim figure, a meagre face, and a shrill voice. He talked a great deal, and was fond of dwelling on controversial points in religion. He was by no means destitute of ability, though the afflictive

* Daughter of Gilbert Wakefield.

disease was lurking in him, which in a few years broke out, and, as is well known, caused a sad termination to his life.

"Mrs. Barbauld bore the remains of great personal beauty. She had a brilliant complexion, light hair, blue eyes, a small, elegant figure, and her manners were very agreeable, with something of the generation then departing. She received me very kindly, spoke very civilly of my aunt, Zachary Crabbe, and said she had herself once slept at my father's house. Mrs. Barbauld is so well known by her prose writings that it is needless for me to attempt to characterize her here. Her excellence lay in the soundness and acuteness of her understanding, and in the perfection of her taste. In the estimation of Wordsworth she was the first of our literary women, and he was not bribed to this judgment by any especial congeniality of feeling, or by concurrence in speculative opinions. I may here relate an anecdote concerning her and Wordsworth, though out of its proper time by many, many years; but it is so good that it ought to be preserved from oblivion. It was after her death that Lucy Aikin published Mrs. Barbauld's collected works, of which I gave a copy to Miss Wordsworth. Among the poems is a stanza on Life, written in extreme old age. It had delighted my sister, to whom I repeated it on her death-bed. It was long after I gave these works to Miss Wordsworth that her brother said, 'Repeat me that stanza by Mrs. Barbauld.' I did so. He made me repeat it again. And so he learned it by heart. He was at the time walking in his sitting-room at Rydal, with hands behind him; I heard him mutter to himself, 'I am not in the habit of grudging other people their good things, but I wish I had written those lines,' and repeated to himself the stanza which I have already quoted,

'Life we 've been long together," etc.

In naming a number of poetesses, Wordsworth himself, in writing to Mr. Dyce in 1830, put Mrs. Barbauld at the head of the list. He mentions Helen Maria Williams, Charlotte Smith, Anna Seward, and others, and adds of Mrs. Barbauld, that, "with much higher powers of mind," she "was spoiled as a poetess by being a Dissenter, and concerned with a Dissenting Academy. . . . . One of the most pleasing passages in her poetry is the close of the lines of 'Life,' written, I believe, when she was not less than eighty years of age," and he quotes it to his friend. "He much admired Mrs. Barbauld's Essays, and sent a copy of them, with a laudatory note, to the then Archbishop of Canterbury, his friend," says the biographer of the poet.

The great Lake Poet appears to have disregarded the fact that his own father was an attorney, and acted as agent to a nobleman, and he himself consented to hold an office of small honor but fair salary,—that of stamp distributor, — and later receive a pension from government; all of which makes it rather unjust in him to blame Mrs. Barbauld for the position in life to which she was born. She was certainly liberal and catholic in her views of life, and evinced in her writings the extent and depth of her study as much as any writer of her time, being very remarkable for her talents and power of thought. She might have been born in a more elevated position in a worldly point of view; but it is to be doubted whether the powers of mind she displayed would have been any better developed and cultivated elsewhere. And prejudices from which she was singularly free might then have greatly detracted from the generous, pure, and simple style of her writings. Worldly position did not dazzle her, nor had wealth and rank alone any charms for her; though she was not insensible to the attractions of mind and amiability of character, when they rose superior to these conditions of life, which develop beauties and charms, or materially detract from them, if allowed to exert too strongly the love of display and of power.

After Mr. Robinson's introduction, he was a frequent visitor at Mrs. Barbauld's house, and nearer intimacy only increased his respect and admiration for her fine talents and amiable, womanly character. In the reminiscences of Sir Henry Holland, he tells the reader that he passed his vacation in the holidays of 1803 at

Stoke Newington. He was then at Dr. Estlin's school at Bristol, and afterwards, for a time, a pupil of the Rev. Mr. Turner of Newcastle, of whom mention has been made. He says of it that the vacation was spent at the house of Dr. Aikin, "a very old friend of my father." "His sister, Mrs. Barbauld, who lived close to him, and his daughter, Lucy Aikin, gave a certain literary repute to this then tranquil village, since absorbed, like so many others, into the huge mass of the metropolis. I met in several parties, at one or the other house, several writers of repute of that day, now almost or wholly forgotten, — the warm admirers of Mrs. Barbauld's masculine understanding and gentle feminine character. She well merited this admiration of the excellence of her English prose style; it is enough to say that I have heard it warmly praised both by Mackintosh and Macaulay. Each specified the essay on the 'Inconsistency of Human Expectations' as an example of this excellence."

This was the first visit of Sir Henry to the great city, of which he has since been an ornament, and where he was honored as a professional and social addition to its already full ranks of brilliant and talented men. Mr. Crabb Robinson also alludes to Mrs. Barbauld's essay on "Inconsistency in Our Expectations" as her "famous essay"; and in writing to his friend Mr. Benecke, in 1835, he says: "I wish Mrs. Benecke would amuse herself, or procure some friend to do so, by translating Mrs. Barbauld's 'Essay on Inconsistent Expectations.' I hold it to be one of the most exquisite morsels of English prose ever written. And it had the most salutary effect on me. When a young man I met with it, and so deeply was I impressed with it, that I can truly say I never *repined* at any one *want* or *loss,* or the *absence* of *any* good that has befallen me."

During the year 1804, Mrs. Barbauld was requested to prepare for publication, and edit with a memoir, such of Richardson's letters, and those of his contemporaries and friends included in his correspondence, as she might consider valuable. This large collection of letters from the hand of the novelist and his friends was bought of Richardson's grandchildren. The correspondence was very voluminous and rather tedious. As one can fancy the letters of the author of Sir Charles Grandison would be found, they prove prosy and dull. The Life and the criticism of his novels are admirable, and probably Richardson owes to the excellence and attractive style of the biography the majority of his readers at the present day. The real value of the six volumes of the "Life and Letters" lies in that one which is the production of Mrs. Barbauld, and the remaining volumes are interesting only from their connection with her bright and pleasant account of his career, and notices of his friends and his novels. In Rogers's "Table-Talk" there is an anecdote of Mrs. Barbauld which may interest the reader, and I add to it her own note, taken from Richardson's Life, on the same subject. She also mentions her meeting with the pilgrim who so greatly admired Clarissa Harlowe that he journeyed to the scene of her residence at Hampstead.

Mr. Rogers's description of the meeting is as follows:— "One day, as she was going to Hampstead in the stage-coach, she had a Frenchman for her companion; and, entering into conversation with him, she found that he was making an excursion to Hampstead for the express purpose *of seeing the house in the Flask Walk* where Clarissa Harlowe lodged. What a compliment to the genius of Richardson!" Mrs. Barbauld, in the life of Richardson, in alluding to the character of Clarissa, and mentioning her flight from London to the celebrated tavern called the Flask, — from its situation in the Flask Walk, at the end of that pleasant path in the village of Hampstead, and long celebrated as the resort of fashion and conviviality, being the meeting-place of the noted Kitcat Club, — also describes the meeting, and the surprise of the foreigner, who evidently had firm faith in the truth of the story of Clarissa, and did not for a moment doubt the veracity of Richardson.

Mrs. Barbauld says of this incident: "The writer of

these observations well remembers a Frenchman who paid a visit to Hampstead for the sole purpose of finding out the house in the *Flask Walk* where Clarissa lodged, and was surprised at the ignorance or indifference of the inhabitants on that subject. The *Flask Walk* was to him as much classic ground as the rocks of Meillerie to the admirers of Rousseau; and probably, if an English traveller were to make similar inquiries in Switzerland, he would find that the *châlets* of the Valais suggested no ideas to the inhabitants but such as were connected with their dairies and their farms. A constant residence soon destroys all sensibility to objects of local enthusiasm."

The "Life of Richardson" was generally admired. Mr. Rogers quotes Charles James Fox's opinion about it: "He thought Mrs. Barbauld's 'Life of Richardson' admirable; and regretted that she had wasted her talents on writing books for children, (excellent as these books might be,) now that there were so many pieces of that description." In the Recollections of the previous year, Rogers speaks of hearing Fox repeating with Mrs. Fox that song of Mrs. Barbauld's,—

"Come here, fond youth, whoe'er thou be," etc.

and criticising the first verse as being exceedingly ungrammatical. This was on the occasion of a visit made by Mr. Rogers to the great statesman at his home, St. Anne's Hill.

To Mrs. Beecroft.

Dorking, September, 1805.

. . . . . We came hither to take lodgings somewhere in this beautiful country, but found none vacant; so we have been some time at Burford Bridge, a little quiet sort of an inn in the centre of the pleasant walks; and a few days with our friends the C——s. This is very much of a corn country, and we are in the midst of harvest: the window at which I am now writing looks into a corn-field, where a family have established their *ménage*. The man and his wife are reaping the corn; a cradle with a young child in it is brought into the field by break of day, and set under a hedge; the mother makes a sort of tent with her red cloak to shelter it from the weather; and there she gives it suck, and there they take their meals; two older children either watch the cradle or run about the fields. A young baronet here has incurred great and deserved odium by forbidding the poor to glean in his fields: and effectually to prevent them, the plough immediately follows the sickle; yet probably this man can talk of the wisdom of our forefathers, and the regard due to ancient observances. This country is remarkable for great richness of wood, which Autumn has as yet only touched with his little finger; in a month's time they will be enchanting. Another *agrément* here is, that you see no soldiers; though I confess you are put in mind of them by a military road lately cut over Box Hill,—I hope, a very needless precaution.

One finds little glimpses of the life of Mrs. Barbauld, at this time, in the letters of Lucy Aikin. In one she writes of the book-club at Stoke Newington, and after describing some of its rules, and the differences of opinion as to its arrangement and management, she adds, "It is a great hobby-horse with my Aunt Barbauld and me." Again she writes: "The Barbaulds are going next week to lodgings in town, which they have taken for a few weeks, in order to see everything and everybody with little trouble. They wish me to go and share their gayety, but I feel by no means equal to racketing at present, and my father shows little inclination to intrust me to the prudence of my aunt, who is at least forty years younger than I am."

In Mrs. Barbauld's correspondence with Miss Edgeworth, there was much about new books and their authors. In one letter she asks Miss Edgeworth if she has yet seen "Mr. Scott's new poem 'Marmion,'" and strongly advises her to obtain it and read it, if she has not already done so.

TO MRS. SMITH.

STOKE NEWINGTON, January 7, 1806.

DEAR MADAM, —I think there is a spell against our profiting by your kind invitations. The occasion on which you now ask us to Parndon is a very interesting one, and we should have had great pleasure in keeping with you your *silver feast*, as the Germans call it when a couple have lived happily a quarter of a century together. But at present it is impossible. . . . .

It is perhaps, after all, as well for me that there is a circumstance which imperiously says "You cannot go"; because, apart from that consideration, if I were tempted by my inclination, a violent cold which I have upon me would, I fear, make me unequal to a winter journey. Meantime my heart is with you, and Mr. Barbauld's, and most cordially do we join in congratulations and wishes that the latter half of your lives may be as happy as the former; for more I think it cannot be, as you seem to me to have all the ingredients, external and internal, of which that precious compound *happiness* is composed; for a compound I maintain it to be, and of a vast many ingredients too, — begging Mr. Harris's pardon, whose dialogue on the subject I read at sixteen with great edification. But your happiness may be *multiplied*, however, as your numerous family spreads abroad into the world, and you have the pleasure of seeing them acquire for themselves in their own families that esteem and consideration which they now derive from yours. May this and every succeeding year increase your satisfaction in them, and find and leave you both happy! etc., etc.

Miss Aikin tells an anecdote which shows the strong feeling of interest and admiration felt for Mrs. Barbauld. When her brother, Arthur Aikin, Esq., was canvassing for votes for the position of secretary to the Society of Arts, "one man, a sword-cutler, to whom he had no introduction, gave his vote to him as Mrs. Barbauld's nephew, and begged to introduce him to his family." She writes of meeting Rogers, the poet, his brother and sister, at the Barbaulds' at dinner. "Nothing," she adds, "could be more agreeable. Mr. Rogers *laid himself out to be entertaining*"; and that he probably always did when with Mrs. Barbauld, whom he respected and loved. The vein of cynicism in him was subdued and quieted by her amiable temper. In another letter to her brother, Miss Aikin describes the efforts of her mother and herself to prepare their minds to teach one of her brother's children. For the benefit of her little nephew, they were studying a work on "Practical Education," at which, she says, "My Aunt Barbauld laughs excessively; she says 'I know that everybody reads works on education as pleasant works,' but this is the first time that ever I heard of anybody's sitting gravely down to study them for use.'" In 1806, Miss Aikin, in writing Mrs. Taylor, tells her that the Estlins of Bristol, whom the Barbaulds had often visited, were there "on a visit to the Barbaulds, and we meet almost daily."

TO MRS. J. TAYLOR OF NORWICH.

1806.

I am now reading Mr. Johnes's "Froissart," and I think I never was more struck with the horrors of war, — simply because *he* seems not at all struck with them; and I feel ashamed at my heart having ever beat with pleasure at the names of Cressy and Poitiers. He tells you the English marched into such a district; the barns were full, and cattle and corn plentiful; they burned and destroyed all the villages, and laid the country bare; such an English earl took a town, and killed men, women, and little children; and he never makes a remark, but shows he looks upon it as the usual mode of proceeding.

Mrs. Barbauld required all the variety of occupation, the cheer of society, and the sympathy of friends, in this period of her life. She had a long and anxious interval of care and distress of mind, arising from the mental condition and excitable temperament of Mr. Barbauld. At length the blow came, — perhaps in a direction which she had dreaded, but it would appear to have been a new phase of the disease from which he suffered. Mr. Barbauld was found drowned in the New River, November 11, 1808. One of his peculiarities was an excessive use of water, and he may have fallen in while prompted with a fancy to use the river for the purpose of ablution; or a sudden seizure of a more violent nature may have caused his unhappy death. The dangers and anxiety which had so long impended over and harassed the feeling heart of Mrs. Barbauld now became a terrible reality, and she was deeply affected by these painful trials, and the distressing event which terminated the life of her husband. She herself, in the sketch of him contributed by her to the

"Monthly Repository of Theology and General Literature," feelingly alluded to the malady of Mr. Barbauld, and there stated that the disease was hereditary. As a touching tribute of unwearied and devoted affection, tempered with impartial judgment and discernment, I quote from her description of his character and mental powers.

"The scenes of life Mr. Barbauld passed through were common ones, but his character was not a common one. His reasoning powers were acute, and sharpened by exercise; for he was early accustomed to discussion, and argued with great clearness; with a degree of warmth, indeed, but with perfect candor towards his opponent. He gave the most liberal latitude to free inquiry, and could bear to hear those truths attacked which he most steadfastly believed, the more *because* he steadfastly believed them; for he was delighted to submit to the test of argument those truths which he had no doubt could, by argument, be defended. He had an uncommon flow of conversation on those points which had engaged his attention, and delivered himself with a warmth and animation which enlivened the driest subject. He was equally at home in French and English literature; and the exquisite sensibility of his mind, with the early culture his taste had received, rendered him an excellent judge of all those works which appeal to the heart and the imagination. His feelings were equally quick and vivid; his expressive countenance was the index of his mind, and of every instantaneous impression made upon him. Children, who are the best physiognomists, were always attracted to him, and he delighted to entertain them with lively narratives suited to their age, in which he had great invention. The virtues of his heart will be acknowledged by all who knew him. His benevolence was enlarged; it was the spontaneous propensity of his nature, as well as the result of his religious system. He was temperate almost to abstemiousness, yet without any tincture of ascetic rigor. A free, undaunted spirit, a winning simplicity, a tendency to enthusiasm, — but of the gentle and liberal kind, — formed the prominent lineaments of his character. The social affections were all alive and active in him. His heart overflowed with kindness to all, — the lowest that came within his sphere. There never was a human being who had less of the selfish and worldly feelings, — they hardly seemed to form a part of his nature. His was truly the charity which thinketh no ill. Great singleness of heart, and a candor very opposite to the suspicious temper of worldly sagacity, made him slow to impute unworthy motives to the actions of his fellow-men; yet his candor by no means sprang from indifference to moral rectitude; for, when he could no longer resist conviction, his censure was decided, and his indignation warm and warmly expressed. His standard of virtue was high, and he felt no propensities which disposed him to lower it. His religious sentiments were of a most pure and liberal cast; and his pulpit services, when the state of his spirits seconded the ardor of his mind, were characterized by the rare union of a fervent spirit of devotion, a pure, sublime philosophy, supported by arguments of metaphysical acuteness. He did not speak the language of any party, nor exactly coincide with the systems of any. He was a believer in the pre-existence of Christ, and, in a certain modified sense, in the Atonement; thinking those doctrines most consonant to the tenor of Scripture; . . . . . but he was too sensible of the difficulties which press upon every system not to feel indulgence for all, and he was not zealous for any doctrine which did not affect the heart. Of the moral perfections of the Deity he had the purest and most exalted ideas; on these were chiefly founded his system of religion, and these, together with his own benevolent nature, led him to embrace so warmly his favorite doctrine of the final salvation of all the human race, and indeed, the gradual rise and perfectibility of all created existence. . . . . His latter days were oppressed by a morbid affection of his spirits, in a great degree hereditary, which came gradually upon him, and closed the scene of his earthly usefulness; yet in the midst of the irritation it occasioned, the kindness of his nature broke forth, and some of his last acts were acts of benevolence."

An affecting "Dirge," written November, 1808, attested to the depth of his widow's grief and the Christian fortitude with which she met this terrible shock and affliction. She touchingly and fervently prays that she may be taught and supported —

"To welcome all that 's left of good,
To all that 's lost resigned."

CHAPTER XII.

Mrs. Barbauld edits "British Novelists." — Prepares a "Selection" for the Young, called "The Enfield Speaker." — Publishes Poem "Eighteen Hundred and Eleven." — Criticisms on this Poem. — Style of it. — Mr. Robinson's Diary. — Letters. — Social Activity of Mrs. Barbauld. — She meets Scott at Dinner. — Mrs. Farrar's Recollections. — Mrs. Barbauld and Byron's Poem. — Miss Edgeworth's Visit. — Mr. Robinson's Picture of Mrs. Barbauld. — Dr. Channing visits her. — Old Age and its Trials. — Loss of her Old Friends. — Death of Dr. Aikin. — Mrs. Barbauld's Cheerfulness and Patience. — Illness and Death. — Miss Aikin's Estimate of her Character. — Miss Edgeworth's Remarks. — Tablet to Mrs. Barbauld's Memory. — Anecdotes. — Mrs. Barbauld's Poetry. — Her Prose Works. — Her Position in English Literature. — Her Character. — Her Influence. — Her Personal Appearance. — The Justice of the Claims to Respect and Veneration her Life inspires.

IN the year 1809, Miss Edgeworth wrote a friend that Dr., now Sir Henry, Holland, in his visit at Edgeworthstown, had much to say of Mrs. Barbauld, and greatly interested her old friends there by his conversation about her. In the same year Miss Edgeworth again refers to her, and mentions correcting "Belinda" for Mrs. Barbauld, who is going to insert it in her collection of novels, with a preface. While still very much prostrated and depressed by the death of Mr. Barbauld, she had the strength of mind and fortitude to busy herself with her beloved pursuits; and being asked to edit a "Collection of the British Novelists," she consented to occupy herself with the arrangement and preparation of their works and lives. She wrote also for the edition an introductory essay which is still of value and interest in connection with the novels. The biographical and critical notices of each writer, and the events of his or her career; their genius, style, and position in the ranks of literature, are admirable, full of life and spirit, and charmingly clear and concise. Sir Walter Scott acknowledged his indebtedness to Mrs. Barbauld for some of his material used in the biographies prefixed by him to the novels in Ballantyne's edition of "British Novelists." This "Collection of the British Novelists" prepared by Mrs. Barbauld consisted of fifty volumes, and appeared in the year 1810.

In Mr. Robinson's diary, he wrote, for the year 1810, of one day: — "In the afternoon I sat with Mrs. Barbauld, still in all the beauty of her fine taste, correct understanding, as well as pure integrity."

June 18, 1810.

MY DEAR MRS. TAYLOR, — A thousand thanks for your kind letter; still more for the very kind visit that preceded it; though short, too short, it has left indelible impressions on my mind; my heart has truly had communion with yours, — your sympathy has been balm to it; and I feel there is no one *now* on earth to whom I could pour out that heart more readily, — I may say, so readily, — as to yourself. Very good also has my dear, amiable Mrs. Beecroft been to me, whose lively sweetness and agreeable conversation has at times won me to forget that my heart is heavy.

I am now alone again, and feel like a person who has been sitting by a cheerful fire, not sensible at the time of the temperature of the air; but, the fire removed, he finds the season is still *winter*. Day after day passes, and I do not know what I do with my time; my mind has no energy, nor power of application. I can tell you, however, what I have done with some hours of it, which have been agreeably employed in reading Mrs. Montague's Letters. I think her nephew has made a very agreeable present to the public; and I was greatly edified to see them printed in modest octavo, with Mrs. Montague's sweet face (for it is a very pretty face) at the head. They certainly show a very extraordinary mind, full of wit, and also of deep thought and sound judgment. She seems to have liked not a little to divert herself with the odd and the ludicrous, and shows herself in the earlier letters passionately fond of balls and races and London company; this was natural enough at eighteen. Perhaps you may not so easily pardon her for having early settled her mind, as she evidently had, not to marry except for an establishment. This seems to show a want of some of those fine feelings that one expects in youth; but when it is considered that she was the daughter of a country gentleman with a large family and no fortune to expect, and her connections all in high life, one is disposed to pardon her, especially as I dare say she would never have married a fool or a profligate. I heard her say — what I suppose very few can say — that she never was in love in her life. Many of the letters are in fact essays; and I think, had she turned her thoughts to write in that way, she would have excelled Johnson.

I have also turned over Lamb's "Specimens of Old Plays," and am much pleased with them. I made a discovery there, — that La Motte's fable of Genius, Virtue, and Reputation, which has been so much praised for its ingenious turn, is borrowed from Webster, an author of the age of Shakespeare, — or they have taken it from some common source, for a Frenchman was not very likely to light upon an English poet of that age; they knew about as much of us then, as we did fifty years ago of the Germans. It is surprising how little invention there is in the world; no *very* good story was ever invented. It is perhaps originally some fact a little enlarged; then by some other hand embellished with circumstances; then by somebody else, a century after, refined, drawn to a point, and furnished with a moral. When shall we see the moral of the world's great story, which astonishes by its events, interests by the numerous agents it puts in motion, but of which we cannot understand the bearings or predict the catastrophe? It is a tangled web, of which we have not the clue. I do not know how to rejoice at this victory, splendid as it is, over Buonaparte, when I consider the horrible waste of life, the mass of misery, which such gigantic combats must occasion. I will think no more of it; let me rather contemplate your family: there the different threads all wind evenly, smoothly, and brightly.

In the year 1811, Mrs. Barbauld prepared for the use of young ladies an excellent selection of prose and poetical works of the best English writers; this was called the "Enfield Speaker," and appeared in one volume.

STOKE NEWINGTON, May, 1811.

MY DEAR MRS. KENRICK, — I have been thinking what to liken our uncertain and unfrequent correspondence to. I cannot liken it to the regular blow of flowers that come out and blossom in their proper season. It is rather like the aloe, that, after having been barren season after season, shows signs of life all on a sudden, and pushes out when you least expect it. But take notice, the life is in the aloe all the while, and sorry indeed should I be if the life was not all the while in our friendship, though it so seldom diffuses itself over a piece of paper. How much I long to see you again! I wish you would come and see me this summer; the journey, I should hope, would not be too much for you, and in coming to see me you would be near all your friends. Do think of it!

.... I believe I am writing you an enormous letter; but I have been in a course of letter-reading. I am wading through the letters of Madame du Deffand, in four volumes. Have you read them? Walpole and she wrote every week, and they were continually grumbling at one another, yet they went on. Walpole, poor man, seems to have been terribly afraid that this old blind lady was in love with him; and he had much ado to reduce her expressions of friendship to something of an English standard. This lady appears to have been very unhappy. She was blind, indeed; but she had everything else that could make age comfortable: fortune, friends, talents, consideration in the world, the society of all the wits and all the people of rank of Paris, or who visited Paris; but she totally wanted the best support of all, — religious feelings and hopes; and I do not know anything that is likely to impress their importance more on the mind than the perusal of these letters. You see her tired of life, almost blaspheming Providence for having given her existence; yet dreading to die because she had no hopes beyond death. A lady told me she would not on any account let her daughter read the letters. I think, for my part, they give in this view as good a lesson as you can pick out of Mrs. More's "Practical Piety," which, if you have not read, I cannot help it.

Adieu! do let me hear from you soon. I wonder, say you, the woman has the face to ask it. That 's true, but I hope you will, notwithstanding. Nothing will give more pleasure to

Your ever affectionate friend.

To Miss F.

Stoke Newington, September, 1811.

"And when did you hear from Miss F.?" "Pray, madam, when did you hear from Miss F.?" "I hope Miss F. is well! Is she got to E—— yet?" This is a specimen of the questions often asked me by those who have been too much interested in the hours they enjoyed of your company while you were in this part of the world not to feel an interest in you when you had left it.

To these I reply, that I have *not heard;* that I shall be most happy at any time to hear, when dear Miss F. feels any inclination to write; that I do not think she is particularly fond of writing letters; and that I have too much of her taste in this respect, and am conscious of too many sins of my own in this matter, to urge any claims on other people, supposing I had them, which in this instance I do not pretend to have. At present, however, I cannot resist taking the *opportunity,* as the children say, of Mr. ——'s conveyance. . . . chiefly to express the affectionate remembrance which must always dwell in my heart of one so dear to me. . . . .

We have had the very beautiful and interesting sight of a balloon sent off from the neighboring fields. The carriages of all sorts, eager countenances exhibited from windows, tops of houses, and church steeples, made a gayer spectacle, I think, than any exhibition within walls could have been made. I saw it like a majestic dome among the trees; it swelled, it rose gently, it vibrated; then it sprang up into the sky, light as — what shall I say? what can I say of a substance that is itself lighter than air? I must say, I believe, as light as thought, — as your thoughts, I mean, for mine are often heavy, etc., etc.

In the year 1811 Mrs. Barbauld wrote the fine poem which the reader will find in the Selections from her works; it being considered the most perfect long poem she wrote. The prophetic gift was certainly not hers; but the fervor and spirit which the poem on the year "Eighteen Hundred and Eleven"[1] displays, and the finished and eloquent descriptions in it, the grand ideas of freedom, and the hope for its future which she expresses, are very powerful. It must impress the reader with the highest sense of the author's genius and style of thought, power of language and imagination. The time at which she wrote this poem was one of the deepest national distress and gloom. War on every side had made Great Britain for years the scene of constant military preparation, and had drawn from her soil the best and bravest of her sons, leaving her with an enormous and exhausting debt and decimated population, in mourning the loss of sons, brothers, and husbands slain in war.

Mrs. Barbauld — with the grand and patriotic purpose of warning her countrymen against the want of national integrity and honor, and the spirit of luxury, after making a beautiful apostrophe to the land she loves, admonishing Great Britain that she cannot escape the consequences of unrighteous war — opens a splendid description of the wealth, culture, science, and art of England, with these lines, which evince very strongly her love of country, and that her very affection for her native land did not blind her to the faults, seeing which she felt forced to reprove and caution. The piece begins, —

> "Yet, O my country, name beloved, revered,
> By every tie that binds the soul, endeared,
> Whose image to my infant senses came,
> Mixt with religion's light and freedom's holy flame."

And continuing this address, she gives her reader a truly magnificent picture of London, and its former greatness, with "the faded glories" which shall draw the future traveller in ages to come from distant lands to muse sadly on the ruins of so much that was once great and renowned. The reader will not fail to be impressed with the strength of energy, power of description, and beauty of language in this poem. Though, happily for the world, England has not fallen under the evil days she predicted, her hope for freedom and true liberty of thought in America, and the vision of the Genius of Freedom, have found a partial realization here, in our great republic, while this has been gained by the horrors of war which she so much deprecated.

The warning voice, which spoke from a mind and heart filled with true patriotism, one would suppose must have affected all who read the grand and elevated words of this poem. But there were those who could not bear with equanimity the thought that others who differed with them in sentiment should express their views freely. Mrs. Barbauld, in common with other liberal and progressive thinkers and writers, was the victim of a reviewer. Under the cover of an anonymous article in the "Quarterly Review," she was made the subject of a most malignant and ungentlemanly attack, personal in its nature and wholly unwarranted by the spirit or opinions contained in her poem.

I have Miss Aikin's authority for stating the author of this unfeeling and cruel attack to be one who should, for the sake of poetry and true literature, have spared the venerable author of so much that has given pleasure and instruction. At the time Miss Aikin wrote her Memoir of Mrs. Barbauld, she was apparently ignorant of the authorship of this review of the poem "Eighteen Hundred and Eleven"; for she speaks of the review and its anonymous nature, but does not hint any surmises about the writer of it. In 1845, in writing to her friend Mr. Mallet, she says: "If you see the last and preceding numbers of the 'Gentleman's

Magazine,' you will find an article on Southey's Life in the first of them, and some pretty sharp comments of mine in the second, exposing the vileness of his conduct to Mrs. Barbauld. It is impossible now to doubt that all the scurrilities of the 'Quarterly' respecting her were his. I am persuaded that he hated most literary women; and latterly all Dissenters."

The article was neither indicative of good feeling nor literary taste and judgment; being full of personalities, and utterly wanting in discrimination as to Mrs. Barbauld's just and acknowledged claims to respect as a poetess and a literary woman of ability. This cutting, satirical notice of the poem "Eighteen Hundred and Eleven" appeared in the "Quarterly Review" for 1812. The reviewer says he had hoped the nation might be saved without the aid of Mrs. Barbauld, but "not such, however, is her opinion; an irresistible impulse of public duty — a confident sense of commanding talents — has induced her to dash down her shagreen spectacles and her knitting-needles, and to sally forth, hand in hand with her renowned compatriot,* in the magnanimous resolution of saving a sinking country by the instrumentality of a pamphlet in prose and a pamphlet in verse." Of her former works he says, "They have been of some utility, though they display not much of either taste or talents: are something

* William Roscoe.

better than harmless." In concluding the article, which is only a repetition of abuse, and the harshest, most narrow criticism, the writer warns Mrs. Barbauld, at her peril, to use satire again, evidently considering that weapon his pet instrument; and certainly in his hands it became one of torture to his victims. Mr. Roscoe's pamphlet, "Occasional Tracts relative to the War between Great Britain and France," was the prose pamphlet which roused the wrath of the reviewer.

Mr. William Turner, the friend and contemporary of Mrs. Barbauld, in his sketch of her speaks of this article as follows: —

"On this poem a critique was published in the 'Quarterly Review,' which, I must think, was anything but creditable to the writer. He had a right to smile at what many of her best friends flattered themselves would prove at least a very premature prognostic of the decline of British glory, and, if he pleased, to sneer at her exultation in the prospect of American freedom; but the contemptible affectation of undervaluing her talents, and placing her before his readers as a mere writer of lessons for children, is disgraceful only to himself. It is agreeable to wish that the article may have been the production of some one who was really as ignorant of the excellent author and her works as he indeed professes himself. At the same time it is satisfactory that she lived to see the Columbian States advanced so near to the realization of all her wishes for them; while none would rejoice more fervently that her apprehensions for her own beloved country were, for the present at least, without foundation."

One of the most displeasing parts of this poem to the critic of the "Quarterly" was the thought which Mrs. Barbauld expressed as to the brilliant future of America, and the transfer of the greatness and prosperity of England to our Western Continent. No critic reprimanded Bishop Berkeley for his poem on that subject, and Lord Macaulay, a few years later, wrote unchallenged two passages which contain this same idea clothed in his magnificent prose. Bishop Berkeley, in his enthusiasm for his New World project, the college which he hoped to start in the Bermudas, wrote the beautiful lines which close his poem "On the Prospect of Planting Arts and Learning in America": —

"Westward the course of empire takes its way;
The first four acts already past,
A fifth shall end the drama with the day:
Time's noblest offering is the last."

And Macaulay, some years later, made use of the very images and metaphors of Mrs. Barbauld, clothing them in his magnificent, sonorous prose, and adding another to the list of those who have predicted, it is to be hoped without foundation, the future downfall of England. I insert here the passages in which Macaulay alludes to the possible destruction of the prosperity and civilization of Great Britain. Speaking of the Catholic Church, in his review of Mrs. Austin's translation of Ranke's history of the Popes, he says: "And she may still exist in undiminished vigor when some traveller from New Zealand shall, in the midst of a vast solitude, take his stand on a broken arch of London Bridge to sketch the ruins of St. Paul's." In his essay on Mitford's "History of Greece," he enlarges on the same idea: "And when those who have rivalled her greatness shall have shared her fate, when civilization and knowledge shall have fixed their abode in distant continents, when the sceptre shall have passed away from England, when, perhaps, travellers from distant regions shall in vain labor to decipher on some mouldering pedestal the name of our proudest chief, shall hear savage hymns chanted to some misshapen idol over the ruined dome of our proudest temple, and shall see a single naked fisherman wash his nets in the river of the ten thousand masts, her influence and the glory will still survive,—fresh in eternal youth, exempt from mutability and decay, immortal as the intellectual principle from which they derive their origin, and over which they exercise their control." Walpole, Volney, Henry Kirke White, and Shelley, have made use of this image, conveying the downfall of Great Britain.

Mrs. Barbauld was deeply wounded by the insults and personal remarks which this poem, her latest publication, received from the prejudice and malignity of a critic who seems to have seen in its gifted and venerable author only a mark for unfeeling sarcasm, and the utterance of party spirit. Her judgment of the future, her spirit of prophecy, may be doubted: her gloomy forebodings have been proved untrue; but the highly patriotic spirit and the just pride with which she feelingly alludes to the heroes whose fame she sings, — the men of learning whose names are Britain's glory, — and the scenes made almost sacred by their influence to the future pilgrim whose progress she describes and whose thoughts she conceives in viewing these grand ruins, should have softened the heart and restrained the hand of the critic from its ungracious and unjustifiable censure. So severely did the aged author feel the treatment she received, that she laid aside all thoughts of collecting and publishing her works, then long out of print and much sought after, feeling that the day would come when her name would secure respect, and her memory be properly honored; and she left it with perfect confidence "to men's charitable speeches, to foreign nations, and to the next ages."

In the following letter to her friend Mrs. Beecroft, Mrs. Barbauld mentions her stay at Bristol, and a day pleasantly passed at the home of her old friend Miss Hannah More, who, with her sisters, was living in her delightful residence at Barley Wood, the cottage which she built after living for a time at Cowslip Green. Mr. Robinson, in 1811, refers frequently to calling on Mrs. Barbauld, and to the pleasure which it gave him. He often went to play chess with her, — a game which they both enjoyed.

TO MRS. BEECROFT.

STOKE NEWINGTON, January 1, 1813.

Many happy New Year's to you, my dear friend, and may they bring you increasing joy in your children and your children's children, and in your circle of friends, and in the various occupations of all sorts which the exercise of your talents or the offices of kindness engage you in! To you I may wish this with cheerful hope of its fulfilment. At my time of life, to look forward to New Year's is to contemplate the prospect of increasing languor and growing infirmities. Not, I am sure, that I have any reason to complain, for time deals gently with me; and though I feel that I descend, the slope is easy, and greatly thankful I am that I have, so accessible and so near me, the friends and relatives that were assembled at Christmas in order to help me to despatch your noble turkey. It was indeed so large that I had some difficulty in persuading them that it came to me *enclosed in a letter;* but I pleaded your known veracity, and they submitted. Accept, my dear friend, my best thanks, and believe me, though my pen (it is a naughty pen) has been idle, I did not want it to put me in mind of so dear a friend.

Yes, I have been at Bristol this summer, and spent there almost the only month that could be called summer in the last year. I spent some days at Bath, some at that delightful place, Clifton; and I spent a day with Hannah More and her four sisters at her charming cottage under the Mendip hills, which she has named Barley Wood, and which is equally the seat of taste and hospitality. We have had a meeting here for an auxiliary Bible Society. Many ladies went, not indeed to speak, but to hear speaking; and they tell me they were much entertained and interested. I honor the zeal of these societies; but it has become a sort of rage, and, I suspect, outgoes the occasion.

In Mr. Robinson's diary for 1812 he alludes to a party at Charles Aikin's where he went "with Wordsworth, and there met Mrs. Barbauld, the Aikins, Miss Jane Porter, Montgomery the poet, Roscoe," and other eminent people. He refers to a call made on the family of Dr. Aikin, where Charles Lamb was warmly praised by the family. He remarked on the universality of taste and freedom from prejudice of this excellent family, to whom, by their own request, he introduced Lamb a little while after. Mrs. Barbauld also desired the acquaintance, and Mr. Robinson speaks of bringing them together. In May of the same year, Mr. Robinson speaks of an ungenerous attack on Mrs. Barbauld which was made by Coleridge in one of his extraordinary rambling conversations, which were termed lectures in the advertisement of them. In this he made some remarks on Mrs. Barbauld, of which Robinson says, "I cannot forgive him for selecting *alone* (except an attack on Pope's "Homer," qualified by insincere praise) Mrs. Barbauld. She is a living writer, a woman, and a person who, however discordant with himself in character and taste, has still always shown him civilities and attentions. It was surely ungenerous." .... In this Mr. Robinson was quite right; Mrs. Barbauld had shown Coleridge much kindness, and her admiration of his talents and anxiety for his future progress were finely expressed in the lines addressed to him in 1797. In these she exhorted him to use with energy the genius and powers of mind which he showed he possessed. But his habits of indolence and the vice of opium-eating were his great misfortunes, and more powerful than the voice of duty and of friendly warning. He rather resented the poem, it is to be believed, and says some rather disagreeable things of Mrs. Barbauld in some of his letters and diaries, — repeating also something said by Charles Lamb, who, when himself, had a high admiration of Mrs. Barbauld. These remarks are unworthy of notice, being evidently the result of a morbid and unhappy state of mind in Coleridge. Lamb used jocosely to call Mrs. Barbauld and Mrs. Inchbald, the novelist, "the two bald women."

To Mrs. J. Taylor.

May, 1813.

. . . . There is certainly at present a great deal of zeal in almost every persuasion; certainly much more in England, as far as I am able to judge, than when I was young. I often speculate upon what it will produce, — not uniformity of opinion certainly; that is a blessing we seem not destined here to enjoy, if indeed it would be a blessing. But will it tend to universal toleration and enlarged liberality of thinking? or, with increase of zeal, will the church spirit of bigotry revive, and unite with the increasing power of government to crush the spirit of research and freedom of opinion? Bible societies, missionary schemes, lectures, schools for the poor, are set on foot and spread, not so much from a sense of duty as from being the real taste of the times; and I am told that Mrs. Siddons's readings are much patronized by the evangelical people, as they are called, of fashion, who will not enter the doors of a theatre. Would that with all this there could be seen some little touch of feeling for the miseries of war, that are desolating the earth without end or measure! One should be glad to see some *suspicion* arise that it was not consistent with the spirit of the Gospel; but this you do not see even in good people.

. . . . Friends at a distance do not want some medium of sympathy, though they do not meet. I have sometimes looked upon new books in that light. When I peruse a book of merit to be generally read, I feel sure, though not informed of it, that precisely the same stream of ideas which is flowing through my mind is flowing through my friend's also; and without any communication, either by word or letter, I know that he has admired and criticised, and laughed and wept, as I have done.

In June of this year Mr. Robinson speaks of a call on Mrs. Barbauld. He says: "Had a pleasant chat with her about Madame De Staël, the Edgeworths," etc. And he then goes on to relate an anecdote of Mr. Edgeworth and Mrs. Siddons, which shows some of Mr. Edgeworth's peculiarities. Mrs. Siddons, perhaps, would have consented to join the society which, I think, was proposed by Lord Byron for the suppression of that excellent man Mr. Edgeworth, who was very trying in many ways; though four agreeable and charming women found him sufficiently attractive and interesting to marry. In the preceding letter to Mrs. Taylor, Mrs. Barbauld comments on the state of religious zeal and the very numerous charitable societies then in vogue, the motive being not a sense of duty so much as the spirit of the times. She questions whether liberality of opinion will go hand in hand with all these benevolent plans, and hopes for it.

TO MRS. FLETCHER.

September, 1813.

MY DEAR MADAM, — I have to thank you for your very entertaining letter. I would have undergone a good wetting, and even a suspicion of danger, to have enjoyed the grandeur of your thunder-storm. Indeed, I am rather partial to a death by lightning, and, were I to choose the mode of my departure, should certainly prefer to be "by touch ethereal slain." However, as I have no right to choose for you, I am glad you got shelter under the roof of your hospitable though penurious farmer. Surely he must be a phenomenon even in the Highlands; but I believe it is rare in all professions for the same person to amass and to enjoy riches. Even with regard to the treasures of the mind, which one should suppose would include the power of using them, the laborious collector of facts and dates produces some ponderous volume, which sleeps on the shelf till some light and airy wit skims it for tale and anecdote, or some original genius shapes and moulds it into a system.

I am now reading the third and fourth volumes of Mrs. Montague's Letters. To me, who have lived through all the time she writes of, they are interesting — independent of the wit and talent — as recalling a number of persons and events once present to my mind; they are also, I think, very entertaining, though, as letters, somewhat studied. With all her advantages she seems not to have been happy. She married not Mr. Montague from affection. It is evident she looked upon him as a wise and kind friend, but nothing more; a little *too* wise sometimes, when he kept her in the country longer than she liked. To a person so married, nothing will fill the mind and give a permanent interest to life but children. She lost her child; and notwithstanding all that nature and all that fortune had given, and high cultivation, and chosen society, and public esteem, she speaks of life as a thing to be got through, rather than to be enjoyed.

In this letter to her friend Mrs. Fletcher, Mrs. Barbauld expresses the interest she has felt in reviving old associations and times past by reading the letters of Mrs. Montague which had recently been published by her nephew. The letters must have brought back to her memories pleasant and sad of the circle whose members had mostly passed away, of which she was one of the few survivors.

To Mrs. Beecroft.

Stoke Newington, September, 1813.

We have had great pleasure in seeing again our friend Dr. H—— after a tour through Spain, Sicily, and Greece. Pray, do you intend to learn modern Greek? I suspect it will grow quite fashionable, from the many tourists to Athens we have had of late; particularly if Eustace succeeds in persuading us to have nothing to do with the French *jargon*, as he is pleased to call the language of Bossuet and of Racine. I suppose you have read Lord Byron's Giaour, — and which edition? because there are five, and in every one he adds about fifty lines; so that the different editions have rather the sisterly likeness which Ovid says the Nereids had, than the identity expected by the purchasers of the same work. And pray do you say Lord Bȳron, or By̆ron, in defiance of the *y* and our old friend in Sir Charles Grandison? And do you pronounce

Giaour hard *g* or soft *g*? And do you understand the poem at first reading? — because Lord Byron and the Edinburgh reviewers say you are very stupid if you don't; and yet the same reviewers have thought proper to prefix the story to help your apprehension. All these, unimportant as you may think them, are matters of discussion here.

Mrs. Barbauld, in the following letter to Mrs. Estlin and her husband, speaks of old age and the false sentiment of Pope regarding the last years of life. She thinks the "idea beautiful, but false," and says the later years of life are usually spent in ill-health or lethargy. But whatever may have been her observation of others, such was not her case. She was interested and animated by all that passed in the world, and though not an active participant in literature and book-making, was a reader of all that was new and valuable. Society had its charms for her, and the circle she graced was often adorned by her genial and kindly presence. Her fine conversation and beautiful face lent an additional attraction to the intelligent and literary gatherings where she was frequently to be seen.

STOKE NEWINGTON, December, 1813.

. . . . If you ask what *I* am doing, — nothing. Pope, I think, somewhere says, "The last years of life, like tickets left in the wheel, rise in value." The thought is beautiful, but false; they are of very little value. They are generally past either in struggling with pains and infirmities, or in a dreamy kind of existence; no new veins of thought are opened; no young affections springing up; the ship has taken in its lading, whatever it may be, whether precious stones or lumber, and lies idly flapping its sails, and waiting for the wind that must drive it upon the wide ocean.

Have you seen Lord Byron's new poem, "The Bride of Abydos?" and have you read Madame de Staël's "Germany?" You will find in the latter many fine ideas, beautiful sentiments, and entertaining remarks on manners and countries; but in her account of Kant and other German philosophers she has got, I fancy, a little out of her depth. She herself is, or affects to be, very devotional; but her religion seems to be almost wholly a matter of imagination, — the *beau ideal* impressed upon us at our birth, along with a taste for beauty, for music, &c. As far as I understand her account of the German schools, there seems to be in many of them a design to reinstate the doctrine of innate ideas, which the cold philosophy, as they would call it, of Locke discarded. They would like Beattie and Hutcheson better than Paley or Priestley. I do not like Lord Byron's poem quite so well as his last; and I cannot see any advantage in calling a nightingale *bulbul*, or a rose *gul*, except to disconcert plain English readers.

To Dr. and Mrs. Estlin.

STOKE NEWINGTON, January, 1814.

Yes, my dear friends, 't is as I said: you are snowed up at the Hyde, very comfortable, I dare say, with a fine library and prints, &c., and I hope a cheerful Christmas party; at least, if the party is there, you will make them so. But whether the enclosed will ever come to your hands is a melancholy consideration; for if you offer to stir, I expect you will be buried in the snow, in which case I intend to write your epitaph, — "Here lies, &c., in candor and purity of mind equalling the snow that covers them"; or "Reflecting light from heaven on the world around them"; or "They were lovely in their lives, and in their deaths they were not divided"; or

"While far from home
They sought to roam,
By wandering fancies seized,
'Twixt earth and sky
They buried lie,
For so the Fates have pleased."

The lines, I own, are not very finished; but it is not worth while to take much pains about them, unless one were sure of the catastrophe. On the supposition, however, that you will be reading this comfortably by Mr. Coates's fireside, accept, my dear friends, my thanks for the pleasant days — very pleasant, but very few — that you were so good as to bestow upon me; if you can enlarge the gift, most thankfully shall I receive it.

STOKE NEWINGTON, January, 1814.

MY DEAR MRS. BEECROFT, — There are animals that sleep all the winter; I am, I believe, become one of them: *they* creep into holes during the same season; *I* have confined myself to the fireside of a snug parlor. If, indeed, a warm sunshiny day occurs, *they* sometimes creep out of their holes; so, now and then, have *I*. *They* exist in a state of torpor; so have *I* done: the only difference being, that *I* have all the while continued the habit of eating and drinking, which, to their advantage, *they* can dispense with. But my *mind* has certainly been asleep all the while; and whenever I have attempted to employ it, I have felt an oppression in my head which has obliged me to desist. What wonderful events have passed during the last few months! How new is the very name of peace to us all; and to those of thirty and under, it is a state that, since they were able to reflect at all on public affairs, they have never known. London seems to have nothing to do now, but to give feasts and pop away all the spare gunpowder in rockets and *feux-de-joie* in honor of its illustrious guests. Everybody has been idle since these royal personages came amongst us. It is in vain even to bespeak a pair of shoes, — not a man will work; and I imagine Alexander must be greatly puzzled, when the concourse in the streets from morning till night shows how many there are that are doing nothing, and the shops and manufactures how much has been done.

In the preceding letter to Mrs. Beecroft, Mrs. Barbauld rejoices most sincerely at the universal peace which then pervaded Europe. She speaks of the strange feeling it must give to the young, to experience this new sensation which they could never have previously known. Here, as everywhere in her writings, she expressed her great horror of war and its attendant evils. In the following letter to Mrs. Fletcher, Mrs. Barbauld is full of excitement on the extraordinary events which succeeded each other with startling rapidity in France. And Spain, she writes, — "Spain has disappointed all our hopes, — 'Down with the Cortes! up with the Inquisition!' being the popular cry there." She thinks that the lesson to be learned from all these changes and revolutions is, "that the concerns and destinies of all the world are too high for us; that we must wait the winding up of the drama, and be satisfied in promoting and enjoying the happiness in our own little circle." She speaks of the three distinguished women then in London, who were the objects of great interest, — Madame de Staël, Miss Edgeworth, and the Duchess of Oldenburgh. "The kings and emperors," then in London after the peace, and the rejoicing at the happy termination of the long struggles, she hopes will bring Mrs. Fletcher and Miss Fletcher to London. In her letter to the same friend, written in August of the same year, she speaks of the quiet of London after the close of this crowded season.

To Mrs. Fletcher.

Stoke Newington, June, 1814.

What do I think of the French! In the first place, it requires some time before one can think at all, events succeed each other with such astonishing rapidity. The constitution held out to the king's acceptance was indeed all one can wish, — the principles of liberty were carried further than even in ours, — but you see he has not signed it; and if he had, it is a jest to talk of a constitution, when three or four foreign armies are in the kingdom.

France, proud France, gallant France, is a conquered country. I do not think we yet know her real inclinations; convulsed by a revolution, tyrannized over by a despot, and owing her deliverance to her very enemies, — how she is humbled, how much she has suffered; but how much she has inflicted! The French, however, have a better chance for happiness with the mild imbecility of the Bourbons than with Napoleon.

This was written a week ago; and now Spain — Spain has disappointed all our hopes: "Down with the Cortes, — up with the Inquisition!" and, as at Naples some years ago, the few fine spirits who would have rejoiced in a better order of things will be consigned to dungeons. I do not know what we can gather from the contemplation of all these revolutions but this: that the concerns and destinies of all the world are too high for us; that we must wait the winding up of the drama, and be satisfied in promoting and enjoying the happiness of our own little circle. . . . .

The three persons who have most engaged the attention of London societies this year have been women: Miss Edgeworth, Madame de Staël, and now the Duchess of Oldenburgh, who shows, they say, a most rational and unsated curiosity. But kings and emperors are now appearing on the stage, and the lesser lights must "pale their ineffectual fires." Dear madam, will not you and Miss F. come to London to see all these sights? You are much mistaken if you think, as you seem to do, that you shall find us anxiously speculating about the liberties of Europe. We shall be squeezing to get a sight of Alexander, and taking tickets for *fêtes*, and looking at the Prince's fireworks, and criticising the Oldenburgh hat, and picking up anecdotes to shine with in the next party. Shall I be equally mistaken, or shall I not, when I suppose that you in Edinburgh are deep in mathematics and metaphysics with Dugald Stewart? I want to know how his work is relished. I am glad he has spoken a good word for *final causes*, the search for which, under the guidance of judgment and impartiality, certainly assists investigation as truly as it is the reward of it.

To Mrs. Fletcher.

Stoke Newington, August, 1814.

. . . . What an alteration a few weeks has made in London! If you but crossed the street a month ago, you had a chance of meeting a prince or an emperor; and now it is empty beyond the usual emptiness of summer, and everybody you meet has been, or is planning to go, across the Channel. I am sorry to say, that among my female acquaintance the joy of bringing home, cleverly concealed, shawls, lace, &c., seems to dwell more upon the fancy than museums of art or new scenes of nature; and truly, some of the young men seem better able to criticise French cookery than French conversation, or the Venus and Apollo. Is there not something strange and rather revolting in speaking of the French, as most have done for these twenty years past, with the utmost abhorrence and contempt, — and pouring ourselves over their country the moment it is accessible, to mix in their parties and bring home their fashions? . . . . We have been full fed with novels lately, and shall be with poems. Think of a thick quarto of ——'s, entitled *Fragments*, being only a taste of the second part of a poem, which I suppose he means to give us some time or other. I should like to supply him with a motto: — "And of the fragments there were taken up *twelve baskets full*."

To Mrs. Estlin.

1814.

My days of travelling are now nearly over; yet I find a little variety as necessary, perhaps, to relieve the tedium of life, as once it was to recruit from its toils and avocations. I do not know how it is with you at Bristol, but in most places there has been lately a migration into France of almost all who could command money and time. I was amused with the contrast between a lively, pleasant-tempered man and a *poco curante*. "How do you like France?" said I to the first. "I have spent," said he, "seven weeks of uninterrupted happiness." "How do you like France?" to the second. "I have been there because one must go, one is ashamed not to have been; it is a thing over." "A lively nation?" "Manners quite spoiled, no agreeable company." "It is possible they may not be partial to the English just now, as we have so lately been with fire and sword into their territory; — but the museums?" "Valuable, to be sure; but they do not properly belong to Paris." "The theatres, sir?" "Now and then, when Talma acts: but to visit all their little paltry theatres, and every evening, as some do, — I had rather sit at home in my chamber and read." And so ended my dialogue with the *poco curante*. Not with such indifference, but with the strong feelings which you who witnessed the destruction of the Bastille can appreciate, Mr. —— says he should *abhor* going to Paris. As to the ladies who go, they think of nothing but smuggling lace and silk shawls.

In the following letter to Mrs. Estlin, Mrs. Barbauld herself alludes to meeting the *lion* of the London season, *Sir Walter Scott;* and Miss Aikin also mentions it in a letter written to her brother.

MY DEAR MRS. ESTLIN, — I have just been reading, as probably you have also, six close volumes of Miss Seward's letters, which she informs us was only a twelfth part of her correspondence in, I think, twenty years. I have also been reading a letter of the poet M——'s to my brother, in which, apologizing for his long silence, he says, "I verily believe that if I had been an antediluvian, I could have let a hundred years pass between every letter, and feel the most violent twinges of conscience every day of that century for my omission, without their working any reformation in that respect." Now I look upon myself to be between both these characters; to which I approximate most, I must leave you to determine.

Everybody has been abroad, this uncommonly fine summer, but my brother and sister and myself. I spent one day only at Hampstead, — where I met Walter Scott, the *lion* of this London season, — and one day at Chigwell. The road to Chigwell is through a part of Hainault Forest; and we stopped to look at Fairlop oak, one of the largest in England; a complete ruin, but a noble ruin, which it is impossible to see without thinking of Cowper's beautiful line, "Who lived when thou wast such." The immovable rocks and mountains present us rather with an idea of eternity than of long life. There they are, and there they have been before the birth of nations. The tops of the everlasting hills have been seen covered with snow from the earliest records of time. But a *tree*, that has life and growth like ourselves, that, like ourselves, was once small and feeble, that certainly some time began to be, — to see it attain a size so enormous, and in its bulk and its slow decay bear record of the generations it has outlived, — this brings our comparative feebleness strongly in view. "Man passeth away, and where is he?" while "the oak of our fathers" will be the oak of their children, and *their* children.

In Miss Aikin's letter to her brother Edmund, in 1815, she tells him of a dinner at the Carrs' in Hampstead, when her aunt and their family were invited to meet Scott. "Nothing could persuade my father to go, so my aunt said she would take me instead, and I had not the grace to say no. A charming day we had. I did not, indeed, see much of the great lion; for we were fourteen at dinner, of whom about half were constantly talking, and neither at table nor after was I very near him; but he was delighted to see my aunt, and paid her great attention, which I was very glad of. He told her that the 'Tramp, tramp,' 'Splash, splash' of Taylor's 'Lenora' which she had carried into Scotland many years ago, was what made him a poet." This interesting anecdote, which Mrs. Barbauld's modesty naturally prevented her telling her correspondent, pleasantly connects her with the "Wizard of the North" as an inspiration and a friend.

STOKE NEWINGTON, January, 1815.

MY DEAR MRS. BEECROFT, — Thanks for your kind letter, and for the finest turkey I ever saw, which arrived without accident, and fulfilled the end of its being — its fattening, at least — last Tuesday amid the commendations of the whole party. I cannot tell where the spirit went; but I hope it is animating some other vehicle, and rising by degrees in the scale of existence, till perhaps it may come at length (who knows) to eat turkeys itself.

I give you joy of the Peace. It ought to last at least for this next twenty years; for though I am afraid war and peace must always take their turns, like day and night in the natural world, I think War ought to be satisfied, as the other dark and unlovely power is, with *share and share alike.* The two striking features of the present times in Britain are *religion* and *charity;* and I should think they are both of them well inclined to pacific measures.

In this letter Mrs. Barbauld again alludes to the happy event which had filled the minds of people, — Peace; and she thinks it should last long to compensate for the terrible times which had passed. In Mrs. Barbauld's letter of 1814 to Mrs. Estlin, she speaks of the people who rushed over to France at the opening of that country, which war had long closed to the English, and tells her of the smuggling done by the ladies, who think of nothing but running in silks and satins; while some of the men who go over seem to have very little taste or enjoyment of the country. She mentions one gentleman, who told her he had "rather sit at home in his chamber and read" than visit the French theatres. And he found fault in the same strain with everything French. In the following letter of condolence with Mrs. Fletcher on the loss of her daughter, one sees the tender feeling and warm sympathy which came directly from the amiable writer's heart. Her friends always found her full of interest and thought for them in the joyful and sad events in which all must have their share.

April, 1817.

DEAR MADAM, — It has been the impulse of my heart to write to you, and yet I hardly know how. What can I say? How can I express the shock this awful, this most affecting event has given me, has given all of us! How are the fairest hopes destroyed! How are the dearest ties severed! When was the uncertainty of life and all its hopes exemplified in a more solemn manner! Dear Grace! I had hoped myself some time, perhaps this summer, to see more of her, — to see her open the stores of her mind, — to see the modest flower expand and show all its lustre; but it is shut up forever here, to blow, I trust, in a happier climate. Young as she was, she has seen, perhaps, the best of life. Like Young's Narcissa, "She sparkled, was exhaled, and went to heaven." No long sickness to wear the mind as well as body; none of the decays incident to a more advanced period; she leaves life, it is true, in all its freshness, but without having tasted its cares or sorrows.

And is it nothing to have raised and cultured such a mind? Is she not fitter for another state, with higher powers, than many a one who has passed sixty years of a drowsy existence! May we not presume that — like a forward schoolboy, who has run rapidly through his classes and left the school, while others of his own age and standing are still drudging on — she will step into a higher form with more advantages? O but, I think I hear you say, the mother's heart must bleed. It must; I know it. God comfort you, my dear Mrs. F., and Mr. F., and all your family. Your mind will turn, I know it will, to the promising children you still have. One jewel has fallen from your maternal crown, but many remain; you are still rich. May God enable you to bear what he has laid upon you!

In Mrs. Farrar's "Recollections of Seventy Years" she mentions Mrs. Barbauld, and says that her mother made her acquaintance while she was writing "for the benefit of her little nephew, Charles Aikin, those hymns and lessons which have since delighted so many children both in the Old and New World." She adds that this acquaintance was kept up: "I remember sitting on Mrs. Barbauld's lap and her asking me if I could read, and what book I was then reading; I answered 'Barbauld's Lessons,' quite unconscious that I was sitting in the lap of their author. She then said 'I suppose you study geography, and can tell me what ocean is between England and America?'" Mrs. Farrar adds that, her mother having relatives in America to whom she wrote often, she was able to answer this question; but fearing that the next might be more difficult, she slid down from the perch, where she was very comfortable, and ran off. She says, "I often met her after I was grown up, and remember her as a sweet-looking, lively old lady, wearing her gray hair, which was then uncommon, reading aloud to a circle of young people on a rainy morning in the country. She read well; the book was 'Guy Mannering,' then just published." Mrs. Barbauld then made them all draw their impressions of the witch, and kept that done by Mrs. Farrar's sister. "The kind old lady" and her pleasant manners made much of an impression on the youthful mind of Mrs. Farrar, who long after recalled with pleasure her venerable friend.

Mr. Robinson, in the diary for 1816, writes of February 11, "I walked to Newington and dined with Mrs. Barbauld and Miss Finch; Miss Hammond and Charles Aikin were there. As usual, we were very comfortable; Mrs. Barbauld can keep up a lively argumentative conversation as well as any one I know, and at an advanced age (she is turned seventy) she is certainly the best specimen of female Presbyterian society in the country. — N. B. Anthony Robinson requested me to inquire whether she thought the doctrine of Universal Restoration scriptural. She said she thought we must bring to the interpretation of the Scriptures a very liberal notion of the beneficence of the Deity to find the doctrine there."

In July of the same year, Mr. Robinson wrote of taking tea and playing chess with Mrs. Barbauld. In the diary of May 26, 1817, he made the following entry: — "After dining with the Colliers I walked to Newington, and took tea with Mrs. Barbauld. I found that Dr. Aikin had been very seriously ill. Mrs. Barbauld herself retains her health and faculties, and is an interesting instance of a respected and happy old age. I played chess with her, and then went to Becher's late." In 1818 he writes, "Mrs. Barbauld speaks contemptuously of Lord Byron's new poem ('Beppo'), as being without poetry and in horrible versification. It may be so." Many of Mrs. Barbauld's sentiments regarding her contemporaries are worthy of note. She said in one letter, of Lord Byron, that he "filled a leaf in the book of fame, but it is a very blotted leaf." Rogers says that she told him "she thought Byron wrote best when he wrote about the *sea* or *swimming*." Curiously enough, William Howitt charges Byron with plagiarizing from her this figure, which is really Shakespeare's,—

"The earth hath bubbles as the water hath,
And this is of them."

In Mrs. Barbauld's poem, "Washing-Day," the same idea had been conceived by her,—

"Earth, air, and sky, and ocean hath its bubbles,
And verse is one of them, — this most of all."

In a letter of Miss Edgeworth's to Mrs. Edgeworth, written October, 1818, she says, "We went to see Mrs. Barbauld at Stoke Newington. We waited some time before she appeared, and I had leisure to recollect everything that could make me melancholy, — the very sofa where you and my father sat. I was quite *undone* before she came in, but forced to get through it. She was gratified by our visit, and very kind and agreeable." In the following letter to Mrs. Beecroft, Mrs. Barbauld is full of enthusiasm for America and its future; and after speaking of the ever new and interesting phases presented by a study of history to the thinker of enlarged and liberal views, she says, "What is the whole field of ancient history, which knew no sea but the Mediterranean, to the vast continent of America, with its fresh and opening glories?"

STOKE NEWINGTON, November 14, 1818.

Our tourists are mostly now returned. Such numbers have resided more or less abroad, that I cannot help thinking the intercourse must influence in some degree the national manners, which I find by Madame de Staël are not yet to the taste of our neighbors. They allow us to be respectable, but they plainly intimate they do not think us amiable. When I read such censures, I cannot help saying in my mind to the author: I wish you knew such a one, and such a one, of my acquaintance; I am sure you could not but love them. Yet, after all, I fear we must acknowledge something about us dry, cold, and reserved; more afraid of censure than gratified by notice; very capable of steadiness in important pursuits, but not happy in filling up the pauses and intervals of life with ingenious trifles, and spontaneous, social hilarity. . . . .

It seems to me that there is more room for authors in history than in any other department. It is continually growing. It is like a tree, the dead leaves and branches of which are continually pruned and cleared away, and fresh green shoots arising. How much less interesting since the French Revolution are the glories and conquests of Louis XIV.! What is the whole field of ancient history, which knew no sea but the Mediterranean, to the vast continent of America, with its fresh and opening glories! Will they be wise by our experience, peaceable, moderate, virtuous? No: they will be learned by our learning, but not wise by our experience. Each country, as each man, must buy his own experience.

To MRS. TAYLOR.

STOKE NEWINGTON, December 8, 1818.

I will write, now my dear friend is better, is recovering, is, I hope, in a fair way to be soon quite well, and all herself again; and she will accept, and so will Mr. T. and Mrs. R., my warmest congratulations. To tell you how anxious we have been, would, I trust, be superfluous, or how much joy we have felt in being relieved from that anxiety. It is pleasant to have some one to share pleasure with; and though I could have had that satisfaction in a degree with every one who knows you, it is more particularly agreeable to me at this time to have your dear Sarah to sympathize with and talk to about you. Among other things, we say that you must not let *mind* wear out *body*, which I suspect you are a little inclined to do. Mind is often very hard upon his humble yokefellow, sometimes speaking contemptuously of her, as being of a low, mean family, in comparison with himself; often abridging her food or natural rest for his whims. Many a headache has he given her, when, but for him, she would be quietly resting in her bed. Sometimes he fancies that she hangs as a dead weight upon him, and impedes all his motions; yet it is well known that, though he gives himself such airs of superiority, he can in fact do nothing without her; and since, however they came together, they are united for better for worse, it is for his interest as well as hers that she should be nursed and cherished and taken care of. — And so ends my sermon.

In the year 1819, Mrs. Barbauld lost one of her

earliest and most intimate friends, Mrs. Kenrick, to whom several of her letters in these pages were addressed.

Miss Aikin, in writing about this time, says, "We are all quite well here; my aunt Barbauld hears as quick as ever." And in writing Mrs. Taylor of Norwich in the same year, 1819, she says, "My aunt Barbauld, though complaining a little occasionally, has continued to make many visits, and enjoy, I think, a great deal of pleasure this summer." In the following letter to Mrs. Fletcher of Edinburgh, her old friend, Mrs. Barbauld writes of making visits, and the pleasure of travelling in a post-chaise with agreeable companions, when "you may sulk in a corner if you choose; nay, you may sleep without offence," and "you talk, and yet you are not bound to talk."

STOKE NEWINGTON, September, 1819.

How good you are to me, my dear Mrs. F., and how kind and how cheering are your expressions of regard! I will not tell you how much you have made me love you by your late visit. Your kindness, your frankness, the interest you have made me take in your family, the thought how much your own feelings have been tried, have made me look on you with mingled reverence and affection. I hope the Misses F.'s visit to London will have made sufficiently favorable impressions to induce them sometimes to repeat it; and yet I fancy I hear them saying that, after all, this great overgrown mass of buildings, these pushing, bustling, crowded streets, this hubbub and hum of the busy hive, that poverty and crime which form the background of the gay picture, are not so attractive as their own Edinburgh, with its picturesque site, — the singularity of the Old, the splendor of the New town, — with the remembrances that attach (softened by being only remembrances) to the decayed palace and the closed doors of the halls of legislation, with taste and the spirit of inquiry emanating from the seat of literature and spreading its influence over society, and with all the romantic stories attached to glen and brook and heath, impressed with the still recent footsteps of a wild and hardy race, but lately brought within the pale of civilized society, — stories the treasure-house of the poet and the novelist. And if they do make this preference, I have not much to say against it, provided you keep your Edinburgh as it is, and do not imitate us too much.

Our weather is still pleasant. I am going to spend two or three days at ——, Mr. and Miss B. and myself in a post-chaise. An agreeable companion in a post-chaise — though I would not advertise for one — is certainly an agreeable thing. You talk, and yet you are not bound to talk; and if the conversation drops, you may pick it up again at every brook or village, or seat you pass, — "What 's o'clock?" and "How 's the wind?" "Whose chariot 's that we left behind?" You may sulk in a corner if you will; nay, you may sleep without offence.

In the following letter to Mrs. Estlin, congratulating her on the happy marriage of her son, she feelingly alludes to the loss of Mrs. Kenrick; and though infirmities had made life less desirable to her, yet she is sensible of the blow to herself in the departure of her old and valued friend.

My dear Mrs. Estlin, — I was just going to write to you when I received your kind letter, for I had heard of your son's marriage, and wished to congratulate you on the event; but I do it with much more pleasure now that I learn from your letter the full satisfaction and pleasure that you feel in the match. You are fortunate, my dear friend, in having so excellent and well principled a son; fortunate in having him married agreeably to your wishes; and very fortunate in having him and your other children within a walk of your door or within it.

We are all pretty much as usual; for myself, indeed, I am sensible I grow weaker both in mind and body, and I am sensible it is natural and right it should be so. How many friends have I survived! A very dear one Mrs. Kenrick was. I had no prospect, indeed, of ever seeing her again, nor, with the privations she suffered, (of which her almost total deafness was the severest) could I wish her to live; yet there is a melancholy in the thought, Gone forever! which no other separation can inspire. But why do I write in this strain to you, when I write on purpose to congratulate you on a wedding? How soon children become, from playthings, subjects of education; then objects of anxiety for their settling in the world; and then, very often, are transplanted wide away from their parents' home, — perhaps to America. The more particularly fortunate you: so I began, and so I conclude.

In Mr. Robinson's diary the entry for January 21, 1821, is as follows: — "I called on the Colliers, and then went to Mrs. Barbauld's. She was in good spirits, but she is now the confirmed old lady. Independently of her fine understanding and literary reputation, she would be interesting. Her white locks, fair and unwrinkled skin, brilliant starched linen, and rich silk gown, make her a fit subject for a painter. Her conversation is lively, her remarks judicious and always pertinent."

In July of the same year he writes, "I went to Mrs. Barbauld's, where I was soon joined by Charles and Mary Lamb. This was a meeting I had brought about to gratify mutual curiosity. The Lambs are pleased with Mrs. Barbauld, and therefore it is highly probable that they have pleased her. Mrs. C. Aikin was there, and Miss Lawrence. Lamb was chatty, and suited his conversation to his company, except that, speaking of Gilbert Wakefield, he said he had a peevish face. When he was told Mrs. Aikin was Gilbert Wakefield's daughter, he was vexed, but got out of the scrape tolerably well. I walked with the Lambs by the turnpike, and then came home."

STOKE NEWINGTON, October, 1822.

MY DEAR MRS. CARR, — I think I never was so long without seeing you since we were acquainted. May I hope that it will not be much longer? I want to know of the health and welfare of every individual of you. . . . . My love to your young ladies; tell them I am sorry they must wait to be married till Parliament meets again; but everybody says it is the most difficult thing in the world. Dr. ——, indeed, has accomplished it, in spite of obstacles; but he is a man of energy and perseverance. Englishmen are said to love their laws; that is the reason, I suppose, they give us so many of them, and in different editions.

Dr. Channing, in writing to Mrs. Kinder of London, in 1823, after his return to America, says of Mrs. Barbauld, whom he had called on with Mrs. Kinder in 1822, "I recollect with much pleasure the visit which we paid with you to Mrs. Barbauld. It is rare to meet with such sensibility, mildness, and, I may say, sweetness, united with the venerableness of old age; and I was particularly gratified with seeing, in a woman so justly distinguished, such entire absence of the consciousness of authorship. I trust that she is still living, for her life seemed to me a blessing, both to herself and her friends; and if so, I beg you to assure her of our affectionate and very respectful remembrances."

In December of 1822, her brother, Dr. John Aikin, the beloved companion of her early years, and the object of her deepest affection through a long life, died, after a long and tedious illness, which somewhat reconciled his family and friends to his loss.

In the following letter Mrs. Barbauld asks, "What does life offer at past eighty (at which venerable age

I arrived one day last June)? And I believe you will allow that there is not much of new, of animating, of inviting, to be met with after that age." With all the disabilities and the failing strength of the long years which bring in their train so many infirmities to all, she was very cheerful; and her last years were passed amidst an affectionate family circle, while she was the beloved object of solicitude to many friends. Her brother's family and his son Charles — her adopted son, "the little Charles" for whom she wrote the "Early Lessons," and whose early years called forth so much affection and thought from her — united in devoted care and attention to her. Friends and kindness she did not lack, though a long life naturally left her in her declining years somewhat lonely, as most of her earlier companions were taken from her by death. In 1823 she lost another very dear friend, Mrs. John Taylor of Norwich. This lady was endeared to her by long intimacy and great excellence of character. She was never very near her for any length of time, but visits exchanged, and a correspondence, kept up a very close friendship. In a letter to one of Mrs. Taylor's daughters, Mrs. Barbauld spoke truly and affectionately of her character and amiable traits. She says, "Receive the assurance of my most affectionate sympathy in those feelings with which you must be now contemplating the loss of that dear woman, so long the object of your respect and affection; nor, indeed, yours only, but of all who knew her. A prominent part of those feelings, however, must be, that the dear object of them is released from suffering, has finished her task and entered upon her reward. . . . . Never will she be forgotten by those who knew her! Her strong sense, her feeling, her energy, her principle, her patriotic feelings, her piety, rational yet ardent, — all these mark a character of no common sort. When to these are added those of relation or friend, the feeling must be such as no course of years can efface."

LETTER TO ——.

STOKE NEWINGTON, October 25, 1823.

. . . . The enigma you do me the honor to ask for will accompany this. But I have first to find it; for though I have looked a good deal, I have not yet been able to lay my hands on it. I beg to make proviso that if I should want myself to insert it in any publication, I may be at liberty to do it. Though, truly, that is not very likely; for well do I feel one faculty after another withdrawing, and the shades of evening closing fast around me; and be it so! What does life offer at past eighty (at which venerable age I arrived one day last June)? And I believe you will allow that there is not much of new, of animating, of inviting, to be met with after that age. For my own part, I only find that many things I knew, I have forgotten; many things I thought I knew, I find I know nothing about; some things I know, I have found not worth knowing; and some things I would give — O what would one not give? — to know are beyond the reach of human ken. Well, I believe this is what may be called prosing, and you can make much better use of your time than to read it.

I saw yesterday two boys, modern Greeks, in the costume of their country, introduced by Mr. Bowring, who has the charge of them, — "*Du Grec, — ah, ma sœur, du Grec; ils parlent du Grec!*" I have been reading one or two American novels lately. They are very well, but I do not wish them to write novels yet. Let them explore and describe their new country; let them record the actions of their Washington, the purest character, perhaps, that history has to boast of; let them enjoy their free, their unexpensive, government, number their rising towns, and boast that Persecution does not set her bloody foot in any corner of their extensive territories. Then let them kindle into poetry; but not yet — not till the more delicate shades and nicer delineations of life are familiar to them — let them descend to novels. But, tempted by writing to you, I am running on till my eyes are tired, and perhaps you too. Compliments to Mrs. ——, and all your family. If I find the riddle, I will send it to you; meantime I am, with the truest esteem and friendship,

Your affectionate friend.

Mrs. Barbauld was well aware of the decline of strength and the fast approaching close to her life. She plainly saw her own increased feebleness and the want of energy which overcame her. Without repining or complaints she cheerfully awaited the day of release. In the following letter to Mrs. Estlin, she speaks of having "arrived at a period when life has no more to give, and every year takes away from the powers both of mind and body."

STOKE NEWINGTON, January, 1824.

MY DEAR MRS. ESTLIN, — I will not say I was not disappointed in being obliged to give up the hope of seeing you this year; but you know best the time that suits you, and I dare say have done what is right and proper. With regard to myself, I do not reckon much upon any enjoyment that has months between it and me. I am arrived at a period when life has no more to give, and every year takes away from the powers both of body and mind; when the great tendency is to inaction and rest, and when all subjects of thankfulness or congratulation must be, not how much you enjoy, but how little you suffer. Then the powers of man strive — how vainly! — to penetrate the veil, to pierce the thick darkness that covers the future; life seems of no value but for what lies beyond it, and even our views of the future are perhaps cheerful or gloomy according to the weather or our nerves.

STOKE NEWINGTON, February, 1824.

MY DEAR MRS. BEECROFT, — The state of my eyes — which have been very weak of late, and are giving me a hint that they have served me nearly long enough — has hindered me for some time from answering your kind letter. Long may you enjoy that activity and flow of spirits which makes life indeed a blessing; and which by conversation, by the very look of a happy and social spirit, communicates pleasure to all within its influence. But, you will say, a social spirit often leads one to mourn. It is very true; we are just now sympathizing with .... But what is all this to you? will you say; these are not your acquaintance or connections. Why, that is very true; but I have so long been accustomed to see you take part with ready and affectionate sympathy in the habits, connections, and trains of ideas of your friends, that I am always apt to suppose that where I am intimate you cannot be a stranger, and that where I am interested you cannot be indifferent. I heard a lady say once, that she should not at all care or interest herself about anything which might happen to her friends or relations when she was out of the world, — I mean, if she were to know it now. How unnatural! I need not tell you, I think, that she was not a parent. Nor do I like those metaphysical moralists, who, by a refinement of subtle investigation, assert that our anxiety for our friends proceeds only from a wish to avoid, *for ourselves*, the pain we are conscious we should feel whenever they suffer. Miserable evasions of Nature's best feelings!

In Mr. Robinson's diary he writes of November 4, 1824, "Walked to Newington; Mrs. Barbauld was going out, but she stayed a short time with me. The old lady is much shrunk in appearance and is declining in strength. She is but the shade of her former self, but a venerable shade. She is eighty-one years old, but she retains her cheerfulness, and seems not afraid of death. She has a serene hope and quiet faith,—delightful qualities at all times, and in old age peculiarly enviable." In Mr. Robinson's reminiscences of past years there is one written in a letter to his brother in 1852, in which he speaks of "the spirit of Mrs. Barbauld's famous essay," that on "Inconsistency." And in another letter, a few days later, to the same person, he says of an incident, "This reminds me of my leave-taking of Mrs. Barbauld on my going to France, *anno* 182–. She was suffering from a severe cold with a cough. 'I hope I shall find you better on my return.' 'Why so?' 'That seems a foolish question; health is better than sickness.' 'Not always; I do not wish to be better. But don't mistake me, I am not at all impatient, but quite ready.' She died a few weeks after my leave-taking. It was her brother who wrote the couplet she might have written, and which I make no apology for repeating as a pious wish:—

'From the banquet of Life rise a satisfied guest,
Thank the Lord of the Feast, and in hope go to rest.'"

STOKE NEWINGTON, November 23, 1824.

It is so long since I heard of you or yours, that I begin to be impatient, and moreover I am disappointed; for you certainly did flatter me some time ago with the idea that I should see you here before this summer was ended. And now, while I had hardly finished my sentence, your kind letter arrives. Let me beg of you to give up your reasons against paying me a visit before this year is concluded. Think of my age, and come to me while my eyes serve me to look on your countenance, and my ears can catch your words, and my heart can be exhilarated by the conversation of a friend.

I think nothing flourishes more in Newington than schools. We have several set up lately, besides charity-schools, of which so many have been established that I should imagine there is not an individual among the lower order who cannot get his son instructed, if he really desires it. We have some little Greek boys here, who, in their national costume, are great objects of curiosity. They are protected by Mr. Bowring. By the way, are you not sorry Lord Byron is dead, just when he was going to be a hero? He has filled a leaf in the book of fame, but it is a very blotted leaf.

It is amazing how building increases everywhere near London, though, as I said, my neighbors decrease. This is the necessary lot of age. One of our ministers prays that when we come to die we may have nothing to do but die. In one sense the petition is rational; but if it means nothing to do for ourselves, nothing to do for others, nothing to do in any of the useful stations of life, — the languor and privations, if not the sufferings, of age, more than balancing its few enjoyments, — then, truly, I do not think the blessing is much to be prayed for. I am rather getting into a melancholy vein, and I ought not, for I have much to be thankful for, and shall have more when your next letter comes to tell me, as I hope it will, such a day, such an hour, I have taken my place for London, thence to proceed to Newington, where you will be sincerely welcomed by, dear Mrs. Estlin, your affectionate friend.

Mrs. Barbauld suffered from an asthmatic complaint for some time before her death, and it greatly limited her activity, though her excellent constitution for a long time resisted the disease. But finally she died rather suddenly, after a few days of severe illness. She had consented, in view of her weak state of health, to become an inmate of her adopted son Charles's family, though it was hard for her to leave her own old home, endeared to her by many associations, for any other. She paid a visit to her sister-in-law, Mrs. John Aikin, previous to leaving Newington for her nephew's house in London; and while with her the illness suddenly manifested itself which terminated her life. She calmly and quietly expired, March 9, 1825, in the eighty-second year of her age.

Miss Aikin says very well and truly of her aunt, "To claim for this distinguished woman the praise of purity and elevation of mind may well appear superfluous. Her education and connections, the course of her life, the whole tenor of her writings, bear abundant testimony to this part of her character. It is a higher, or at least a rarer, commendation, to add, that no one ever better loved 'a sister's praise,' even that of such sisters as might have been peculiarly regarded in the light of rivals. She was acquainted with almost all the principal female writers of the time; and there was not one of the number whom she failed frequently to mention in terms of admiration, esteem, or affection, whether in conversation, in letters to her friends, or in print. To humbler aspirants in the career of letters, who applied to her for advice or assistance, she was invariably courteous, and in many instances essentially serviceable. The sight of youth and beauty was peculiarly gratifying to her fancy and her feelings; and children and young persons, especially females, were accordingly large sharers in her benevolence. She loved their society, and would often invite them to pass weeks or months in her house, when she spared no pains to amuse and instruct them; and she seldom failed, after they had quitted her, to recall herself from time to time to their recollection, by affectionate and playful letters or welcome presents. She passed through a long life without having dropped, it is believed, a single friendship, and without having drawn upon herself a single enmity which could properly be called personal." This is just and not partial praise, dictated by the writer's connection with Mrs. Barbauld. It appears to be a plain statement of facts, and amply borne out by her own writings, her letters, and the testimony of her other contemporaries.

The praise of one "sister" and friend is worthy attention here. Miss Edgeworth, in a letter written March 15, 1825, says, "You have probably seen in the papers the death of our admirable friend, Mrs. Barbauld. I have copied for you her last letter to me, and some beautiful lines written in her eightieth year. There is a melancholy elegance and force of thought in both. Elegance and strength — qualities rarely uniting without injury to each other — combined most perfectly in her style, and this rare combination, added to their classical purity, forms, perhaps, the distinguishing characteristics of her writings. England has lost a great writer, and we a most sincere friend." In the year 1840, Mrs. Barbauld's adopted son and nephew, Charles Rochemont Aikin, placed a tablet in the Newington Green Chapel. This tablet is of white marble, of a simple form, laid on a black ground; and the monument is placed on the wall opposite another, which was erected to the memory of Samuel Rogers, the poet, who for many years was a trustee of the Chapel. A tablet to Dr. Price's memory also has a place in the edifice. The inscription which I copy is from the pen of Mrs. Barbauld's eldest nephew, Arthur Aikin, Esq., Secretary to the Society of Arts, Adelphi, for many years. It must be admired for its simplicity, its truth, and the point and elegance of the language. The inscription is as follows: —

IN MEMORY OF
ANNA LÆTITIA BARBAULD,
DAUGHTER OF JOHN AIKIN, D. D.
AND WIFE OF THE REVD. ROCHEMONT BARBAULD,
FORMERLY THE RESPECTED MINISTER OF THIS CONGREGATION.
SHE WAS BORN AT KIBWORTH IN LEICESTERSHIRE, 20TH OF JUNE, 1743,
AND DIED AT STOKE NEWINGTON, 9TH MARCH, 1825.
ENDOWED BY THE GIVER OF ALL GOOD
WITH WIT, GENIUS, POETIC TALENT, AND A VIGOROUS UNDERSTANDING,
SHE EMPLOYED THOSE HIGH GIFTS
IN PROMOTING THE CAUSE OF HUMANITY, PEACE, AND JUSTICE,
OF CIVIL AND RELIGIOUS LIBERTY,
OF PURE, ARDENT, AND AFFECTIONATE DEVOTION.
LET THE YOUNG, NURTURED BY HER WRITINGS, IN THE PURE SPIRIT
OF CHRISTIAN MORALITY,
LET THOSE OF MATURE YEARS CAPABLE OF APPRECIATING
THE ACUTENESS, THE BRILLIANT FANCY, AND SOUND REASONING
OF HER LITERARY COMPOSITIONS,
LET THE SURVIVING FEW WHO SHARED
HER DELIGHTFUL AND INSTRUCTIVE CONVERSATION,
BEAR WITNESS THAT THIS MONUMENT RECORDS
NO EXAGGERATED PRAISE.

In conversation with Mr. James Martineau recently, he spoke to the writer very affectionately of Mrs. Barbauld and her charm of manner, her kindly nature, and her interest in the young. This eminent man received what may be termed an inherited friendship from Mrs.

Barbauld, who, to the last, was peculiar in her ability and power to interest herself in the rising generation, and in that way kept up her own freshness of thought and vivacity. Once he called on her in the little, old-fashioned house where she lived, in Newington, and found with her two gentlemen who had risen to take leave. After a few affectionate parting words, they went, saying, as they handed her a package, "Well, we will leave these with you, as you can make them useful." When they had gone, she turned to Mr. Martineau, then fresh from his academic studies, and asked if he knew who these gentlemen were. Then she told him one was Samuel Rogers, the poet; the other, Sir James Mackintosh. The package she gave him, saying it would interest him, and her eyes were too sensitive for her to read much, and especially Greek characters. On opening it, he found it consisted of a number of Greek newspapers, sent by Lord Byron from Greece, and containing some description of the struggle there, into the midst of which he had thrown himself with so much impetuosity and zeal, costing him his life in the same year, 1824. One cannot help thinking with interest of that little group, — the aged poet, Mrs. Barbauld, Mr. Rogers, Sir James Mackintosh, and the young man, — now one of the "great, half-recognized philosophers of the day," as the Spectator lately termed him, — the Rev. James Martineau. That brilliant thinker, philosophical and finely cultivated writer and talker, Sir James Mackintosh, said of the essay "On Inconsistency in Our Expectations," that he considered it the finest in the language for the depth of thought, clearness of the reasoning, and perfect finish of style which Mrs. Barbauld displayed in its composition. He was a warm friend and sincere admirer of Mrs. Barbauld for many years.

In Mr. Robinson's Diary for 1825, he writes: "This morning I read to the young folks Mrs. Barbauld's 'Legacy.' This delightful book has in it some of the sweetest things I ever read. 'The King in his Castle,' and 'True Magicians' are perfect allegories in Mrs. Barbauld's best style. Some didactic pieces are also delightful." This "Legacy," of which he speaks, was printed several months after Mrs. Barbauld's death, and intended particularly for the young. Several of the allegories and tales will be found among the "Selections" from her works given at the close of the volume; "True Magicians" being placed first, as it was in the original volume.

In Mr. Rogers's "Reminiscences" he says of Mrs. Barbauld, that, "strangely enough, in spite of her correct taste, Mrs. Barbauld was quite fascinated by Darwin's *Botanic Garden,* when it first appeared, and talked of it with rapture; for which I scolded her quite heartily." Rogers would not have thought her admiration so odd, had he known that Cowper even was fascinated by the "Botanic Garden," and addressed some complimentary verses to Dr. Darwin, written in connection with Hayley, his friend, and afterwards his biographer. Wordsworth once said, "Darwin had not an atom of feeling; he was a mere eye-voluptuary. He has so many similes, all beginning with '*so*,' that I used to call the 'Botanic Garden' so-so poetry." Miss Aikin says that Mrs. Barbauld criticised "Lalla Rookh" somewhat. "As my aunt Barbauld says," she writes, " 't is my flower-dish, sweet and gay, and tastefully arranged, but the flowers do not *grow* there; they are picked up with pains here and there." Mrs. Barbauld was extremely simple in her taste, and preferred classical purity and natural description to the novel and startling. When Byron published his "Bride of Abydos," she wrote to Mrs. Estlin, "I cannot see any advantage in calling a nightingale *bulbul*, or a rose *gul*, except to disconcert plain English readers." In 1818, Mr. Robinson says, "Mrs. Barbauld speaks contemptuously of Lord Byron's new poem, ['Beppo'] as being without poetry, and in horrible versification. It may be so." This was on an occasion when he dined with her, and found a number of people there, and saw young Mr. Roscoe, who was calling on her. The conversation turned on Byron's new poem, which he had been reading as he walked, — a habit of Mr. Robinson's.

Lord Brougham, in one of his speeches, made an eloquent tribute to Mrs. Barbauld's memory. In his "Discourse on the Objects, Advantages, and Pleasures of Science," he writes: "Children's books have at all times been made upon the pernicious plan of exciting wonder, generally terror, at whatever risk. The folly and misery occasioned by this error it would be difficult to estimate. The time may come when it will be felt and understood. At present, the inveterate habits of parents and nurses prevent the children from benefiting by the excellent lessons of Mrs. Barbauld and Miss Edgeworth."

In one place we find Mrs. Barbauld's hymns spoken of as follows: — "In devotional poetry she never has been, and probably never will be, excelled." And the writer then praises very highly the "Address to the Deity," and "A Summer Evening's Meditation," as very elevated in sentiment and feeling. In a charming review by W. O. B. Peabody of Miss Aikin's edition of her aunt's works, he says of Mrs. Barbauld: "Endowed with a mind masculine in its grasp, and no less fitted to be the communicant than the recipient of knowledge, she devoted, through an unusually long life, every faculty of her soul to the most hallowed purposes. Whether we look at her as a poetess inculcating moral lessons in harmonious strains; as an essayist, seldom beneath, and not unfrequently equal to, our most classical writers; as a theologian, the powerful and consistent supporter of its tolerant and reasonable side; or as a politician denouncing despotism and advocating a wise and philosophic freedom, — we confess we know not in which character to admire her most."

Mrs. Barbauld's poems are characterized by her easy versification, — the smooth and polished style, which leads the reader from thought to thought without startling the mind, — and their influence is elevating and pleasing. Her high tone of thought, pure and deep sentiment, her powers of description and imagination of things seen, and aspirations towards the unknown, the beautiful, and the grand, are her peculiar charms as a poet. Mrs. Barbauld's poetry places her among the writers of that English school which has for its head Cowper, — named as "the most popular poet of his generation" by Southey, — the school of descriptive, didactic, and picturesque versification. The writers of this style of poetry are distinguished for their high tone, religious feeling, and love of the beautiful and true in nature and man. Calm and unexciting in their style, they present no glaring or startling effects of the terrible or tragic, relying on simple and natural word-pictures of scenes and characters to interest and attract the reader. In the peculiar powers of mind Mrs. Barbauld displayed, her devotional and beautiful hymns, her long poems on various subjects of interest which called them forth, — "Corsica," the "Epistle" to William Wilberforce, and "Eighteen Hundred and Eleven," the "Address to the Deity," and "A Summer Evening's Meditation," — excel; and these poems convey to the mind an idea of her range of thought. She loved liberty and toleration for all men, and this feeling prompted the "Address to the Corsicans," and the "Epistle" to Mr. Wilberforce, — the first being an animating voice of encouragement to a patriotic and struggling people, the second a fervent expression of hope and sympathy for the slaves. She wrote many bright and witty verses, which show that humor, fancy, and sentiment went hand in hand, and combined to make a rare union of strength and imagination in her writings. There is a pleasing and noticeable variety in Mrs. Barbauld's poems, and she ranges over a wide field of thought, which Dryden tells us is well for a poet: —

> "Happy who in his verse can steer
> From grave to light, from pleasant to severe."

Though Mrs. Barbauld was gifted with great facility of expression, and wrote very easily, she was very particular about the preparation and composition of her works published; and many very pretty and pleasing poems have never been printed, as she did not consider them of sufficient interest for the public, and properly finished in their style. "To a friend who had expressed his surprise at not finding inserted in her volume a poem which he had admired in manuscript, she well and characteristically replied, 'I had rather it should be asked of twenty pieces why they are not here, than of one why it is.'" The works, when first prepared, after her reluctance to appear before the public had been overcome, were issued on this plan. Miss Aikin followed it out most conscientiously, and I have omitted many poems and prose pieces not of present interest, as being suggested by passing events, or addressed to one or another friend.

In Mr. Turner's sketch of Mrs. Barbauld, from which I have just quoted, he names the following poems as being among his treasures, and given him by Mrs. Barbauld in manuscript: "A Fragment of an Epic Poem, occasioned by the Loss of a Game of Chess to Dr. Priestley, in Consequence of an Unreasonable Drowsiness"; "Verses on the Birth of Dr. Priestley's Son" (Joseph Priestley, Esq., of Tindale, near Dudley, who continued and published his father's Memoirs); "Verses written on the Back of an old Visitation Copy, of the Arms of Dr. Priestley's Family, with a Proposal for a new Escutcheon." Also he mentions another, "'An Invocation to the Muse' for help to describe the various romantic scenes to which she had been taken while in Yorkshire," — in a letter to Mrs. Priestley. This had been in his possession, but was lost. In his list he included "The Inventory of the Furniture of Dr. Priestley's Study," which Mrs. Barbauld did not print; and this poem, with the lines on "The Deserted Village," were the only pieces first printed by Miss Aikin, — the only exceptions to the rule made by Mrs. Barbauld. Miss Aikin assigns as her ground for this departure from her aunt's arrangement of her plans the fact that no reason existed at the date of her publication for retaining the *jeu d'esprit* on Dr. Priestley's furniture. The lines on "The Deserted Village," she gave "partly for the sake of connecting the name of their author as a contemporary with that of a poet who has so long been enrolled among the classics of his country. It may also be mentioned, that Goldsmith, whose envy is well known, bore involuntary testimony to the merit of these lines by exhibiting no sentiment but mortification on hearing them read in a London circle." Dr. Goldsmith was able neither to control nor to conceal his envy, and the amusing scenes described by Boswell will show this. The lines were exceedingly graceful in their allusion to him, and should have pleased the warm-hearted but eccentric poet. Long after this poem was written, Mrs. Barbauld told Mr. Robinson, "I never shall be tired of reading Goldsmith's 'Deserted Village.'" Among the poems omitted there are some beautiful lines. Those on the death of Mrs. Martineau, the ancestress of Mr. James Martineau, contain a fine thought about the death of the aged: —

"'T is Virtue's triumph,
Nature's doom."

And in a poem addressed to Miss Rigby she has commemorated the filial devotion of this young lady, who was in attendance on an invalid mother at Buxton. To her and of her she says, —

"Thus some tall column graceful rears its head
To prop some mould'ring towers with moss o'erspread;
Whose stately piles and arches yet display
The venerable graces of decay."

The prose works of Mrs. Barbauld are varied in style and character. We must consider her as an essayist, a biographer, a critic, and a writer of charming allegories and tales. The "Prose Hymns" and "Early Lessons" also give her another title to the reader's attention, as one who had a peculiar and happy talent for adapting thought, and simplifying, not degrading, ideas, so that young children might early learn to think. It is not worth while here to question how many books written for children teach them to use their reasoning powers, but certainly there are very few. Amusement, excitement, and novelty or wonder, perhaps terror, form the marked characteristics of a large part of this class of literature. Mrs. Barbauld's books for children formed an era, gave a new direction to the range of books intended for the young, and formed the basis of all our present standard works for children, and some of which we owe to several of Mrs. Barbauld's contemporaries and friends, — Dr. Aikin, Miss Edgeworth, Mr. Day, and others. The "Prose Hymns" of Mrs. Barbauld I have already spoken of at length, and need only add that these beautiful hymns are as unique in their style and execution as they are original and perfect in thought and simplicity.

As an essayist, Mrs. Barbauld was very felicitous in her clear, forcible, and thorough investigation and comprehension of her theme, in her grasp of thought, and in the calm, judicial, yet graceful and animated, treatment of the subject she had before her. In her prose as well as her poetry she never offered her work to the public without the most perfect finish which it was possible to give it. She felt that the most self-commending and noble thought could not dispense with the added lustre of the choice and elegant language in which she carefully clothed her sentiments and opinions. As I have said, the essay "On Inconsistency in Our Expectations" has an acknowledged and prominent rank, being thought by those whose opinions are of value to stand at the head of that class of literature.

In Mrs. Barbauld's "Life of Richardson," she proved herself a faithful and judicious narrator of facts, and chronicler of the novel-writing bookseller, Richardson. It was not an easy life to present to the world. Dullness, one feels, must have been its marked characteristic, and yet she was able to draw from the dull and prosy little man's life, and his relations with the small circle who admired him and made much of him, an exceedingly attractive and yet true picture of his career. The writing, reading, and publishing of his novels, and afterwards the perusal of them by the world of fashion, formed the great events of his daily life. Yet from these simple materials Mrs. Barbauld wrote a biography which is charming, animated, and spirited. The memory of Richardson is but a name when one tries to wade through his prolix, tedious "Sir Charles Grandison"; but his biography almost vivifies him for the present generation.

In Mrs. Barbauld's critical essays she showed discrimination and taste. As the train of thought was dictated by the work to be considered, less scope was allowed her for originality or freedom of design; but these articles are models of that kind of writing, and of enduring and permanent interest, taken in connection with the works of which they serve as an introduction and study. Her political pamphlets — which gave her a high and deserved reputation for liberality of thought, and an honest, fearless expression of her views and sentiments — were called forth by arbitrary and narrow legislation; and her earnest protest against injustice, intolerance, and inhumanity, must gain the respect and admiration of this later age. It is plainly to be seen that this fearless protest was dictated by conscience, for she had no personal gain to expect by the success of her party, and exposed herself to ungenerous and impertinent criticism and attacks, in her noble efforts for the unfortunate and oppressed.

The allegories and tales of Mrs. Barbauld present her in another light to our attention. They are bright, fanciful, and imaginative; full of airy flights of fancy, and graceful in their conception, turn of thought, and expression. Through this apparently unstudied and figurative style of writing she conveyed many truths and ideas to the minds of her readers, and while they thought they read for pleasure and amusement, great and important ideas insensibly influenced and affected them. The allegories for the young are delightful specimens of this class of writing, and in the "Hill of Science" Mrs. Barbauld "tried her strength with Addison, and sustained no defeat." She showed in that piece her power of imagination and perfect ability to sustain and complete her imaginary dream by clothing it in the language of fancy and giving it an air of natural and unstudied description. The tales partake of this figurative, allegorical style, and convey always some good ideas, some profound yet simple truths, adapted to the age of those for whom they were prepared. Miss Aikin very justly thinks "the allegorical or enigmatical style" "peculiarly adapted to her genius," and says "even her conversation was often enlivened with these graceful sports of wit and imagination." The reader will observe the tendency to the allegorical and fanciful in several of her letters, and her "Dialogues" and "Riddles" also prove her an adept in this species of writing.

I have spoken of Mrs. Barbauld's mental characteristics, her genius, and her devotion to learning. Shall I not do the reader injustice by forgetting that interest may be felt in her personal appearance, her manners, and her character? Few women of learning have left an impression on the memory of those who knew them intimately and socially more pleasing and attractive than Mrs. Barbauld. She was very small and perfectly formed. Her figure was fine, and she carried herself with dignity and elegance. Her hair, which was abundant, was in early life light, and in her later years became gray. Her complexion was fair and brilliant, her features were very regular and finely formed, and her air and manner was that of a person favored by perfect health, — for which she was remarkable during her long life. There are several portraits of Mrs. Barbauld, which are now in the possession of her great-niece, Mrs. Le Breton of Hampstead, who kindly showed them to me. One of these, a silhouette, had a peculiar interest, as it was the work of Mrs. Barbauld, when, as Lætitia Aikin, she charmed and adorned the Warrington society. In this manner she took portraits of almost all of the tutors, scholars, and her friends at Warrington, and of these many are still in possession of her nieces. This picture gives her quite marked features, and the classic arrangement of the hair shows the fine shape of her head. After Mrs. Barbauld's death, an old friend sent the family a miniature taken from memory by a young man who was deeply in love with Miss Aikin, and he thought, under the agitating circumstances of that state of mind, being convinced that his suit was hopeless, that the portrait was quite good, and did justice to the attractions which had made him a worshipper at a distance. This picture is colored, and represents Miss Aikin in full evening dress, and her very profuse light and wavy hair is arranged in an elaborate manner. The features are quite decided, and the whole character of the face would seem to show that it must have been a fair likeness of this eminent woman at that time. The third portrait is quite small, but very distinct, and evidently conveys an excellent idea of the subject. This is a miniature medallion in bas-relief, done by Mr. Wedgwood. It is about an inch in length, and an oval, being intended to be set and worn as a brooch. The treatment of the head is thoroughly classical, and the simple arrangement of the hair and the delicate lines of the face indicate great attention and care in its execution. Mr. Wedgwood did this little portrait by his own prompting, and it adds another to the long list of great and distinguished men and women whose faces are known to the present generation in this form.

The silhouette of Mrs. Barbauld which formed the portrait published in her Collected Works prepared by Miss Aikin was done by Mrs. Hoare of Hampstead. It was considered an excellent portrait by her brother, Dr. John Aikin, and her adopted son, Charles Aikin, and undoubtedly, for those who knew her well, the likeness was good; but, very naturally, it has not the merit of a regular portrait. It is delicate in execution, and certainly has wonderful expression for a silhouette. It has a slight stoop of the shoulders, which the family remember as characteristic of Mrs. Barbauld late in life; and this picture pleased them so much that they used it in preference to the charming portrait by Miss Smirke, which I have had engraved and placed at the beginning of this volume. This portrait, of which Miss Catherine Aiken, her great-niece, allowed me to have a copy, hangs in Mrs. Le Breton's house at Hampstead; and having carefully studied the original picture I can assure the reader of the excellence of the engraving. The portrait was done by Miss Smirke, daughter of Robert Smirke, R. A., and is in pencil. It is perhaps twice as large as the engraving, and has an extraordinary delicacy of touch and finish, well suited to the character of the subject and the refined, beautiful features and expression of Mrs. Barbauld. Mrs. Le Breton possesses also a pencil sketch simply done in outline by her father, Charles Rochemont Aikin, Esq. This was evidently very good, and like his aunt in feature, though, of course, there are no details of shade to complete the effect and give character to the expression. In the Exhibition of Deceased Masters of the British and Foreign School, held a year or more since in London, there was a portrait by George Romney, — whose fame, never small, has greatly increased of late, till he is considered second only to Sir Joshua Reynolds in his style of painting. This portrait purported to be one of Mrs. Barbauld, and it is not impossible that it should have been the work of Romney, who was a native of Dalton in Lancashire, and as Warrington is in that county he might have known Mrs. Barbauld and sketched her. It is a beautiful portrait, and her family desired to buy it; but as no authentic information was possessed by them of such a painting having ever been done of Mrs. Barbauld, nor were they able to obtain any as to its history from its owners, they could not feel certain that it was a portrait of their aunt.

I have touched upon Mrs. Barbauld's position as a poet and prose writer, and noted the varied powers of mind, the genius, the elegance, the learning and study, she displayed. I have placed before the reader the simple, yet it is to be hoped not uninteresting, study of the events of her career, the social and literary claims she has upon the attention and regard of the present generation, and the merits of her title to an enduring and elevated place in English literature. The great mass of books written now renders it almost impossible for the ordinary reader to study even the works of authors which are now classic, as Mrs. Barbauld should be justly considered. But she has other claims to the admiration and high regard which the world owes her, besides her rank as a writer. Mrs. Barbauld was a thinker, a student, a lover of progress and humanity, and a noble, true-hearted woman, who did a genuine and active work. She was a true friend, an affectionate sister, a devoted and tender wife. Mind and heart formed a rare union and well balanced her character. She was governed in her views by reason, and her enthusiasm, though not wanting, was restrained by common-sense and practical judgment. Her heart was warm, full of love and sympathy for all mankind; but the expansion of her interest did not make her overlook the claims of those around her, and her duties to her own little circle. In "the little, nameless, unremembered acts of kindness and of love" she was most charming and attractive; as the author and poet she was respected and admired; but as a woman, a friend, and a relation, she was beloved and revered. Her greatest opponents could not find anything to say against her motives, her honesty, or her character. They might scorn her opinions, doubt her judgment, differ with her in her conclusions; but malice and envy found no mark in her pure and simple integrity of purpose, her open and free expressions of the love of religion, humanity, and progress which formed part of her character and influenced her career.

Mrs. Barbauld exhibited in her life her principles and convictions. She was liberal in her religious views, and tolerant in her estimate of others. A lover of liberty, she desired it for all, and used her influence and her best efforts to secure justice, religious freedom, and liberty for all men. She was one of the earliest opponents of slavery in England, and made her voice of protest heard when the question was agitated by Mr. Wilberforce, that the boast might be true, which was made, that the laws of England knew no slavery. She had "the generous shame,"

> "The unconquerable mind, and Freedom's holy flame,"

which Gray describes as attending the love and progress of poetry. Mrs. Barbauld was one of the great minds which belong to all time for their catholic spirit, their enlightened faith, their love of freedom, their hope for humanity, their communion with nature, and their appreciation of truth and beauty in human life and the great possibilities for the future of the world which characterize them. Born in a station of life which opened to her very limited opportunities for greatness, she has left an indelible impress upon the literature of which her works form a very small portion; but the spirit which animated her writings, — that lives, and will continue to have its influence. Her

> ". . . . life has flowed
> From its mysterious urn a sacred stream,
> In whose calm depth the beautiful and pure
> Alone are mirror'd ; which, though shapes of ill
> May hover round its surface, glides in light,
> And takes no shadow from them."

INDEX.

INDEX.

Aberdeen, University of, 8.
Academy at Kibworth, 7.
Academy at Northampton, 7, 8.
Academy at Warrington, 5, 18-20, 29-33, 55, 111, 112.
Academy proposed to Miss Aikin, 56.
ADAMS, MR. JOHN, 117.
ADDISON, 11, 247.
Address to Mrs. Priestley, 28.
Address to Mr. William Turner, 37, 38.
Address to the Corsicans, 45-49, 208, 326.
Address to the Deity, 35, 36, 326.
Address to the Opposers of the Repeal of the Corporation and Test Acts, 52, 53, 186.
Advertisement to Early Lessons, 86.
AGHRIM, LORD, 113.
AIKIN, ANNA LÆTITIA.
Birth, 7.
Parentage, 7, 12.
First studies, 12.
Precocity, 12, 13.
Anecdote by Mrs. Cappe, 13.
Domestic education, 14.
Early impressions, 15, 16.
Classical education, 16, 17.
Removal to Warrington, 18.
Life there, 26-29.
Her Address to Mrs. Priestley, 28.
Extract from letter, 29.
Her Ode to Wisdom, 29.
Admiration expressed by A. H. Rowan, 32.
AIKIN, A. L. (*continued*).
Takes silhouettes, 33.
Writes Mouse's Petition, 33.
Visits Dr. and Mrs. Priestley, 33-38.
Writes Address to the Deity, 35, 36.
Her character of Dr. Priestley, 36.
Poem addressed to William Turner, 37, 38.
Letters, 39, 40.
Poems printed, 44, 45.
Extracts from Corsica, 45-49.
Groans of the Tankard, 49.
Miscellaneous Pieces published, 50.
Fox's praise of them, 51.
Her imitation of Dr. Johnson, 51, 52.
The Vision of Anna published, 52, 53.
Her marriage to Mr. Barbauld, 54.
See Barbauld.
AIKIN, ARTHUR, 243, 244, 259, 319.
AIKIN, CHARLES ROCHEMONT, 85, 86, 249, 299, 300, 310, 317, 319, 335, 336.
AIKIN, EDMUND, 296.
AIKIN, JOHN, M. D.
His Memoir, 2, 14, 21, 23.
Settles at Warrington, 42.
His character, 42.
Prints his sister's poems, 44.

AIKIN, JOHN, M. D. (*continued*).
Publishes Miscellaneous Pieces with his sister, 50, 86.
Essay printed, 92.
Removal to Yarmouth, 111, 112, 117, 121, 124, 131, 141, 165, 169, 176.
Address to Mrs. Barbauld, 125.
Sonnet to her, 183, 184.
Character of Dr. Johnson, 196, 200, 201.
Visits Dorking, 214, 215.
On sugar, 222, 223.
His character by Mrs. Barbauld, 229.
He visits Kibworth, 233, 234.
Removal to Newington, 237, 238.
Address to his sister, 238, 239, 243, 253, 281, 301, 329, 335.
Death, 309.
A couplet by him, 315.
AIKIN, MISS LUCY, 1, 2, 13, 27-29, 36, 45, 50, 64, 66, 96-99, 111, 112, 201, 204, 221, 229, 231, 232, 244, 247, 250, 253, 257-260, 274, 275, 295, 296, 305, 317, 318, 323, 324, 327, 328, 332, 335.
AIKIN, MRS. C. R., 249, 308.
AIKIN, REV. JOHN, D. D., 4.
Assistant of Dr. Doddridge, 8.
Character of him by G. Wakefield, 8, 9.
Settles at Kibworth, 8, 9.
Anecdote of him, 13, 14.
Teaches his daughter, 17.
Removal to Warrington, 18.
Classical tutor, 20.
Theological tutor, 20, 25.
Letter to him from Mr. Seddon, 25, 26.
AIX, 111-113, 141, 142.
AKENSIDE, 173, 206.
An Inquiry into those Kinds of Distress which excite Agreeable Sensations, 51.
Animal Magnetism, 142.
Annual Review, 243, 244.
Anti-saccharists, 222, 223.
Archbishop of Canterbury, 251.

BAILLIE, MISS AGNES, 231.
BAILLIE, MISS JOANNA, 5, 230-232.
BARBAULD, ANNA LÆTITIA.
Academy buildings, 23, 24.
Meets Mr. Barbauld, 55.
Answers the proposal for Young Ladies' College, 56-59, 60, 61.
Visits London, 62.
Sees Strawberry Hill, 62.
School at Palgrave, 62, 64.
Scholars, 64, 65.
Studies, 65, 66.
Her own account of school life, 70, 71, 73.
Dr. Johnson's remarks, 73, 74.
Devotional Pieces printed, 74.
Her contemporaries, 75-81.
Meets Miss More, 81.
Visited by her, 81.
Adopts her nephew, Charles Aikin, 85.
Early Lessons printed, 86.
Comments on Autumn, a Fragment, by Horace Walpole, 88.
Prose Hymns written, 97-99.
Visits London, 102.
Mrs. Montague's new house, 102, 103.
Visit to Norwich, 105-107.
Addressed by Miss More in her poem Sensibility, 109-111.
Address to Dr. Enfield, 112, 113.
Vacations, 113.
Visit to London, 113, 114.
Meets Miss Burney, 116, 117.
Leaves Palgrave, 121.
Sails from Dover, 121.
Returns to England, 165.
Removal to Hampstead, 172.
Life there, 176, 177.
Takes a pupil, 177.
Poem on French Revolution, 182.

Barbauld, A. L. (*continued*).
Address to the Opposers of the Repeal of the Corporation and Test Acts, 186.
Poetical Epistle to William Wilberforce, 188-191.
Remarks of H. Walpole on it, 192, 193.
She writes Reply to G. Wakefield's Inquiry, 200, 201.
Writes Discourses, 201.
Pieces for Evenings at Home, 201.
She visits Scotland, 201-204.
Writes Essays on Akenside and Collins, 206.
Meets Paoli, 208.
Visits Bristol, 212, 213.
Visits Dorking, 214, 215.
Visits Madame D'Arblay, 215.
Visits Clifton, 220-222.
The Edgeworths, 220-222.
Letter to Miss More, 223.
Characters, 229.
Address to Dr. Priestley, 230.
Miss Joanna Baillie's Call, 231, 232.
Visits Isle of Wight, 235.
Removal to Newington Green, 237.
Anxiety about Mr. Barbauld, 240.
Contributes Critique to Annual Review, 244.
Selection from Spectator, etc., with Essay, 246-248.
Compared to Addison, 247, 248.
Mr. Robinson's introduction to her, 248-250.
Wordsworth's remarks on her, 250, 251.
She writes Life of Richardson, 254-256.
Meeting with the Frenchman, 255, 256.
Life at Newington, 257, 258.
Visit to London, 258.

Barbauld, A. L. (*continued*).
Death of Mr. Barbauld, 261.
His character by his wife, 262-264.
Dirge, 264.
Edits Collection of British Novelists, with Essay, 266.
Edits Enfield Speaker, 269.
Mrs. Barbauld writes Eighteen Hundred and Eleven, 272-274.
Review of it, 274-279.
Attack on her by Coleridge, 281, 282.
Death of her brother, 309.
Her character of Mrs. Taylor, 310, 311.
Her own declining years, 312-315, 317.
She dies, 317.
Her character by Lucy Aikin, 317, 318.
Inscription on monument, 320.
Reminiscence by Mr. Martineau, 320, 321.
Her Legacy, 322.
Her Criticisms, 322, 323.
Her Hymns, 324.
Her Poems, 325-329.
Unpublished Poems, 327, 328.
Her position as a writer, 329-332.
Her personal appearance, 333, 334.
Portraits of Mrs. Barbauld, 333-336.
Her claims to notice and respect, 336-338.
Conclusion, 338, 339.

Barbauld, Mr. Rochemont.
His descent, 54.
His parents, 54.
Birth, 55.
Early years, 55.
Marries A. L. Aikin, 55.
Settles at Palgrave, 55.
Resigns his parish, 121.

BARBAULD, MR. R. (*continued*).
Continental visit, 122.
Returns to England, 165.
Called to Hampstead, 172.
Chapel, 179, 201.
Visits Dorking, 214, 215, 231.
Becomes pastor of Newington Green Chapel, 237, 239, 240.
Peculiarities of character and appearance, 249, 250.
His death, 261.
Tribute to him by Mrs. Barbauld, 262-264.
BATHURST, Bishop of Norwich, 106.
BECHER, MR., 301.
BEDDOES, DR., 212, 213.
BEECROFT, MRS., 196, 201, 208, 279, 290, 302.
Belinda, 265.
BELSHAM, MISS, 29, 40. *See* KENRICK.
BENECKE, MR. and MRS., 253.
BENT, CAPTAIN, 202.
BERKELEY, BISHOP, 277.
BERRY, MISS, 192, 193.
Birmingham riots, 20, 208.
Bishop of Landaff's Address, 21.
Bookham, 215.
BOSCAWEN, MRS., 77, 78, 109.
BOSWELL, JAMES, 45, 73, 196.
Branghtons, 116.
Bristol, 212.
BROUGHAM, LORD, 323, 324.
BROWN'S Amusements, etc., 11.
BRYANTON, MR., 202.
BÜRGER, 204.
BURKE, HON. EDMUND, 77, 79, 116, 179, 187, 193.
BURNEY, DR., 73.
BURNEY, MISS. *See* D'ARBLAY.
BURNS, 168.
BURROWS, MR., 117, 215.
BYRON, LORD, 301, 302, 321, 323.

CALAMY, DR., 176.
CAPPE, MR., 13.
CAPPE, MRS., 13.
CARR, MRS., 209, 212, 296.
CARTER, MISS ELIZABETH, 79.
Cecilia, 116.
CHANNING, DR., 36, 229, 309.
CHAPONE, MRS., 117.
Chapter of Modern Apocrypha, 52, 53.
CHARLES II., 176, 186.
Christian Miscellany, 52.
Christian Reformer, The, 52.
Clifton, 220.
COLERIDGE, S. T., 5, 281, 282.
Collected Poems, Mrs. Barbauld, 208.
Collection of British Novelists, 266.
COLLIERS, 301, 308.
COLLINS, WILLIAM, 206.
CONTARINE, REV. THOMAS, 203.
Corsica, 45-49, 326.
COWPER, WILLIAM, 114, 322, 323, 325.
CROKER, JOHN WILSON, 52.
Crown and Anchor Tavern, 192, 193.
CURRAN, JAMES, 32.

DAER, BASIL, LORD, 113.
D'ARBLAY, MADAME, 79, 80, 215-218.
DARWIN, DR., 212, 322, 323.
DAVY, SIR HUMPHRY, 213, 227.
DAY, THOMAS, 329.
Declaration of Indulgence, 9.
DELANY, MRS., 79.
DE MORVEAU, M., 130, 131.
DENMAN, THOMAS, LORD, 96, 97, 113.
DE ROHAN, CARDINAL, 162.
Deserted Village, 203, 328.
DE STAEL, MADAME, 284, 291.
DEVONSHIRE, DUCHESS OF, 119.
Devotional Pieces, 74.
Diamond Necklace, 162.
Dissenters, 9-12, 251.
Dissenting Academy, 251.
DIXON, MISS, 88. *See* Beecroft.
DODDRIDGE, DR., 4, 7, 8, 13.
Dorking, 214, 215.
Dover, 122.
DRYDEN, JOHN, 326.
DYCE, MR., 251.

Early Lessons, 73, 99, 329.
EDGEWORTH, MISS ANNA, 212.
EDGEWORTH, MISS MARIA, 212, 220-222, 258, 265, 284, 291, 302, 319, 329.
EDGEWORTH, R. L., 212, 220-222, 284.
Edinburgh, 204.
Eighteen Hundred and Eleven, 272-274, 326.
ELDON, LORD, 107.
ENFIELD, DR., 21, 24, 105.
Enfield Speaker, 269.
Epistle to William Wilberforce, 179, 188, 192, 326.
ESTLIN, DR., 21, 212, 213.
ESTLIN, MRS., 253, 260, 287, 295, 297, 306, 313, 323.
Etruria, 24.
Evelina, 116.
Evenings at Home, 43, 201.
Exhibition of Deceased Masters, 336.

FARADAY, PROFESSOR, 227.
FARR, DR., 21.
FARRAR, MRS., 299, 300.
FERRIER, DR., 22.
FINCH, MISS, 301.
Flask Walk, 255.
FLETCHER, MISS, 291.
FLETCHER, MRS., 285, 290, 291, 298.
Foliage, 173.
FORDYCE, DR., 41, 42.
FOX, CHARLES JAMES, 51, 119, 187, 256.
French Emigrants, 206, 207.
French Protestants, 251.
French Revolution, 182, 183, 193.

GELL, SIR WILLIAM, 64, 97, 113.
General Biographical Dictionary, 42.
Geneva, 126.
Gentleman's Magazine, 274.
GEORGE II., 54.
GEORGE III., 80.
GIBBON, E., 30, 31, 34.
GIBSON, DR., 22.
GODWIN, WILLIAM, 115.
GOLDSMITH, DR., 202, 203, 328.
Grandison, Sir Charles, 254, 331.
GRAY, THOMAS, 338.
Groans of the Tankard, 49.

Hackney, 176.
HAMMOND, MISS, 300.
Hampstead, 172, 173, 176, 177.
HARLOWE, CLARISSA, 255.
HASTINGS, WARREN, 179.
HAWKINS, SIR JOHN, 11.
HAYLEY, WILLIAM, 323.
HERVEY, LORD, 186, 187.
Highlands, 202, 203.
Historical Society Cheshire and Lancashire, 23.
HOADLY, DR., 186, 187.
HOARE, MRS., 335.
HOLCROFT, T., 115.
Holland, 203.
HOLLAND, SIR HENRY, 213, 252, 253, 265.
HOWARD, JOHN, 5, 22, 141, 142.
HOWITT, WILLIAM, 239.
HUNT, LEIGH, 173.
HUXLEY, PROFESSOR, 227.

INCHBALD, MRS., 281, 282.

JENNINGS, MISS, 7.
JENNINGS, REV. JOHN, 7.
JOHNSON, DR., 6, 11, 45, 76, 77, 195, 196.
JOHNSON, JOSEPH, 44, 114, 115.

KEMBLE, MR., 232.
KENRICK, MRS., 227, 230, 305-307.
Kibworth, 7, 8, 233, 234.
KINDER, MRS., 309.
Kitcat Club, 255.

Lalla Rookh, 323.
LAMB, CHARLES, 5, 281, 308.
LAMB, MARY, 308.
LAMOTTE, MADAME, 162.
LE BRETON, MRS., 333, 335.

Leeds, 28, 33.
LEGUET, MADEMOISELLE, 162.
Letters of Mrs. Barbauld.
To Dr. Aikin, 62, 63, 67-69; 72, 73-75; 81-85; 87, 88; 92-94; 99, 100; 100-102; 115, 116; 117, 118; 119, 120; 123, 124; 127-130; 131-133; 133-138; 143-146; 151-154; 154-158; 162-164; 165-167; 177-179; 198-200.
To Mrs. Beecroft (Miss Dixon), 89, 90; 90-92; 94, 95; 147-151; 167, 168; 180, 181; 184, 185; 197, 198; 204,-206; 207, 208; 240, 241; 242, 243; 257; 280, 281; 286; 289, 290; 302; 313, 314.
To Mrs. Carr, 210, 211; 232, 233; 235, 236; 308, 309.
To Dr. and Mrs. Estlin, 224, 225; 287, 288; 288, 289; 294, 295; 295, 296; 307; 313; 315-317.
To Mrs. Fletcher, 291-293; 293, 294; 305, 306.
To Miss F——, 271, 272.
To Mrs. Kenrick (Miss Belsham), 40-42; 49, 50; 138-141; 225-227; 230; 232; 269, 270.
To Miss More, 107-109; 219, 220.
To Mrs. Smith, 241, 242; 258, 259.
To Mrs. Taylor, 122; 158-161; 266-269; 282, 283; 304.
To Miss Taylor (Mrs. Reeve), 244-246.
Leyden, 203.
Lichfield, 106.
Life, 250, 251.
London, 62, 102, 172.

MACAULAY, LORD, 9-12, 179, 194, 253.
MACAULAY, MRS., 193.
MACKINTOSH, SIR JAMES, 5, 123, 321, 322.
Magdalen College, 30, 31.
MALLET, MR., 274.
MALTHUS, 21.
Manchester New College, 22.
MARTINEAU, PROFESSOR RUSSELL, 22, 23.
MARTINEAU, REV. JAMES, D. D., 22, 23, 320, 321, 328.
MASON, REV. WILLIAM, 88.
Medical Memoir, 42.
METEYARD, MISS, 3.
Miscellaneous Pieces, 51.
MONTAGUE, MRS. ELIZABETH, 5, 56, 75-78, 102, 103, 116, 286.
MONTGOMERY, JAMES, 281.
Monthly Magazine, 43, 214, 215.
Monthly Repository of Theology and General Literature, 261.
MORE, LORD, 113.
MORE, MISS HANNAH, 3, 5, 76-81, 86, 102, 109-111, 192, 223, 279, 280.
Mouse's Petition, 33.
MURCH, MR., 204.

Ode to Wisdom, 29.
Odes of Collins, 206.
OLDENBURGH, DUCHESS OF, 291.
On Inconsistency in Our Expectations, 51, 253, 254, 322, 330.
On the Prospect of planting Arts and Learning in America, 277.
On Romances, 52.
On Monastic Institutions, 51.
OPIE, MRS., 105.
OSSORY, COUNTESS OF, 63.
Oude, Begums of, 179.
Oxford, 30, 31.

Palgrave, 55, 62, 64, 121.
PAOLI, GENERAL, 47, 208.
Paris, 161, 162.
PEABODY, W. O. B., 324.
PEEL, SIR ROBERT, 187.
PERCIVAL, DR., 21.
Percy, 102.
PHILANTHROPUS, R. FRANK, 203.
PHILLIPS, MRS., 215.

PHIPPS, HON. AUGUSTUS, 113.
PIOZZI, MRS., 74.
POPE, 287.
PORTER, MISS JANE, 281.
PORTLAND, DUCHESS OF, 79.
Practical Education, 221.
PRICE, DR., 176, 196, 197, 237, 239, 240, 319.
PRIESTLEY, DR. JOSEPH, 5, 19, 20, 24, 25, 27, 28, 33-36, 176, 179, 196, 227-229.
PRIESTLEY, MRS., 5, 27, 28.
PRIOR, 79.
Prose Hymns, 97-99, 329, 330.

Quarterly Review, 274-279.

Recollections of Seventy Years, 299, 300.
REYNOLDS, SIR JOSHUA, 116, 336.
RICHARDSON, SAMUEL, 254-256, 330, 331.
RIGBY, MISSES, 29, 329.
ROBINSON, MR. H. C., 5, 177, 218, 248-254, 266, 280-282, 284, 308, 314, 315, 322, 323.
ROGERS, MR. SAMUEL, 5, 51, 218, 219, 255, 256, 259, 260, 319, 321.
ROMNEY, GEORGE, 336.
ROSCOE, WILLIAM, 5, 22, 275, 276, 281, 323.
ROWAN, A. H., 32.
Royal Institution, 227.
RUMFORD, COUNT, 227.

Sacred Dramas, 109.
SADLER, DR., 177.
SALISBURY, BISHOP OF, 186, 187.
SAYERS, DR., 64, 65, 105, 106, 113.
School for Scandal, 102.
Scotland, 201-204.
SCOTT, SIR WALTER, 5, 204, 244, 266, 295, 296.
SEDDON, MR., 23-26.
Selâma, 51.
SELKIRK, EARL OF, 113.
Sensibility, 109-111.
Ser Bertrand, 51.
SEWARD, MISS ANNA, 251.
SHELLEY, P. B., 278.
SHENSTONE, WILLIAM, 169.
SHERIDAN, R. B., 102, 116.
SIDDONS, MRS., 232, 284.
Silhouettes, 33.
SMIRKE, MISS, 325.
SMIRKE, R., 325.
SMITH, DR. ADAM, 30.
SMITH, MISS C., 251.
Society of Arts, 259, 325.
SOUTHEY, ROBERT, 274-279, 325.
Spectator, 11, 321.
STEWART, DUGALD, 5, 169, 204.
Strawberry Hill, 61, 62.
Surrey, 214, 215.
SWIFT, DEAN, 79.

TALBOT, MISS, 79.
TALLEYRAND, PERIGORD, 162.
TAYLOR, DR. JOHN, 20, 21.
TAYLOR, MISS, 244.
TAYLOR, MRS. JOHN, 158, 260, 305, 310, 311.
TAYLOR, WILLIAM, 64, 65, 106, 113, 204, 296.
TAYLORS, 105.
Tempest, 92.
TEMPLETOWN, LORD, 113.
Test Act. *See* Corporation, etc.
TURNER, MR., 35-38.
TURNER, WILLIAM, 35, 37, 38, 253, 276, 277, 327, 328.
TYNDALL, PROFESSOR, 227.

VAUGHAN, MR. B., 229.
VAUGHAN, MRS., 229.
VESEY, HON. A., 77.
VESEY, MRS., 77, 78.
Vision of Anna, etc., 52, 53.
VOLNEY, 278.

WAKEFIELD, GILBERT, 8, 9, 20, 21, 176, 200, 201, 249, 308.
WAKEFIELD, MISS, 249.

Walpole, Hon. Horace, 61, 62, 88, 192-194, 278.
Walpole, Sir Robert, 186.
Warrington, 21-26, 44.
Watts, Dr., 6.
Wedgwood, John, 21, 24.
Wedgwood, Josiah, 3, 24.
Wedgwood, Thomas, 213.
West, Lady Mary, 44.
White, H. K., 278.
Wilberforce, William, 179, 188, 192.
Williams, H. M., 193, 251.
Williams, Miss, 76.
Willoughby, Lord, of Parham, 18.
Wingates, 12.
Wordsworth, William, 5, 15, 250-252, 281, 323.

THE END.

www.ingramcontent.com/pod-product-compliance
Lightning Source LLC
LaVergne TN
LVHW021251110826
845151LV00002BA/387